About the author

Dr Julia Buxton is Senior Research Fellow in the Centre for International Cooperation and Security in the Department of Peace Studies at the University of Bradford, UK. Her research field covers Latin American politics; conflict prone countries and regional capacities in democracy promotion and conflict resolution. Her publications include *The Failure of Political Reform in Venezuela* (Ashgate, 2001) and the edited collections, with N. Phillips, *Country Case Studies in Latin American Political Economy* (Manchester University Press, 1999) and *Developments in Latin American Political Economy* (Manchester University Press, 1999).

JULIA BUXTON

The political economy of narcotics

Production, consumption and global markets

Fernwood Publishing
NOVA SCOTIA

Zed Books
LONDON | NEW YORK

The political economy of narcotics: Production, consumption and global markets was first published in 2006.

Published in Canada by Fernwood Publishing Ltd, 32 Oceanvista Lane, Site 2A, Box 5, Black Point, Nova Scotia BOJ 1BO

Published in the rest of the world by Zed Books Ltd, 7 Cynthia Street, London N1 9JF, UK and Room 400, 175 Fifth Avenue, New York, NY 10010, USA

www.zedbooks.co.uk

Cover designed by Andrew Corbett
Set in Arnhem and Futura Bold by Ewan Smith, London
Index: <ed.emery@britishlibraty.net>
Printed and bound in the United Kingdom by Biddles Ltd, King's Lynn

Distributed in the USA exclusively by Palgrave Macmillan, a division of St Martin's Press, LLC, 175 Fifth Avenue, New York, NY 10010.

A catalogue record for this book is available from the British Library.
US CIP data are available from the Library of Congress.

Library and Archives Canada Cataloguing in Publication
Buxton, Julia
The political economy of narcotics: production, consumption and global markets / Julia Buxton.
ISBN 1-55266-198-9
    1. Drug traffic. 2. Drug control. 3. Drug abuse. I. Title.
HV5801.B89 2006   363.45   C2006-900909-0

ISBN 1 84277 446 8 | 978 1 84277 446 8 hb (Zed Books)
ISBN 1 84277 447 6 | 978 1 84277 447 2 pb (Zed Books)

Contents

Tables and figures

Tables

Figures

Acknowledgements

Researching and writing this book was a tortuous process, particularly for those around me. I would consequently like to thank my long suffering partner, whose tolerance and support extended beyond the line of relationship duty. I am also grateful to Anna Hardman and Robert Molteno of Zed for their patience and encouragement of my endeavour to explain narcotic drug policies. I would like to extend enormous thanks to those students at Kingston University who followed my Political Economy of Drugs course (1999–2003) as part of their undergraduate degree studies. Their enormous enthusiasm for the subject matter and pertinent questioning of the material provided a real insight into contemporary conceptualization of the 'drug problem' and helped me to identify gaps in our knowledge of drug-related issues. They also bombarded me with books, articles, policy documents and newspaper cuttings, all of which helped me to immerse myself (at times too deeply) in the subject. Many thanks also to Terry Sullivan and Wendy Stokes for their support and interest and to Mike Hawkins and Keith Weightman for helping me to find a balance between teaching commitments and research. I am also grateful to colleagues at the Centre for International Co-operation and Security, in the Department of Peace Studies at the University of Bradford, for enabling me to finalize the work for publication.

Researching drug-related issues is sensitive and difficult. The majority of people prepared to share their experience of drugs, either from within the trade, enforcement services or policy implementation requested anonymity. Very little of the 'fieldwork' was consequently brought into the book, but it provided a valuable opportunity to experience and understand the drugs trade. I am therefore thankful to all who were prepared to share their perspectives on narcotic drugs and for trusting in the value of the research, including officials from countries including the US, Nepal, Colombia and Venezuela, who allowed me to incorporate a discussion of drugs into meetings on completely unrelated matters.

When friends and acquaintances know that you are working on drugs, they feel somehow compelled to discuss their own drug experiences and views on drugs, so many thanks for these insights, which by my own calculation, ran into their hundreds. I am also grateful to my sister Kate for kicking my drug 'hobby' off by buying me a book on cocaine in relation to my work on South America. Finally, humble thanks to Steve 'magnet man' Every who recovered five chapters of the book after my fatal encounter with a memory stick.

For Ruby Harper Buxton Bisset
A lesson in life

'Virtue is more to be feared than
vice, because its excesses are not subject
to the regulation of conscience.'

Adam Smith, 1723–90

Introduction

If the United Nations meets its deadline, we should be living in a 'drug-free world' by 2008. Within the UN there is a large bureaucracy that monitors trends in the production and consumption of drugs such as cocaine, cannabis and heroin. The reports produced by these bodies show the 2008 target to be hopelessly unrealistic. In fact, even a cursory reading of the drug-related documentation produced by the UN leads to the conclusion that a 'drug-free world' is itself an unachievable and utopian objective.

All countries are united in the goal of eliminating the production, distribution and consumption of harmful drugs. There is also a global consensus that the cultivation of plants such as coca and opium poppy that can be used in the manufacture of harmful drugs should be eliminated. This international agreement is enshrined in a series of conventions that are administered and monitored by a dedicated UN bureaucracy. The conventions oblige signatory states to act against the trade in harmful drugs in co-operation with each other.

There is strong international pressure on states to fulfil their commitments under the conventions and implement anti-drug legislation and strategies in line with the thrust of the conventions and the UN's recommendations. This is because the model of controlling drug availability is dependent on global unity. Any weak link in the chain of consensus is a potential centre for drug production and trafficking, and this would undermine the efforts of other states to restrict public access to drugs. So, while there might be a lively debate on changing aspects of the national drug laws in some countries, the reality is that national governments have very limited room for manoeuvre in terms of developing domestic drug strategies.

This situation is regrettable because the system of international drug control does not work. All the statistical information shows that, rather than decreasing, the number of people who are producing, distributing and consuming harmful drugs is increasing. This expansion of the trade in drugs has been particularly pronounced since the collapse of Soviet communism in the early 1990s and it has accelerated in line with the globalization process. On that basis alone, drug control policies have failed. Not only have they failed, they are also counter-productive and this was recognized by critics at an early stage of the control model. There is a substantial literature on the contradictions inherent in pursuing current strategic approaches. More problematically, and the main contention of this book, the current control model has not adapted to the enormous changes that have occurred in production and consumption trends during

1

the 1990s and 2000s. As a result, drug control strategies are no longer simply counter-productive; they are now doing more harm than good.

This book is an examination of the international system of drug control and the social, economic, environmental and political problems that it has created. It was motivated by the concern that, at the beginning of the twenty-first century, the international community faced unprecedented challenges from terrorism, violence and disease. Current control strategies are completely inappropriate for the problems ahead and, if maintained, are likely to exacerbate the threats posed by HIV/AIDS, civil conflict, underdevelopment and social injustice. Three key problems with the current model are identified. The first is the ideology of prohibition that informs drug control strategies and which has been institution-alized within the international drug control apparatus. Prohibitionists believe that the state should step in to prevent people from voluntarily consuming substances that might cause them harm. However, as the book demonstrates, it is impossible to enforce prohibition. Even though prohibition is shown to be flawed and inappropriate as a basis for drug policies, the principle is difficult to jettison. This is because of the power and influence of the USA.

The USA emerges as the second explanation as to why drug control policies have failed and why they cause harm. A key argument of this book is that international drug control policies have been intertwined with US foreign policy goals since the launch of the control system nearly a century ago. The principle of prohibition that informs the control model emerged from a unique and specifically American worldview that was influential in the nineteenth century. In promoting prohibition as the guiding principle of drug policy, the USA has moulded the control system to its own values, interests and aspirations and locked the international com-munity into an arcane view of drugs and drug users. The strategies for achieving prohibition have been determined by the USA and prohibition thinking. As a result, all countries have to pursue reductions in drug consumption through a set of universalized policies that emphasize supply elimination and criminalization of the trade, even if these approaches are not appropriate in distinct national contexts. Drug control has consequently failed because it is very much a tool of the USA and because the US controls international drug policy institutions.

Structure of the book

In order to demonstrate how the USA has crafted control of international drug policy and why prohibition thinking exerts such a powerful influence over drug policy and drug control institutions, the first five chapters of the book explore the historical context of the control system. Chapter 1 assesses the history of drugs, from the period when they were a freely traded commodity through to the beginnings of regulation. This provides an historical context for the emergence of prohibition thinking, which is assessed in the second and third chapters. These demonstrate how alternative drug policy approaches, such as regulation and treatment of users, were sidelined by the USA as the country assumed control of the drug policy agenda and, through this issue, an increasingly influential role on the international stage. Chapters 4 and 5 outline the evolution of the international control system and explore the dilemmas and tensions inherent in establishing an international policy consensus and unity of policy action. They demonstrate how the USA was able to gain control of the 'idea' and institutional framework of drug control and the origins of the national and international drug policies that are pursued today.

The sixth and seventh chapters are a statistical analysis of trends in drug consumption and production in the 1990s and 2000s. The aim of the two chapters is to provide the reader with clear evidence that drug policies have failed and also to underscore the scale and nature of the emerging problems faced by the control framework. In Chapters 8 and 9, the reasons for failure are considered in detail. Chapter 8 examines the utopian nature of prohibition as an ideology and guiding principle and the counter-productive results of pursuing it as an end goal. Chapter 9 shifts the focus of analysis away from ideology towards institutions. The chapter examines how drug control is operationalized and it argues that policy strategies have compounded rather than alleviated the problems inherent in following prohibition-based strategies.

The book then proceeds with an exploration of the 'more harm than good' thesis. It focuses on three areas: politics, HIV/AIDS and the environment. While it is acknowledged that the production and use of illicit drugs have damaging consequences for political stability, public health and environmental protection, it is argued that the harm caused is a result of drugs being illegal, rather than production and consumption being damaging per se. This section then demonstrates how, in seeking to curb the negative impact of prohibition, drug polices compound the scale and impact of the problems that they have created in the first place. This book, then, is a study of iatrogenic policy, institutional sclerosis and the organizational and intellectual tools of US foreign policy.

Because this book seeks to provide the reader with a rounded understanding of the drug dilemma that the international community faces in the current period, it approaches the study of drugs from different disciplinary perspectives. As such, it also serves as a guide to the existing literature on drugs. Drugs are an enormously difficult topic to research. Each discipline, from medicine to economics, has its own drug studies; there is also an extensive historical and cultural literature of each of the main drugs; and each country has a unique drug history. For somebody new to drug debates, the range and quantity of material can be daunting. The book therefore aims to provide a guide to some of the key writings and analyses that have been conducted, thereby allowing readers to follow up in any area covered that they find to be of particular interest. While there is a large body of work on drugs, this book aims to break new ground in integrating the study of history, ideology, institutions and policy.

3

1 | Intoxicating substances in historical perspective

The role of drugs in global society

People have ingested naturally-occurring intoxicating and hallucinatory substances since the beginning of civilization. There are approximately 4,000 plants containing psychoactive substances and sixty of these have been consumed throughout world history. The most widely used naturally-occurring drugs are opium from the opium poppy (*Papaver somniferum*), the flowers, leaves and resin of the cannabis plant (*Cannabis sativa*) and the leaves of the coca plant (*Erythroxylum*). The earliest surviving written accounts of these three drugs date back to the third century BC (Austin 1979).

Naturally-occurring drugs were an important and persistent element of cultural, social, economic, medical and spiritual evolution. Only four out of 237 cultures worldwide have no record of intoxicating substance use, these being societies that are isolated and incapable of cultivating psychoactive plants, such as the Inuit community (Blum 1969). So omnipresent is drug use in global history, one commentator claimed that it: 'must represent a basic human appetite [...] analogous to hunger or the sexual drive' (Weil 1972).

The functions of drug use Drugs were consumed in ancient and modern societies for five main purposes (Inglis 1975). They were first used for pain relief and this was particularly the case with cannabis and opium. The smoking, inhalation or eating of cannabis was recommended in ancient Indian and Chinese manuscripts for the relief of sickness and diseases such as gout, cholera, tetanus, neuralgia, depression and for pain relief in childbirth. The leaves and flowers of the marijuana plant (*Cannabis sativa* or *Cannabis indica*) were prized for their psychoactive properties and used in medicines and religious ceremonies for over 3,000 years. From 1850 to 1937, cannabis was the primary treatment for more than 100 illnesses or diseases in the US pharmacopoeia. Queen Victoria's personal physician, Dr John Russell Reynolds, prescribed cannabis to the royal family for over thirty years, describing it in an 1890 edition of the medical journal *The Lancet* as one of the most valuable medicines known to man (Abel 1980).

Opium was highly valued for its medicinal properties. It contains forty-six alkaloids including the analgesics codeine and morphine and, like cannabis, it was used for the treatment of a wide range of illnesses and relief of bronchial problems (Booth 1999; Scott 1969). Knowledge of the opium poppy and its cultivation techniques was passed from Lower Mesopotamia, where it was first cultivated, to the Assyrians, Babylonians, Egyptians and the Greeks. In 330 BC, Alexander the Great extended opium poppy cultivation to Persia (Iran). Arab traders, who were believed to have acquired their knowledge of the medicinal properties of opium from the Greeks, introduced opium from Persia to South Asia and by AD 400 opium was used in medical practice in India and China. These two countries subsequently became the world's leading opium poppy cultivating countries.

Intoxicating substances were also consumed for physical stimulation by those engaged in arduous employment. This was the case in a wide range of country contexts and, across time, extended from the practice of coca leaf chewing by indigenous Indian societies in the Andes (Allen 1981) to cannabis smoking among labourers in Jamaica and South Africa. Cannabis use was thought to have developed in Jamaica after it was transported to the island by indentured labourers from India, while the use of cannabis in Africa was introduced by Arab traders in Mozambique (Brecher et al. 1972). A range of other natural plant-based stimulants such as betel, khat and tobacco were also used as 'work' drugs because their consumption increased stamina, reduced the appetite and boosted physical endurance (Courtwright 2002). Drug use also played an important role in religious, pagan, shamanic and cultural ceremonies across the world (Schultes and Hoffman 1992). Coca leaves, opium, cannabis and hallucinogenic plants such as peyote and psilocybin were used as religious sacraments and venerated as gifts from nature or the gods. Their consumption or inhalation was promoted as a means of communing with the divine and achieving spiritual enlightenment (Davenport Hines 2001; Russell 1998; Walton 2001).

Drugs were also consumed for the purpose of relaxation. In some cultures this was the preserve of the elite, as was the case in the Peruvian Inca and Indian Mughal empires. In other historical and country contexts, social drug use was an integral element of community and tradition. This was particularly the case with cannabis. Social cannabis use was an integral element of tribal life among African Dagga (cannabis) cults in both the ancient and modern period and the drug was recreationally consumed across the continent, from South Africa, through Central African countries such as the Congo up to Northern states such as Morocco (Abel 1980; Brecher et al. 1972). There is no evidence of drug 'abuse' in ancient or traditional societies. This is attributed to cultural mores that regulated patterns of use. If over-indulgence occurred, sanction was the domain of the family or community elders (Escohotado 1999). Cultivation of 'narcotic' plants was also limited and balanced by the production of other agricultural goods such as potatoes and maize in the coca cultivating areas of the Andes in South America and cotton and wheat in the opium poppy cultivation areas that stretched from the Mediterranean to South Asia.

Cannabis, coca and the opium poppy were also cultivated as a food source. This was the case with opium consumption in China and cannabis use in India during political and demographic upheavals in the eighteenth and nineteenth centuries

(McCoy 1972; Michaud 1997). The Indian Hemp Commission convened by the British government in 1893 to examine cannabis use in India concluded that: 'the supporting power' of cannabis 'brought many a family through famine' (Indian Hemp Drugs Commission 1969). Hemp, a member of the *Cannabis sativa* family, produces highly nutritious hemp seed and seed oil. These have been consumed in China since 6000 BC and they formed a staple of rural diets in South and Central Asia, Russia and the Balkan region for centuries (Roulac 1997).

In addition to consumption purposes, these drug plants were also cultivated so they could be used as a means of exchange in early trading systems and they were bartered for spices, dyes and precious metals. The hemp plant was also cultivated for its durable stalk, used for the making of paper, textiles, rope and rigging. The great value of the plant was first recognized in China and its cultivation spread to Central Asia and Europe in the thirteenth century. It was spread to South and North America by the Spanish conquistadors and the Pilgrims in the sixteenth and seventeenth centuries (Herer 1998: Roulac 1997).

Repression and resurgence Around the eleventh century AD, systematic campaigns against the use of cannabis and opium were initiated. This has been linked to the rise of monotheistic religions (Escohotado 1999; Hitti 1967; Walton 2001). Religious authorities, beginning first in Islamic regions and extending into Christian areas by the thirteenth century, viewed the spiritual and cultural practices associated with drug use as a threat to the authority of religious elders and a challenge to their monopoly of religious understanding. Psychoactive substance use was condemned as a short-cut to a 'higher state' that religious authorities maintained should be achieved only through fasting, prayer or meditation. Intoxication and drug use was therefore linked at a very early stage to the idea of deviance, rebellion and heresy.

The move to suppress spiritual pluralism forced knowledge and use of naturally-occurring drugs underground, until the barbarity of the 'Dark Ages' gave way to the European Renaissance of the fifteenth century. Investigation into the properties of drugs was socially and politically re-legitimized and opium and cannabis reappeared in the medical literature. Although religious authorities in Christian areas maintained a hostile stance towards the use of intoxicating substances, even for medical purposes, their authority to pronounce on these matters was increasingly marginalized by the central state.

Beyond the impetus given to research into the medical use of drugs, the social and political changes that occurred in Western Europe during the fifteenth and sixteenth centuries catalysed a radical transformation of drug use and the trade in drugs. The driving force of this change was the European quest for empire, the spread of early capitalism and the emergence of the international trading system. These changed patterns of consumption and production of coca and the opium poppy and transformed these crops into internationally traded commodities.

THE EARLY GLOBAL TRADE IN DRUGS: THE CASE OF COCA Following the conquest of South America by the Spanish in the early sixteenth century, coca leaf consumption and production surged in the traditional Andean cultivation areas of the Yungas in Bolivia and Huanuco, Libertad and Cuzco in Peru. In their drive to exploit the precious metals of the region, the Spanish conquistadors forcibly relocated indigenous peasants from highland areas to work in silver mines. Despite pressure from the Roman Catholic Church, the Spanish monarchy encouraged the cultivation and chewing of the coca leaf by miners, a practice that was central to indigenous culture, as it improved endurance levels.

The Spanish transformed coca leaves into one of the most highly commercialized products in the Andes by using coca as means of payment. They profited further from the coca economy by taxing the trade in coca leaves. However, they did not assume control of coca cultivation, which remained in the hands of the indigenous Indian population, and while coca leaf consumption among the indigenous population did increase, its use did not spread among the Spanish. Because the leaves were perishable, markets for coca were geographically limited and, as a result, demand for coca was initially confined to indigenous labourers in neighbouring South American territories (Walker 1996).

THE CASE OF OPIUM The process by which opium became a globally traded commodity was markedly different from that of coca. Having encountered tobacco during earlier explorations of the Americas, Portuguese merchants shipped it from Brazil to Europe and along new trading routes in the Middle East and South Asia in the early 1600s. In Europe, tobacco was smoked on its own but in South Asia the Portuguese introduced the practice of smoking tobacco mixed with opium (Booth 1999; McCoy 1972). The Portuguese had first discovered opium poppy cultivation and opium production in India after their arrival in the country in 1501. Cultivation was concentrated in two main areas: to the north of the Ganges in Bengal where Patna opium was produced and in the western region around Bombay, the home of Malwa opium. As social preference shifted away from the smoking of tobacco and towards smoking opium on its own, Portuguese merchants concentrated on the sale of Indian opium to the Chinese market. The Portuguese were therefore responsible for transforming the context of opium use from pain relief to leisure activity.

The Dutch and more specifically the British revolutionized the trade in recreational opium in the eighteenth and nineteenth centuries. During this period, opium became one of the most important globally traded goods on the international market.

Opium and empire

In the sixteenth century, the Dutch merchant fleet began to challenge the Spanish and Portuguese for control of their overseas possessions and trading routes. Dutch commercial dominance was stepped up with the formation of the Dutch East India Company (Vereenigde Oost-Indische Compagnie, VOC) in 1602. Created for the purpose of discovering a sea route from the Netherlands to Asia, by the 1640s the VOC had pushed Portugal out of Indonesia and consolidated control of the profitable trade in spices such as tea, pepper, cinnamon and nutmeg that were prized in Europe and which dominated the Asian economy (Courtwright 2002; Schivelbusch 1993).

Western demand for Asian spices, in addition to ceramics, silks and textiles, came at a high economic cost to European countries and they ran a substantial deficit on their foreign trade (Gunder Frank 1995; Maddison and Johnston 2001). The economies of the East and specifically China during the Third Commercial Revolution (1500–1800) were more productive and specialized. China's prosperity increased after the conversion of its fiscal system to the silver standard in the early sixteenth century. The country accumulated vast amounts of silver that had been mined in South America and which had become the standard global trading currency of the period (Flynn and Giráldez 2002).

This pattern of economic growth and capital accumulation in the East and West was reversed towards the end of the eighteenth century, with the trade in opium making a significant contribution to the reshaping of trade balances. Opium was significant because of the direction of the trade flow. While the trade in eastern goods had gone in one direction, from east to west, the trade in opium went from east to east through western intermediaries. Eastern opium payments in silver to western merchants and trading interests helped to redirect the accumulation of silver to Western Europe.

Opium as a commodity: the Dutch VOC and British EIC trade in opium After the Dutch conquest of Indonesia there was a large increase in opium imports from Bengal, which the Dutch traded in the Far East. In the 1660s, Bengal opium exports to Indonesia totalled 0.6 metric tons (mt). By 1699 this had increased to 87 mt. The VOC developed an enormously lucrative trade in the re-export of opium to China, with profits from re-sales estimated to be in the region of 400 per cent. As a result of the enormous profitability of the sector, the trade in opium gradually displaced the trade in spices (McCoy 1972; La Motte 2003).

Initially it was Indian opium merchants, landowners (the *zamindars*) and the emperor of the Mughal state of North India who benefited from the inflow of opium export revenues from the trade with the Dutch. As the sector expanded it became vulnerable to British commercial interests seeking a foothold in the thriving Bengal economy (Chaudhury 2003). The British East India Company (EIC), which had been established in 1600 to increase British access to the spice trade, served as the vehicle for British commercial expansion in India. The EIC arrived in the country in 1608 and gradually increased its control over the opium sector through military confrontation with the *zamindars* and the Dutch and

Indian merchants they supplied. Cultivation areas that fell under EIC control were incorporated into a loose syndicate system, based on advanced opium purchases from peasants, which was inherited from the Indian merchants. After the British conquered Bengal in 1764, the EIC established a monopoly system and asserted the exclusive right to purchase and export Patna opium (Ul Haq 2000). The initial strategy of the East India Company was to maintain low levels of opium poppy cultivation in order to keep the opium price high. Production was divided into two classes. Akbari opium was sold to Indian consumers and Provision opium was prepared for the export market and sold through the EIC's auction houses in Calcutta. Competition from Malwa opium, which continued to be produced in the princely states outside British control, combined with rising demand from China, led the EIC to revise its policy and increase export volumes in the second half of the eighteenth century.

Critics of British policy in India argue that the EIC was rapacious in its drive to maximize opium revenues after this policy change, with devastating consequences for the Indian peasantry. The EIC exploited the coercive capacity of 40,000 British and 200,000 South Asian soldiers in the North of India to enforce cultivation in the Sikh areas of the Punjab, Jammu and Kashmir. Even in years of food shortages, the EIC maintained intensive cultivation, a strategy that was continued by the British governor general after the EIC's charter expired and Britain assumed direct control of India in 1773. It is claimed that the destruction of food crops to make way for poppy cultivation reduced food availability and contributed to the famine of 1770 in which one-third of the population of the Bengal region died (Chaudhury 2003; Ul Haq 2000). However, the charge that intensive poppy cultivation led to famine has been disputed on the ground that the total area under cultivation in the Bengal region constituted less than 2 per cent of all land (Cohen 1990; Richards 2003). It is also argued that the 1.3 million peasants engaged by the British in Patna opium production benefited from a system of interest-free advances and guaranteed prices. Rather than being exploited, peasants received reasonable returns on poppy cultivation and the number who benefited from this system increased as the area under cultivation expanded from 90,000 acres in 1830 to 176,000 ten years later, reaching a high of 500,000 acres by 1900 (McCoy 1972; Richards 2003).

The utility of opium revenues By 1800, British exports of Bengal opium were an estimated 127 mt. By 1857, this had increased to 6,372 mt (Ul Haq 2000: 27). The British also sought to maximize the revenues from the sector by encouraging domestic opium consumption in India. Opium could be purchased only through government-administered shops, of which there were 10,000 by 1893, and retail sales were heavily taxed (Trocki 1999; Ul Haq 2000).

While there is a lively debate on the morality of the opium policy, there is consensus that the opium monopoly was a crucial revenue source for the British authorities. By the end of the 1830s, opium sales contributed 11 per cent of total revenues accruing to the British administration in India. By the 1850s, this had increased to 17 per cent (Richards 2003; Trocki 1999, Ul Haq 2000). Opium revenues made a vital contribution to the maintenance of the colonial structure in India and the financial importance of the sector rose as Britain was forced to increase defence expenditures in the country to counter challenges to the British presence in Asia from Russia (Gilbert 2003; Trocki 1999).

The Dutch, Spanish, Portuguese and the French also exploited the opium trade in order to finance their colonial administrations in Southeast Asian countries such as Laos, Cambodia, Indonesia, Vietnam and the Philippines. Opium poppy cultivation was introduced in these non-traditional cultivation areas through a system of government-sponsored opium 'farms' and this served to expand opium cultivation across Southeast Asia. The colonial administrations taxed opium imports, and monopoly retail sales systems were established for domestic consumers. In Java, Indonesia, the Dutch administered 1,065 opium retail outlets and obtained between 14 and 16 per cent of their revenues for the administration of the colony from opium sales. The British also extended the system of opium outlet licensing to other colonial territories including Burma (Myanmar), Singapore and British Malaya (Malaysia). In Malaysia, taxes on opium contributed 53 per cent of Britain's administrative costs (McCoy 1972). This European colonial policy of encouraging opium smoking ran counter to the practice of restricting use that had prevailed under the pre-colonial indigenous authorities and it went against traditionally strong cultural resistance to the recreational use of opium within these countries.

Opium in Turkey and Iran Turkey and Iran emerged as important sources of global opium supply during this period. Three factors accounted for this development. First, American merchants and Dutch traders in Smyrna (Izmir) began shipping opium cultivated in Anatolia, Turkey, to South Asia via a circuitous route around the tip of Africa beginning in 1805. This followed the decision by the EIC to bar American merchants from its auctions in Calcutta. During the period of America's exclusion, which was lifted in 1834, Turkish opium exports to China increased from 7 tons in 1805 to 100 tons by 1830 (McCoy 1972).

Central authorities in Iran and Turkey also sought to capitalize on their comparative advantage in opium production independently from Dutch and American traders. In the Ottoman region, incentives were introduced to encourage cultivation, such as a waiver on land tithes for one year if farming was turned over to opium poppy planting (Cole 1999). Opium exports subsequently increased in economic importance to Iran and Turkey because of developments in the international economy. Domestic manufacturing was negatively affected by the export of cheap, manufactured goods from Europe in the second half of the nineteenth century. Rising unemployment forced Iranian and Turkish workers to cultivate cash crops such as tobacco, cotton and opium poppy. The opening of the Suez Canal in 1869 was a further boost to European-manufactured exports and, conversely, to opium poppy cultivation (ibid.). This, in conjunction with the Raj opium policy in India, made the second half of the nineteenth century a high-point for global opium production.

The Chinese opium market

The Chinese empire was the motor of the opium trade. Opium was smoked at all levels of Chinese society, from the Court of the Emperor down to peasants. Domestic cultivation in Yunnan and Szechwan was insufficient to meet rising demand and western merchants sought to fill the vacuum of supply with Indian, Turkish and Iranian opium. However, the spread of recreational opium smoking was viewed as offensive to Confucian morality and in 1729 Emperor Yung Cheng issued an edict that restricted the sale and use of opium to medical need (Beeching 1975; Holt 1964; Waley 1985). Demand was sustained despite the decree and European merchants competed aggressively to supply the illicit market. By the late 1790s, an estimated 4,000 chests of opium were being smuggled into China annually (La Motte 2003).

In an attempt to address a sustained problem of recreational use and widespread addiction, the Emperor Kia King issued a second edict in 1799. This prohibited domestic opium poppy cultivation and, as the supply of opium from Yunnan and Szechwan collapsed, European merchants stepped up contraband exports to the country (Janin 1999). By 1838, 20,000 chests per year were being smuggled into the empire through Canton, the only port open to foreign trade under the *cohong* system. By 1858, this had risen to 70,000 chests as continued demand and the addictive quality of opium made suppression of consumption, smuggling and domestic cultivation difficult for the weak and ineffective Qing dynasty (La Motte 2003).

Opium as a Trojan horse Aside from the vast profits that European merchants such as the British firm Jardine and Matheson made from exporting opium to China, there was a second rationale for targeting the empire with opium. There was demand in Britain for highly prized Chinese goods but the Chinese were reluctant consumers of British-manufactured products and hostile to external and free trade (Marchant 2002). The Chinese market remained closed, as did the country, with foreign merchants forbidden from trading outside Canton. Diplomatic efforts to cement a trading agreement were repeatedly rejected and Britain, along with other imperial powers, was frustrated in its efforts to gain a commercial foothold in the country. There was, however, a Chinese market for opium and, in supplying this demand, British merchants were able to construct a triangular trade under which the cost of imported tea and other Chinese products was offset by the export of textiles and machinery from Britain to India and then exports of opium from India to China (McCoy 1972; Trocki 1999). The UK consequently acquired a powerful economic interest in the illicit opium trade with China and, underscoring this, the British government went to war with Chinese authorities in 1839 and 1857 in order to defend British smugglers.

The catalysts for both Sino-British conflicts were relatively minor incidents that prompted full-scale military deployments by the superior British navy. In the resulting peace agreements, Britain gained important territorial and commercial concessions. The 1842 Treaty of Nanking, concluded after the first conflict, opened the treaty ports of Amoy, Tinghai, Chunhai and Ningpo to the British and Britain gained Hong Kong. The Chinese did not, however, legalize the opium trade until after their second devastating defeat and peace negotiations in 1860.

Britain therefore succeeded in gaining control of the largest opium-producing country, India, and access to the largest opium-consuming country, China, through force and the exploitation of internal political weaknesses. In China, the Qing dynasty was vulnerable owing to its weak grip over the vast, unwieldy and ethnically diverse territory. The empire was plagued by banditry, the rise of secret societies and rebellions (Beeching 1975; Waley 1985). These included the Hakka revolt of 1855–58, the Taiping rebellion (1851–64) in which 20 million people died, the Nian rebellion (1853–68), the Miao rebellion (1855–57) and the Muslim rebellion (1862–73). These upheavals led to the displacement of peasants from the Shan, Wa and Miao ethnic groups from the opium poppy cultivating regions around Yunnan into neighbouring Myanmar, Thailand and Laos, where they subsequently introduced opium poppy cultivation and opium production for distribution back in mainland China and Southeast Asia (Michaud 1997).

The beginning of the end of the trade in opium China's legalization of opium had dramatic implications that were not anticipated by the European merchants. Having accepted opium as a legitimate commodity, the Chinese authorities allowed the cultivation and production of opium to re-establish itself in China. Demand for Indian opium consequently declined as Chinese production expanded and saturated the domestic market. This had devastating social consequences in China, where one in every four males was addicted to opium by the end of the century (Yongming 1999). As Indian opium lost its share of the market, the fiscal benefits accruing to the British from the trade declined. This led to a financial weakening of the Raj, a development that coincided with the rise of the independence movement within India (Ul Haq 2000; Trocki 2002). A second important development was the emergence of a class of Chinese entrepreneurs who invested heavily in domestic opium production and distribution. By contrast, European merchants were inadequately positioned in the Chinese cultivation and internal distribution chain to take advantage of legalization. Having previously concentrated on shipping and wholesale, they found themselves rapidly displaced from the distribution market (Rush 1990; Trocki 2002).

Legalizing opium did reduce the external pressures on the Chinese dynasty, but it exacerbated its internal problems. The weakness of the regime allowed the opium revenues to be 'captured' by regional warlords and political movements in cultivating areas that were opposed to the dynasty. As the economic and political importance of opium increased in the regions, so did cultivation levels. By 1906, China was producing an estimated 35,000 mt of raw opium, equivalent to 85 per cent of the world's supply (McCoy 1972). This marked a significant reversal of opium trading patterns, with the profits from cultivation, production and export shifting from the West to the East, a trend exacerbated by the sharp increase in the demand for opium in the West and North America. It was at this point that the USA launched its opium or 'drug diplomacy'. This was the first US initiative on the international stage. The USA pressed for an end to the opium trade, which it condemned as immoral and unethical. This position had significant support from Christian-based lobby groups around the world and it went against a long global history of unregulated opium use.

Drug consumption in the western world and the origins of US drug diplomacy are examined in the following chapter.

2 | The drift to regulation and the idea of prohibition

Drug consumption in the western market

Although China was the key opium consumer market, the commercialization of opium also had a dramatic impact in Europe and North America, where opium use increased from low levels in the sixteenth century to mass consumption by the end of the nineteenth century. The use of intoxicating substances in the western markets was based on the 'medical drug' and 'work drug' model. Opium poppy, for example, was produced in the Fens region in the east of England and it was consumed for pain relief.

The commercialization of opium use in Britain began with the launch of Sydenham's Laudanum in the 1680s. This early 'medicine' was a mixture of opium and wine and its popularity encouraged competition among apothecaries. A range of opium-based products subsequently emerged as increased volumes of raw opium became available and the cost of opium imports fell. By the mid-nineteenth century, opium-based patent medicines such as Gowan's Pneumonia Cure, Godfrey's Cordial, Dr. Moffett's Teethina and McMunn's Elixir were available without restriction and sold in commercial outlets such as grocery shops. Self-medication with opium was common to all social classes and the drug was routinely administered to babies and children. The wage-earning labour sector was a key market for these products. The opium preparations were used for the alleviation of diseases and infections that flourished in the overcrowded and squalid conditions of mass urbanization and factory labour (Berridge and Edwards 1981; Hodgson 2001).

The chemical revolution

OPIATES In the early nineteenth century the active principles in opium and coca were isolated, manufactured and commercialized and this dramatically redefined the scale and purpose of drug use as well as the range of intoxicating substances available. In 1803, the German chemist Friedrich Sertuerner isolated the opium pain-relieving analgesic. The alkaloid was called morphine and, in 1827, the German pharmaceutical firm E. Merck and Company began its commercial manufacture. Morphine-based products such as Winslow's Soothing Sirup, Children's Comfort, Dr. Seth Arnold's Cough Killer and One Day Cough Cure, the latter a mixture of morphine and cannabis, were marketed as a form of pain relief superior to opium. Morphine was also routinely administered to combatants in the American Civil War (1860–65) and the Franco-Prussian War (1870–71).

14

The opiate revolution progressed with the identification of diacetylmorphine by C. R. Wright in 1874. Synthesized from boiling morphine, it was ten times stronger than morphine. After the German scientist W. Dankwortt refined the work of Wright, the German company Bayer began commercial production in 1898. Diacetylmorphine was sold under the brand name Heroin and it was marketed as a cure for 'over-reliance' on morphine and a remedy for bronchial problems related to tuberculosis and pneumonia. Heroin was available as powder, lozenges, salts or tablets and it was initially a bigger commercial success than Aspirin, another pain-killing drug launched by Bayer in 1899. The market for opiates was not limited to Europe. The emerging pharmaceutical sector in Germany, Britain, Italy, the Netherlands, Switzerland and America competed aggressively for 'medical' markets in Asia and South America. Bayer, for example, sold Heroin in twenty-three countries, including China, which imported 10 tons from Germany in 1898. The chemical revolution consequently produced a new group of interests in the drug trade, with the pharmaceutical sector emerging as an important player in the global drug market. This in turn created new distribution and manufacturing chains and more complex relationships between cultivators, manufacturers, producers and consumers (McAllister 2000). Pharmaceutical interests in the drug trade extended from opiates and into cannabis. Parke Davis, Squibb, Lilly and Burroughs Welcome manufactured and marketed extracts of Indian cultivated cannabis (Brecher et al. 1972). Cocaine was also an important revenue generator for the pharmaceutical sector.

COCAINE Preceding the identification of diacetylmorphine, Albert Niemann isolated the active constituent of the coca leaf in 1859 and named it cocaine. Cocaine was commercialized by two pharmaceutical companies, Merck and the American firm Parke, Davis. By 1885 Merck was producing 30 kilograms (kg) of pure cocaine per year from Peruvian and Bolivian leaves; as production increased, prices declined and this made pure pharmaceutical cocaine widely available in Europe and America (Gootenberg 1999; Spillane 2000; Streatfield 2000). It was marketed as a cure for illnesses and 'psychological' problems ranging from nymphomania to morphine dependence. Following experiments in pain relief by Sigmund Freud, who publicly endorsed Merck's cocaine, the *British Medical Journal* recommended the drug for anaesthesia in eye surgery in 1884. As with developments in the opium sector, there was a flood of cocaine-based patented medical products. They included Ryno's Hay Fever and Catarrh Remedy and Agnew's Powder. Containing 99 per cent and 35 per cent pure pharmaceutical cocaine respectively, these two products were marketed as a cure for nasal congestion (Constable 2002; Streatfield 2000).

Before the cocaine market could develop, a central problem in the production process had to be overcome. Unlike opium, which was durable in transit, coca leaves rotted on transhipment from the Andes to manufacturing centres in

Europe and America. To overcome this, American and German pharmaceutical companies invested in coca paste manufacturing facilities in Latin America. This enabled them to complete the first stage of cocaine manufacture overseas. As it requires 100 kg of coca leaves to produce 1 kg of paste, by concentrating paste production in South America, the pharmaceutical companies were able to export higher volumes of coca paste to manufacturing facilities in the West, increasing the total volume of cocaine produced and available.

As the western cocaine market took off, the sector became highly lucrative for cultivator countries in South America. Seeking to exploit its comparative advantage in coca leaf cultivation, the Peruvian government devised a strategy for national development based on the promotion of the coca paste export sector. In Bolivia, the surge in demand for coca triggered changes to the scale and structure of cultivation as *criollos*, South American-born descendants of the Spanish, began to invest in the sector. There was also significant *criollo* encroachment into indigenous coca-cultivating territories and indigenous cultivators were forced off their land to make way for large-scale commercial cultivation (Walker 1996). This attempt to capitalize on the commercialization of cocaine was counter-productive. The increase in cultivation and coca paste manufacturing depressed prices. British and Dutch commercial interests added to these price pressures by transplanting coca leaf cultivation to Jamaica, Sri Lanka, Malaysia, India, Indonesia and British Guyana. The Dutch streamlined the process further, set-ting up cocaine manufacturing facilities in Indonesia following the introduction of the coca leaf to Java in 1900. By the turn of the century, the Dutch were the world's leading cocaine producer (Ashley 1975; Gootenberg 1999).

Sales of cocaine-based products surged in the second half of the nineteenth century. In 1863, the Corsican chemist Angelo Mariani introduced Vin Mariani, a mixture of coca leaves, wine and spices that was hugely popular in Europe, particularly France (Streatfeild 2000). Mariani also manufactured coca lozenges, pastels and tea. Coca-based stimulants found a receptive market in the United States, where they spawned imitators such as French Wine Coca, a mixture of wine and cocaine manufactured by the Atlanta pharmacist John Pemberton. Marketed as a 'brain-tonic', French Wine Coca was re-launched in 1886 as Coca-Cola after the alcohol prohibition movement objected to the wine content of the product (Pendergast 1993).

The recreational market The invention of the injecting syringe by the Scots doctor Alexander Wood in 1843 diversified and expanded the drug consumer market. The syringe revolutionized the administration of opiates and cocaine. Intra-muscular injection allowed the drug to cross the blood–brain barrier quickly, thereby producing a more intense and immediate effect. While the medical profession was the key market for the syringe, there was also consider-able consumer demand. For example, in the 1890s, the Sears Roebuck catalogue offered a syringe and vial of cocaine for the discerning cocaine consumer for $1.50.

Patent medicines, in addition to pure cocaine, opium, morphine and heroin, were freely available through retail sales in Europe and America for snorting, injecting and smoking. There was also a booming catalogue trade, with mail order ensuring that geography did not impede expansion of the market. Recreational drug taking did remain something of an elite and fringe pastime, with the lower classes looking to alcohol rather than opiates, cannabis or cocaine for intoxication and relaxation. Although drug use continued to be modelled on medical need, there was some recreational experimentation by elite, bohemian groups, literary and artistic figures and secret societies. This transformed non-medical use of drugs into a 'social signifier' that indicated rejection of mainstream society values (Keire 1998).

There were exceptions to the model of elite recreational drug use. In Western Europe, North and also South America, opium smoking was prevalent among Chinese migrant labourers who lived in the main port areas such as London, Rotterdam and San Francisco. The first opium 'dens' were opened in San Francisco at the end of the 1860s, with American opium imports rising in line with Chinese and domestic medicinal demand. Underscoring the scale of opium demand in the USA, opium imports increased from 32.8 mt in the 1860s to 298.1 mt by 1907 (Ul Haq 2000). The introduction of opium smoking and the advent of dens were not restricted to the USA. In all areas where there was a sizeable migrant Chinese community, from London and the port regions of the Netherlands to Mexico City, opium dens and recreational smoking existed.

The advent of control: Britain and America contrasted

The British experience The unregulated mass distribution, widespread use and intensive marketing of cannabis, opium and cocaine were gradually called into question. Somewhat ironically, given the country's role in the opium trade, Britain was at the forefront of moves to regulate the domestic distribution of drugs. The regulatory initiative was a product of the nascent welfare state system. In 1864, the remit of the British registrar general was extended from the registration of civil marriages to births and deaths. This revealed an underlying problem of accidental opiate poisoning, particularly among young children and babies. This in turn prompted government intervention (Berridge and Edwards 1981).

The resulting Pharmacy Act of 1868 did not restrict the sale or use of drugs; it simply required that opiates and cocaine be clearly labelled as poisons on products that contained them. The measure built on an earlier piece of legislation, the 1852 Apothecary Act, that had sought to professionalize pharmacology by creating the first statutory register of pharmacists. The 1868 legislation prevented individuals from calling themselves pharmacists or chemists unless they were registered with the Pharmaceutical Society. Pharmacists consequently acquired a professional vested interest in preventing breaches of the labelling requirements introduced in 1868 and as a result they became 'an unpaid, but interested, drug enforcement cadre scattered throughout Great Britain' (Musto n.d.). The subsequent decrease in opiate-related morbidity and drug consumption in the UK was linked to the 1868 legislation (Berridge and Edwards 1981; Musto n.d.).

The US experience: addiction and inaction Federal authorities in the USA did not move to regulate the distribution and consumption of opiates and cocaine in the second half of the nineteenth century. This was despite indications of drug-related problems in users, underpinned by a rise in per capita opiate consumption, which increased from 12 grains in 1840 to 52 grains in the mid-1890s. One grain of opium constituted an average single dose (Musto n.d.).

Public and medical understanding of dosage, addiction, tolerance, habituation and withdrawal were only just developing at this time. The English writer Thomas De Quincey's 1822 *Confessions of an English Opium Eater* was one of the first published accounts of drug dependence but as his experience was viewed as a product of individual debauchery, it did not prompt broader inquiry. Firmer evidence of the addictive potential of routinely administered drugs emerged in the USA following the Civil War of the 1860s. In the aftermath of the conflict, a phenomenon dubbed 'soldier's sickness' or the 'army disease' was identified. This was a craving for morphine after its administration for injury on the battlefield and it affected an estimated 400,000 former combatants of the Northern army (Ul Haq 2000: 40; Whitebread 1995). The largest constituency of addicts in the USA were white middle-class women. Addiction here stemmed from the prescription and intramuscular injection of morphine for 'problems of mood'. This was a catch-all term for a range of physical and psychological problems that included gynaecological infections and disease and depression (Courtwright 1982; Morgan 1981; Walker 1996: 39). By the end of the nineteenth century, addiction rates in the USA peaked, with an estimated 250,000 to 313,000 people addicted to opiates out of a population of 76 million (Courtwright 1982; Musto n.d.). Two-thirds of these were women and this created the perception that addiction was a specifically female problem (Keire 1998).

There was growing awareness of the toxic nature of these new medicines and their abuse potential in Western Europe and this supplemented information emerging in the USA. The potential for cocaine poisoning was revealed in a number of deaths that followed the administration of cocaine anaesthesia in Britain. The drug's habit-forming potential also became apparent, particularly in those prescribed cocaine as a cure for opiate abuse. Sigmund Freud revised his earlier belief, as published in the 1884 work *Über Coca*, that cocaine had no problematic side-effects after his friend and patient, the mathematician Ernst von Fleischl-Marxow, developed a dual addiction to cocaine and opium (Spillane

2000; Streatfeild 2000). By 1886, the *British Medical Journal* had retracted its earlier endorsement of cocaine in medical practice.

Problems associated with the use of heroin were identified within a year of the drug's launch, when Horatio Wood noted that the dosage had to be increased for the drug to remain effective in regular users. European and American medical journals began to address problems of habituation and addiction to heroin, termed 'heroinism'. By 1905 there was an accumulation of evidence that showed terminating heroin use was difficult and that dependent users would quickly graduate from sniffing to injection. The prescription of heroin for morphine dependence was also recognized as having created a large problem of heroin addiction (*Bulletin on Narcotics* 1953). When the American Medical Association approved heroin for medical use in 1906, it explicitly emphasized the habit-forming potential of the drug.

Understanding the US (non-)response Although the USA emerged as the champion of global drug prohibition in the first decade of the twentieth century, the federal government did not intervene to regulate the domestic market in the nineteenth century. This was linked to four factors. The most important was the constitutional separation of power between federal and state government. This limited the authority of the federal administration to foreign policy, inter-state commerce and revenue-raising measures such as taxation. All remaining powers, including policing, criminal and civil law and the regulation of trade and transport, fell under the jurisdiction of the individual states. The states zealously guarded their legislative autonomy, particularly those in the south of the country, and this impeded the introduction of national, federal legislation to regulate cocaine and opiates (Whitebread 1995).

Further obstacles to the development of regulatory initiatives were the organizational weakness of the American Medical Association and the American Pharmaceutical Association and the economic leverage of the patent medicine sector. Patent medicine manufacturers were the largest advertiser in the US print media in the nineteenth century and they used their financial influence to block the introduction of labelling requirements. In advertising contracts signed with publishers it was stipulated that contracts would be voided if drug regulations were introduced in the state where printing took place (Berridge and Edwards 1981; Musto n.d.). A final but significant explanation for the lack of regulation was that drug use and drug-related problems were not seen as significant in the USA at this time. Addiction was viewed as a tragic but private problem. The real issue of concern in nineteenth-century America was alcohol.

The US modernization experience: tension and protest

An understanding of the campaign to prohibit alcohol led by Christian groups in the USA in the nineteenth century is pivotal to an understanding of the later campaign to prohibit drugs that developed in America and which was internationalized through US drug diplomacy (Bewley-Taylor 2001). The campaign for alcohol prohibition overlapped significantly with the later campaign against drugs in terms of group membership and leadership, message, mobilization strategy and the imagery of substance misuse evoked in the two campaigns.

Alcohol prohibition in America was a specific response to the unique tensions generated by the economic modernization process. It was influenced by the religious and ideological values of the period and it was inspired by an idealized vision of the American nation. Although other countries, such as Finland and Sweden, experimented with alcohol prohibition, the US prohibition movement had specific, indigenous characteristics that shaped its religious, political and economic worldview (Levine 1993). The subsequent global extension of drug prohibition despite the unique roots of prohibition thinking within American culture raises questions about the appropriateness and legitimacy of the strategy in other country contexts. Further to this, although prohibition ideas and values developed in the USA in the nineteenth century, the principle was institutionalized in the control regime that developed in the twentieth century. Prohibition thinking remains the cornerstone of international drugs policy in the twenty-first century. The conceptual frameworks that are used to understand and respond to drugs and drug consumption are therefore over a century old and they were framed in a period of colonial enterprise, social tension, racism and a lack of medical and scientific understanding (Sinha 2001).

Modernity in the USA: progress and conflict The alcohol prohibition movement thrived in the uncertainty and chaos of the American modernization process (Goode and Ben Yehuda 1994). As the country shifted from a rural-based agricultural economy towards urbanization and industrialization in the latter half of the nineteenth century, acute tensions based on class, race, the rural–urban divide, religion and gender were generated. These in turn catalysed the emergence of numerous lobby groups, including the alcohol prohibition movement that pressed for federal government regulation of the economy and society.

THE ECONOMIC DIVIDE Instability and lobby group activity were particularly pronounced during a dislocating spurt of economic growth between 1870 and 1900 known as the Gilded Age. During this period a small number of politically connected entrepreneurial families, such as the Vanderbilt, Carnegie, Rockefeller, Hearst and Duke dynasties, assumed control of the emerging transport, energy, manufacturing and media sectors. This accumulation of wealth by the so-called 'robber barons' ran parallel with the emergence of stark inequalities within American society (Josephson 1962; McCraw 2005; Porter 1992). Amid concerns that economic divisions would destabilize the country, the anti-trust movement successfully pressed for federal government regulation of the economy. The movement built popular support for its campaign through the use of powerful imagery that equated the vulnerability of the population at the hands of monopoly economic interests to the enslavement of African Americans. Economic regulation by the federal government was presented as a necessary and fundamentally moral act that was equivalent to manumission.

RACIAL TENSIONS AND PIG-TAILED YELLOW DEMONS Racial antagonisms and anti-immigrant hostilities were potent during this period. By 1880, the population of North America was 50.1 million, of whom 6.6 million were foreign born. African Americans and immigrants from countries such as Ireland, Italy, Russia and China produced an abundance of cheap labour and capital but while immigrants were easy to absorb during economic expansion, social problems emerged during downturns. During these periods, racial tension and suspicion of foreign cultures were mobilized by white Americans opposed to immigration on racial, economic and philosophical grounds. Social Darwinist and eugenicist ideas stressing the naturalness of racial hierarchy and the dangers of racial intermingling that were popular during this era combined with deep-seated racial prejudices to produce a backlash against the African American and immigrant communities.

Racism was institutionalized through the introduction of legislative measures that discriminated against minority groups. Despite the formal abolition of slavery in 1865 and the introduction of supporting legal and constitutional rights, the southern states passed the 'Jim Crow' laws that neutered progressive federal reforms and segregated blacks from whites (Vann Woodward 1974). The Chinese community was a particular focus of anti-immigrant and racist mobilization. Chinese immigration to the USA had increased as a result of the 1868 Burlingame Treaty. Lauded at the time as a breakthough in US–Chinese relations, this provided US commercial interests with access to the Chinese market, and in exchange the USA allowed unlimited Chinese immigration to America. Burlingame faced stiff domestic resistance. The American Federation of Labour was active in the campaign against the treaty and Chinese immigrants. The organization's president Samuel Gompers, author of the 1902 publication *Some Reasons for Chinese Exclusion: Meat Versus Rice; American Manhood Against Asiatic Coolieism – Which Shall Survive?*, argued that the Chinese were an inferior race and that their presence had to be resisted for the benefit of the American nation. This built on earlier anti-Chinese arguments such as Dr Arthur Stout's 1862 work *Chinese Immigration and the Physiological Cause of Decay of a Nation* that portrayed the Chinese as dirty, diseased and a threat to the racial integrity of the USA.

The Workingmen's Party also promoted fear of the 'yellow peril'. The platform of the group was 'The Chinese Must Go!', and after it won control of the mayor's office in San Francisco in 1879, 'Chinatown', a term coined for the neighbourhood where Chinese immigrants made their home, was declared a health menace. Hundreds of Chinese businesses were burnt and ransacked and there were anti-Chinese riots in Washington in 1886 and in Los Angeles in 1871, during which fifteen Chinese men were lynched (Hill 1973). The 'scare' campaign around the Chinese extended to warnings against their employment in domestic service as this would allow them to spread their Oriental diseases and unnatural habits among American children (Miller 1969). American Protestant missionaries in China were influential in developing the stereotype of the 'godless', dirty Chinese. Writings in missionary publications such as the *Herald Missionary* and *North China Daily News* portrayed the Chinese as sexually perverted, violent and idolatrous (Metzger 2003).

AMERICA'S FIRST DRUG LAWS In response to the wave of anti-Chinese feeling, over thirty pieces of legislation restricting the right of Chinese people to marry, own property and practise certain professions were introduced at the state and federal level in the 1870s and 1880s, but it was the Chinese practice of opium smoking that was the focus of particular opprobrium and legislative action. Starting in San Francisco in 1875, eleven states banned the use of opium for smoking by Chinese nationals. Federal legislation introduced in 1880 prohibited Chinese people from importing opium and a second law ten years later forbade Chinese nationals from processing opium for smoking, a measure intended to prevent opium dens from operating. The issue of general opiate and cocaine use was not addressed and the legislation did not apply to non-Chinese people. While the UK government regulated the market in dangerous drugs to prevent public harm, the first anti-drugs legislation introduced in the USA was motivated by racial prejudice. Although the majority of American opiate addicts were middle-class white females, the drug became intimately associated with the Chinese and its use was linked to sexually perverse acts and the degradation of white women. The media played an important role in disseminating the image of the 'pig-tailed yellow demon' and the release of films like *Chinese Opium Den* by Thomas Edison's company in 1893 cemented the popular view of the Chinese lifestyle as dangerous, lurid and opium-fuelled.

THE RURAL–URBAN DIVIDE Mass immigration and industrialization posed a serious challenge to traditional values and community structures and a deep cleavage between rural and urban areas developed. Rural communities were suspicious of expanding new towns such as New York, Chicago and San Francisco. These were populated by immigrants and male labourers and were notorious for prostitution, drinking and gambling, all of which were associated with the rise of a new institution, the saloon bar (Asbury 2002). The rapid growth of the alcohol industry in the 1870s, the introduction of the saloon and the relationship between drinking and vice catalysed the emergence and radicalization of puritan Christian groups committed to abolishing the trade in alcohol.

The alcohol prohibition movement and experience

Evangelical Christian organizations provided a sense of stability, certainty and unity for white Americans when national identities and the nation itself were undergoing the profound transformations discussed. The alcohol prohibition campaign was an integral element of this Christian organizational network and it fed off and into a broader search for those responsible for perverting and destabilizing the American way of life (Behr 1996; Pegram 1999).

The history of the anti-alcohol movement in America is divided into two phases. The 'early' phase started in the late eighteenth century. During this period concern over consumption of spirits led church authorities to preach restraint in alcohol use. The message of responsible drinking reflected a broad popular concern with the spread of drunken and disorderly behaviour among men. The American Society for the Promotion of Temperance, formed in 1826, sought to educate people about the dangers of alcohol and to persuade men not to drink.

There was a dramatic departure from classical Christian thought on drinking in the second half of the nineteenth century. This occurred as more puritanical values gained influence and public debate shifted away from post-Civil War reconstruction and towards consideration of the national destiny (Bischke 2003; Clark 1976). Concluding that moderation was impossible for the individual to achieve and a false concept when applied to alcohol, evangelical Protestant leaders called for a legal ban on the production and sale of alcohol. This was informed by 'causality attribution', in which the danger of alcohol was seen to stem directly from the nature of the substance (Cohen 2003a). Alcohol was perceived as an evil liquid that was quite literally diabolical. The evangelical movement claimed that once alcohol had been consumed, it sapped men of their power, dignity and morality. Drinking alcohol was not only portrayed as unchristian, it was also un-American, with those truly committed to a Christian America impelled to join a patriotic fight against the satanic force of alcohol (Asbury 1950; Cohen 2003a; Pegram 1999).

In order to achieve its goal of a complete ban on alcohol, the evangelical movement adopted new organizational structures, political strategies and mobilization techniques. In 1869 the Prohibition Party was formed and this was followed by the creation of the Women's Christian Temperance Union in 1874 and the Anti-Saloon League in 1893. These organizations pressured for government action against the alcohol industry and mobilized public awareness campaigns and speaking tours to build support. In an early form of direct action, prayer meetings were convened outside government offices, saloons and alcohol manufacturing plants. Women played a central organizational and participatory role in these vigils, with the prohibition campaign serving as a channel for political engagement before the introduction of female suffrage in 1920 (Gilbert Murdock 1998).

In terms of ideology, the prohibition movement rejected individualism and liberal political values. Stress was placed on the importance of the nation and the community over the rights of the individual. A central theme was that freedom of choice had to be restricted for the greater good of American society (Austin Kerr 1973). For critics, this value system went against the fundamentals of the American constitution and the liberal philosophy underpinning it. Opponents argued that the campaign to ban alcohol was a Trojan horse that shielded the evangelical movement's real aim of redefining the values and direction of American society. According to one critic: 'Prohibition is merely the title of the movement. Its real purpose is of a religious, sectarian character' (Andreae 1915).

The prohibition movement borrowed liberally from the imagery of other lobby groups. The symbolism of slavery developed and disseminated by the anti-trust movement had a particular utility in the alcohol prohibition campaign (Keire 2001). The notion of individuals being unwillingly shackled and enslaved by coercive forces was subsumed by prohibition's leading figures such as Richmond P. Hobson of the Anti-Saloon League. Hobson talked of 'five million' Americans coerced into drinking by the brewing industry in his stock congressional and public speech against alcohol, 'The Great Destroyer'. A second key theme of the prohibition campaign was that the 'immoral' alcohol industry was deliberately targeting innocent American youths, with the aim of ensnaring them into a life of alcoholism. The prohibition movement also mobilized racial antagonisms to build support. Social Darwinist ideas ran through the speeches and literature of the campaign. Hobson claimed that: 'Liquor will actually make a brute out of a Negro, causing him to commit unnatural crimes. The effect is the same on the white man, though the white man being further evolved it takes longer time to reduce him to the same level' ('The Great Destroyer'). Lager beer drinking was also linked to European immigrants, further developing the idea that alcohol consumption went against the national interest and the national character (Behr 1996; Gray 2000; Kobler 1993).

Prohibition in practice: lessons not learned The constitutional separation of powers between federal and state authorities prevented the government in Washington from introducing a national ban on alcohol, so the only route to national legislation was amendment of the constitution. This was achieved in 1919 when a two-thirds majority in favour of alcohol prohibition were elected to the 1916 Congress and the Eighteenth Amendment was introduced. This paved the way for national prohibition through the Volstead Act. The production and distribution of alcohol was banned in the USA from 1919 until 1933, when the Eighteenth Amendment was repealed. Supporters of prohibition did not interpret repeal as a repudiation of the principle that dangerous substances should be banned and even though there were important lessons to be learned from the alcohol prohibition experience, these were not accepted by Protestant

Christian groups which focused their energies on achieving the prohibition of 'narcotic' drugs.

The alcohol prohibition experience demonstrated that the criminalization of private acts did not prevent them from continuing. The ban on alcohol served only to create a thriving illicit trade, with illegal supply meeting illegal demand. Testifying before the judicial hearings on the National Prohibition Law in 1926, the New York congressional representative Fiorella H. La Guardia argued: 'I will concede that the saloon was odious but now we have delicatessen stores, poolrooms, drug stores, millinery shops, private parlors, and 57 other varieties of speak-easies selling liquor and flourishing' (Bailey 1968). The incentive to produce and supply alcohol illegally stemmed from the lure of high profits, and illicit alcohol production was only lucrative because it was illegal and therefore carried a financial risk 'premium'. Because the trade operated underground, it was also not subject to federal taxation and this increased the profits accruing to illicit producers and suppliers. In his testimony, La Guardia estimated that state and federal authorities lost in the region of $1 billion in taxes on alcohol to criminal organizations. A key lesson in this respect was that prohibition could not prevent the market dynamics of supply and demand from operating.

Another lesson was that policing alcohol prohibition was impractical unless it took the form of constant and highly intrusive surveillance. Even large increases in the enforcement budget did not enable those responsible for policing prohibition to reduce consumption or supply. Between 1921 and 1930, the alcohol enforcement budget rose from $7 million to $15 million but the trade in illicit alcohol continued to expand. Enforcing prohibition was also tactically challenging. Even when officials from the Internal Revenue Service identified and closed down illicit drinking venues, new ones opened and when small-scale illegal distributors were arrested, larger criminal syndicates moved in to absorb the vacated market share. This in turn led to the emergence of large-scale Jewish and Sicilian criminal syndicates that were infinitely harder to police because they had the financial capacity to protect their markets through violence and corruption. When alcohol prohibition ended, these large criminal groups moved into another lucrative enterprise, the supply of illicit drugs. A fourth vital lesson in this context was that enforcement officials were highly susceptible to corruption. La Guardia calculated that at least one million dollars a day was paid in graft and corruption to federal, state and local officers, a situation that was 'not only intolerable, but [...] demoralizing and dangerous to organized government'.

Alcohol prohibition in the USA also demonstrated that criminalizing consumable substances increased rather than reduced the risk of harm to society. It was estimated that 30,000 people died, were paralysed or blinded following the consumption of methyl alcohol-based concoctions. Prohibition also showed that there had to be effective multilateral co-operation between countries for a national ban on alcohol to be enforceable. This was acutely difficult to achieve owing to the powerful financial incentives created by the massive and illicit US market. Major alcohol smuggling networks into the USA developed through Canada, the Caribbean and Mexico and although the Mexican government did support US prohibition, with the administrations of President Alvaro Obregon (1920–24) and Plutarco Elias Calles (1924–28) decreeing prohibition of alcohol production in Mexico in the 1920s, by the middle of that decade Mexico was one of the largest beer producers in the world.

There was a weight of historical evidence that showed that the prohibition of any substance, be it coffee, tobacco or alcohol, was counter-productive (Wild 2005). Despite this, and the evident failure of alcohol prohibition in the USA, evangelical Christian groups continued to promote prohibition as a viable solution to modern social problems.

3 | From regulation to control: the internationalization of drug prohibition

The anti-opium campaign in Britain

While the campaign against alcohol preoccupied Christian organizations in the USA, in Britain it was the trade in opium that was the focus for Christian-based political agitation. Lobby groups committed to ending 'the trade in misery' emerged in the second half of the nineteenth century. The most influential of these was the Anglo-Oriental Society for the Suppression of the Opium Trade (SSOT), founded with the patronage of the Quaker movement in 1874.

The society's opposition to the trade was based on moral and ethical arguments. It claimed that Britain's promotion of the opium trade in South Asia degraded the physical and spiritual health of Asian societies. The anti-opium campaigners urged the British government to end its role in the 'ungodly' enterprise and forgo the revenues accruing to the colonial administration in India (Johnson 1975). Society members distributed pamphlets, published their arguments in book form (Lodwick 1996; Brereton 1882; Ormerod 1876) and convened public meetings to raise awareness and understanding of the British government's opium policy in Asia. The society's president, Joseph Pease, also encouraged prayer vigils known as the 'worship strategy' as used by the alcohol prohibition movement in the USA.

The SSOT generated popular support but lacked the influence in Parliament necessary for policy change. British politicians did not have a generally favourable view of the trade in opium and both of the opium conflicts with China were condemned in Parliament on the grounds that they would destabilize China and the international balance of power. The Prime Minister, Lord Palmerston, narrowly survived a censure motion during the first Opium War and he was defeated by a second motion introduced during the second war of 1856 (Gilbert 2003). The moral debate as to whether or not it was acceptable to export an addictive substance to an unwilling recipient state gained momentum only after China was flooded with domestically produced opium and dependency and addiction had spiralled.

Ending Britain's role in the opium trade: the obstacles It was profoundly difficult for Britain to withdraw from the opium trade. The first problem was financial. If the colonial administration in India ceased or restricted opium poppy cultivation and opium export, this would have meant the loss of a vital public revenue stream and it would have affected private British commercial interests (Brook and Tadashi Wakabayashi 2000; Trocki 1999; Ul Haq 2000). Alternative ways of financing the British presence in Asia would have to be devised and private investors and traders compensated. This was an unpalatable proposition in the context of the *laissez-faire* economic philosophy of the period. These financial considerations also led politicians to change their views on the trade from one of opposition to support once they moved into government and this further weakened the leverage of the Society in Parliament (Sanello and Travis Hanes III 2002).

A second challenge was the pervasive influence of British opium trading companies such as Jardine, Matheson and Co. and Dent and Co. They enjoyed privileged access to government and were highly effective at 'spinning' the virtues of the opium trade through their own pamphlets and mass meetings. The defence of the trade was premised on two claims: that it contributed to the prosperity of Britain and that the ill effects of mass opium use in China were exaggerated. It was argued that even if Britain ended opium exports, rival suppliers would fill their position in the market and the 'trade in misery' would persist. The intellectual dominance of free trade ideas worked in favour of the existing opium policy. Even if politicians found the trade in opium unethical, they could not support restrictions on the grounds of economic principle. This was the case with the Liberal Party and it prevented prominent anti-opium politicians such as Samuel Smith and William Caine from building party support for their campaign. Legislative initiatives to reform Britain's role in the opium trade consequently floundered, as did Bills presented in 1875, 1876, 1880, 1881, 1883, 1886, 1891 and 1893 (Gilbert 2003).

Internal schisms further weakened the international anti-opium campaign that the SSOT had been successful in developing in collaboration with Christian missionary groups in Asia. The centrality of the missionary groups to the Asian anti-opium campaign was underscored by the fact that no lobby emerged in those countries where missionaries were not permitted to work such as Tibet, Bhutan or Sikkim (McKay 2003). The British campaign did not, however, endorse the Asian movement's proposition that the British government should compensate Indian cultivators in the event that the trade was terminated. This prevented a more effective international campaign from taking shape.

The anti-opium lobby in India Indian opposition to the British trade in opium developed in the 1870s. Philosophers such as Keshub Chandra Sen and Dadabhai Naoroji questioned the morality of the trade and drew this into a wider critique of British colonialism and its impact on Indian society. The anti-opium campaign was subsumed within a broader temperance movement and the priority of that organization was regulation of the alcohol trade. The British had stimulated the development of the Indian brewing industry and taxes on alcohol were as important a revenue stream as the taxes on opium. They contributed in the region of

15 per cent of administrative revenues (Gilbert 2003; Gusfield 1986; Trocki 1999). By 1904 there were 301 temperance associations across the country and these ultimately evolved into the movement for independence from the British that was led by Mohandas Karamchand Gandhi. Parallel anti-opium organizations also sprang up in other British colonies such as Sri Lanka and Burma. In Sri Lanka, where there were an estimated 20,000 opium addicts by 1903, hostility to opium retail outlets united Singhalese Buddhist, Tamil and other minority ethnic and religious groups into a single anti-opium campaign (Ul Haq 2000).

The South Asian campaign had no chance of success independent of the European anti-opium movement as its influence over the colonial administration was negligible. It also lacked popular support, particularly in India where opium was viewed as a valuable and relatively harmless substance. Temperance agitation and by default the anti-opium campaign were also countered by a strong lobby in defence of existing alcohol policy led by Indian private sector interests. The private sector was in turn protected by the Indian National Congress Party, which was working with the British government (Gilbert 2003).

The Royal Commission on Opium The Final Report of the Royal Commission on Opium published in 1895 was a serious blow to the international anti-opium campaign. The Commission had been established in 1893 in response to agitation by the SSOT. Its terms of reference were limited to an assessment of the impact on cultivators, producers and revenue streams of restricting opium exports to medical and scientific need. The Final Report supported continuity of opium policy in its existing free form and dismissed concerns over recreational opium use in India, which it found to be 'comparatively rare and novel' (Reports of Commissioners 1895).

The tone and conclusion of the Report reflected the continuity of British drug policy in its colonies. The Indian Hemp Commission of 1893 had concluded that moderate cannabis consumption had no injurious effect and it rejected the need for regulation. The findings of the Opium Commission legitimized the British government's position and, despite the lobbying of the international anti-opium campaign and criticism that the Report was a whitewash, there was no immediate change in policy.

Enter America: the anti-opium campaign of the US government

Twelve years after the Royal Commission had reported, Britain negotiated a bilateral opium export reduction agreement with China. But as incremental moves were made in the direction of diplomatically negotiated agreements to regulate the trade, the opium debate was transformed by the entry of the USA. This intervention had revolutionary consequences. Through the opium question, the USA came to define international policy not only on opium but on all naturally-occurring and synthetic drugs. The position that the country took was prohibitionist. The USA rejected the possibility that there could be any compromise with the opium 'evil' and it did not accept that a gradual reduction in supply was a viable or morally correct strategy. The US intervention consequently prevented experiments in the regulation of the trade from developing and it shifted the international community towards a model of drug prohibition and control.

The importance of the anti-opium issue to the US government was significant given that the issue generated negligible domestic interest. Further to this, the federal government had no colonial interest in, or experience of, the trade in opium, unlike the Europeans. However, this situation changed in 1899 when the USA acquired its first territorial possession in Southeast Asia and this provided the USA with an important opening into the politics of the opium trade.

The dawn of US imperialism Like their British counterparts, American missionaries in China publicized the opium-related social problems they encountered throughout the nineteenth century. Hyperbolic claims of 'opium devils' failed to inspire the US government to engage with the issue on moral grounds and served only to fuel anti-Chinese sentiment within the USA. The American government was forced to address the opium question when the country assumed control of the Philippines following America's defeat of Spain in the Spanish American War of 1898. The physical conflict was focused in the Caribbean but under the terms of the ensuing Treaty of Paris the Spanish ceded the Philippines and Guam to the USA in addition to Cuba and Puerto Rico.

It was expected that the US government would grant independence to these territories after their centuries-long struggles against Spanish colonialism. Cuba was granted independence under a congressional resolution of 1898 but on the Philippines and Puerto Rico, the Republican president William McKinley adopted a different tack. He declined to grant their independence and the USA assumed direct control. This was legitimized on the grounds that the USA had a responsibility to 'civilize' the inferior people of these territories and therefore should assume the 'white man's burden'. In McKinley's view, these countries had been entrusted to the USA 'by the providence of God' (Presidential address, February 1899).

The decision was imposed on an ideologically divided US society and it polarized an already intense partisan debate on foreign policy (Ignatieff 2003; *Monthly Review* 2003). Prior to the Spanish American War, the USA had been preoccupied with the unification of the national territory. Although the USA maintained an inward focus, it guarded its South and Central American 'backyard' from European challengers; the Monroe Doctrine, issued in 1832, excluded European powers from the American hemisphere. This did not constitute territorial aggrandisement and no South American country was incorporated into an American empire on the lines of the British, French, Spanish or Dutch models. But by the close of the nineteenth century, powerful agricultural and manufacturing interests within the Republican Party sought to reshape US foreign policy and they lobbied for overseas expansion on the lines of the European colonial model.

The Spanish American War galvanized public interest in foreign policy questions and it stimulated concern over external threats to the American nation. Magazines such as William Randolph Hearst's *New York Journal* proselytized in favour of the empire-building campaign and whipped up fears of invasion by inferior foreign nations to pressure federal government action. In response to criticism by supporters of the imperial project that he was weak and ineffective, President McKinley ordered the annexation of Hawaii in 1898. This secured American control of territory outside of the mainland for the first time in US history (Coffman 2003).

The Democratic Party and William Jennings Bryan, the party's unsuccessful candidate in the presidential contest of 1900, opposed empire-building. For Jennings Bryan, the pursuit of empire was dependent on the use and glorification of violence. This was perceived as having damaging consequences for the USA as 'militarism will inevitably [...] turn the thoughts of our young men from the arts of peace to the science of war' (Democratic National Convention, 1900). The Anti-Imperialist League emerged as the main campaign organization for those opposed to the pretensions of empire. It rejected colonialism as a profoundly amoral and unethical enterprise and argued that the concept of American imperialism went against the Republic's foundational ideas of democracy and freedom (Adler 1898; Bouvier 2001).

The Philippines Opium Commission, 1903 When the US government assumed control of the Philippines, it inherited an opium retail system that had been administered by the Spanish for centuries. There were 190 government-licensed opium smoking dens in Manila alone (Ul Haq 2000: 45). Because administration of the Philippines came directly under the authority of the federal government in Washington, it was forced to decide, for the first time, a national position on opium sales and consumption.

The initial response of the American Governor of the Philippines, William Howard Taft, was to renew the licences of the opium outlets, with the revenue they generated to be used for education spending. The proposal provoked a backlash from the American missionary movement, including from the Protestant Episcopal Bishop of Manila, Charles H. Brent, and the Reverend Wilbur Crafts, the president of the International Reform Bureau (IRB), the main American missionary organization. The IRB had been outraged by the findings of the British Royal Commission on Opium and, in response to its Final Report, had collated data from 700 US-educated doctors in China to demonstrate the injurious effect of opium consumption. This IRB report became the foundation of a vigorous campaign against Taft's proposal that succeeded in prompting President Theodore Roosevelt, who assumed office after McKinley's assassination, to convene an Opium Commission to determine US policy in the Philippines.

The commission comprised a three-man panel headed by Brent. It had a wider mandate than the British Royal Commission on Opium, with its remit extending to consideration of the social harm caused by opium use, which the commission investigated in nine Southeast Asian countries. Contradicting the Royal Commission, the Philippines Commission found that the unregulated sale of opium had grave effects on the health and moral capacity of users and it recommended that the import, sale and use of opium should be strictly regulated and dispensed on the basis of medical need only (McAllister 2000).

The recommendation was adopted by the US administration and a three-year transition timetable was put in place during which US authorities gradually phased out the unregulated use of opium. Over 12,000 non-Filipino residents, largely Chinese migrants, registered for the rehabilitation scheme. This was a triumph for the prohibition lobby and it enhanced the influence of the Christian missionary organizations over the Roosevelt administration (McAllister 2000: 27; Musto 1991; Ul Haq 2000).

US drug diplomacy After the Philippines Opium Commission had concluded, the missionary network successfully lobbied Roosevelt to convene an international opium conference with Britain and China. Brent and Crafts argued that without action to stem the flow of opium imports into the Philippines, the US administration would not be able to eliminate non-medical use. This emphasis on 'supply-side' solutions was of enormous significance in terms of the future shape of the international drug control model. It also had implications for the conduct of US policy as it de facto provided a rationale for US intervention in supply countries. The supply-side-focused argument developed by the prohibition lobby was based on the idea that the USA could 'call upon the world to choke off at the source substances we wanted to keep from flowing inward across our boundaries' (King 1972). Demand for drugs was not seen to be the primary driver of consumption. Instead, it was the supply of available drugs that was conceptualized as causing demand.

There were two additional benefits stemming from US engagement in the international opium campaign. First, by criticizing the opium trade on the international stage, the Republican government was able to demonstrate that imperialism could serve a higher moral end and that the US empire worked in the interests of its subjects. Second, drug diplomacy provided the Roosevelt administration with an opportunity to construct an alliance with the Chinese that could be in the commercial interest of America. Brent's proposal followed the signing of a new trade agreement between China and America in 1903 but tensions between the two countries persisted as a result of the treatment of Chinese nationals in the USA (Bewley-Taylor 2001). In the view of Hamilton Wright, the

US Opium Commissioner in the State Department, an anti-opium alliance with the Chinese could be 'used as oil to smooth the troubled water of our aggressive commercial policy there' (Musto 1991). Strengthening Chinese–American relations was considered imperative due to the increased presence of Russia and Japan in the region and a dramatic change in Anglo-Chinese relations that threatened to deepen ties between the two countries. The Sino-British Ten-Year Agreement of 1907 catalysed this change.

The triumph of the British anti-opium lobby: the Ten-Year Agreement Indignation over the Final Report of the Royal Commission on Opium, and the release of the Final Report of the Philippines Opium Commission, reinvigorated the anti-opium campaign in Britain. The British parliamentary elections of 1906 reflected this change, with 250 supporters of the anti-opium campaign returned to Parliament. The new Liberal Government flagged its intention to re-examine British participation in the opium trade in the context of strong domestic and Southeast Asian political pressure and a decline in Indian opium export revenues. Concurrent with this development in Britain, the Empress of China launched a ten-year campaign to suppress opium poppy cultivation and opium consumption. This reversal of the post-Opium War policy was initiated in 1906. It was supported by Chinese anti-opium groups that were mobilized by the political elite and utilized by the Qing dynasty to extend its influence in remote provinces where its authority was under threat (Yongming 1999).

In order to prevent Indian-produced opium imports supplanting domestic supplies, the Chinese looked to negotiate a reduction in Indian opium exports to China with the British. This advance came at an opportune time given developments in Britain, and it resulted in the Ten-Year Agreement of 1907. Under the accord, Britain undertook to reduce opium exports from India to China by 10 per cent per year from 1908. This was conditional upon the Chinese authorities reducing domestic opium poppy cultivation at the same rate and independent verification of Chinese progress in meeting its targets (McAllister 2000). The bilateral agreement was enormously successful, with the Chinese making substantial progress in reducing opium supplies and consumption through a campaign that drew heavily on nationalist rhetoric and slogans (Yongming 1999). President Taft, successor to Roosevelt, was moved to congratulate the Chinese government on its 'remarkable progress and admirable efforts toward the eradication of the opium evil' in his first annual message in December 1909.

The Shanghai Conference of 1909 and its impact

As the British government was already re-examining its national opium policy, it was willing to attend the proposed US conference on the opium trade initiated by Bishop Brent, but two conditions were set for attendance. First, all countries with an interest in the trade had to be invited on the basis that any agreement negotiated by Britain, the USA and China would fail as rival suppliers would absorb the British export share. Ultimately, all of the main international powers attended including France, Italy, Germany, Japan, Persia, the Netherlands, Portugal, Siam, Austria Hungary and Russia. The only significant absence was the Turkish Ottoman Empire, which refused to participate. A second American concession to the British was that any agreement reached in Shanghai would be non-binding.

It is worth considering the size of the opium sector when the USA convened this breakthrough conference. Opium poppy cultivation had been commercialized for nearly three hundred years and it extended across a vast arc of territory from Asia to the Balkan and Mediterranean regions of Europe. Opium production was at an all-time high, with 41,624 mt produced in 1907. The bulk of this originated in China, which produced 35,364 mt with the remainder supplied by the Southwest Asian countries of Turkey, Iran, India and Afghanistan (6,258 mt). A small quantity, less than 2 mt, was produced in Southeast Asia. Local, regional and central economies in these cultivation and production areas were reliant on the opium export revenues and participation in the opium economy was an important source of employment and security in these agricultural-based societies.

Conflicts of interests: prohibition or regulation? The Shanghai Conference revealed fundamental divisions between the USA and European countries on the question of how the damage caused by the opium trade could be contained. These divisions 'remained central points of contention for decades' (McAllister 2000: 29). Bishop Brent assumed the presidency of the Shanghai meeting and another prominent prohibitionist, the US Opium Commissioner Dr Hamilton Wright, led the US delegation. The aim of the USA was to gain recognition from opium-exporting countries for the opium control policies that it had imposed in the Philippines. The American delegation pressed for global opium poppy cultivation, opium production and use to be limited to medical and scientific need. Illustrating the prohibitionist thrust of the US delegation, Hamilton Wright went so far as to propose that non-medical use of opium be made a criminal offence.

There was support for the principle of regulation of the trade and, in the nine non-binding resolutions that emerged from the meeting, delegates agreed to consider controls on opium production and smoking in colonial Asia. Consideration of the issue did not translate into a commitment to action and this reflected the gap between the USA and other countries. The majority of states attending Shanghai were either cultivating countries or had a large domestic pharmaceutical lobby. As a result, they had a financial vested interest in an unregulated opium market and this diminished enthusiasm for controls on the trade. The USA by contrast was a consumer country. Aside from a comparatively small pharmaceutical sector, it had no major interest in the opium market and, unlike the other countries, would have incurred only minor revenue losses if restrictions on opium were implemented. The Europeans also rejected the idea that the trade could be prohibited. Their experience of prohibition demonstrated that limiting supply encouraged smuggling and the growth of illicit markets (McAllister 2000).

The significance of Shanghai As conference delegates did not have plenipotentiary powers, Shanghai did not catalyse changes to the structure of the international opium trade, but the conference was of enormous importance for the following reasons. First, it laid the foundations for international dialogue on opium and other drugs, with Brent successfully pushing for a follow-up international meeting that was held in The Hague in 1911. Shanghai also allowed the American prohibition movement to shape the terms of the international debate on drugs. In this respect, the prohibition lobby established two crucial principles that were subsequently institutionalized: (i) that the use of opium should be limited to legitimate medical need; and (ii) that a reduction in non-medical use could be achieved through a reduction of supply. A final important aspect of the Shanghai meeting was that it catalysed domestic federal drugs legislation in the USA, where the prohibition movement was positioned to shape the legislative response in that country.

Regulating consumption: US federal drug laws The federal government was compelled to regulate the domestic patent medicine market in the run-up to the Shanghai meeting. It was recognized that the USA would have no credibility in pressing for controls on opium if none existed in the USA (McAllister 2000; Bewley-Taylor 2001). The constitutional separation of power between the states and federal authorities that impeded the introduction of alcohol prohibition was also an obstacle to the introduction of national drug regulation. The anti-opium lobby within the federal administration found a legal route around this constitutional barrier in 1906. Despite strong opposition from the patent medicine sector, the Pure Foods and Drug Act was introduced as an exercise in the right of federal government to regulate interstate commerce. The driving force behind the legislation was Dr Harvey Wiley of the Bureau of Chemistry. He was a close associate of Wright and Brent and a leading figure in the Anti-Saloon League (Gaughan and Barton Hutt 2004).

The Pure Foods and Drug Act followed the passage of the 1897 Tea Importation Act, the first move by the Congress to regulate food standards during the so-called Progressive Era. Like the Tea Act, the Pure Foods and Drug Act regulated standards in much the same way as the British Pharmacy Act had done forty years earlier. It required that alcohol, morphine, opium, cocaine, heroin, chloroform and cannabis contents were labelled on all medicines and tonics and it prohibited the manufacture and sale of 'adulterated or misbranded' foods, tonics and medications. The law did not restrict access to drug-based products or their use but, like the British Pharmacy Act, it was effective in making people aware of what they were consuming. In the immediate aftermath of the law's introduction, the purchase and use of patent medicines declined dramatically (Musto 1973; Courtwright 1982). Despite this, the anti-opium lobby within the federal administration wanted stricter controls, specifically legislation to prohibit non-medical distribution and use. There was progress towards this end in 1909, when the federal government introduced the Smoking Opium Exclusion Act in line with its constitutional right to regulate overseas trade. The legislation prohibited the importation of opium for non-medicinal purposes, making the 1909 law the first federal measure banning the non-medical, 'recreational' use of a substance.

The utility of racism After the Shanghai meeting, Wiley, Brent and Hamilton Wright explored ways of introducing federal legislation that would extend the prohibition of recreational opium use to all drugs, in line with the position that was to be assumed by the US delegation at the Hague conference. To achieve this, two domestic obstacles had to be overcome: public apathy towards the drug 'menace'; and the resistance of individual states to the expansion of federal controls.

In the absence of a grassroots lobby in favour of drug prohibition, anti-drug campaigners in Washington used racist and anti-immigrant hostilities as a tool to build support for their campaign for stricter drug laws. This was achieved with the support of William Randolph Hearst's newspaper empire. In his role as the first US drugs 'tsar', Hamilton Wright focused public and media attention on what he claimed to be two dangerous new drug consumption trends in the USA, a country that he argued was the 'worst drug fiend in the world' (*New York Times*, 15 March 1911). The first was the abuse of cocaine by African Americans. This was presented as a threat to law and order and the safety of white American society, particularly in the south of the country where, he claimed, 'the use of cocaine among the lower order of working negroes is quite common'. In magazines such as *Literary Digest* and *Good Housekeeping*, Wiley and Wright elaborated on the danger posed to white women by 'negro cocaine peddlers' and 'cocainised nigger rapists'. 'Negro fiends' easily substituted for the opium-wielding Chinese 'devils' and terrifying images of African Americans with cocaine-induced superhuman strengths received prominent news coverage.

It was somewhat peculiar that cocaine rather than opium dominated the anti-drugs discourse in the USA. This has been explained through reference to the constitutional obstacles posed by the separation of federal and state powers. By emphasizing cocaine use among African Americans, the drug prohibition movement in Washington aimed to overcome the resistance of states in the south to further federal legislative initiatives (Musto 1991; Whitebread 1995). This emphasis on race, crime and drugs to legitimize anti-drugs legislation in the USA was not unique to the USA. The British government in Australia introduced legislation in 1897 that restricted access to opium by Aborigines. But, as discussed in the following chapter, the use of race in the US context was important because US drug control strategies and narratives became internationalized and institutionalized. As a result, the control system that emerged and the manner in which drug control was operationalized was heavily informed by these early ideas of race, violence and drug use that had emerged in the specific context of America's modernization process.

4 | The beginnings of international drug control

From principle to policy

After the Hague Conference of 1911, multinational co-operation to regulate the trade in dangerous and addictive substances gained concrete form through the creation of an international system of drug control. This developed out of six multinational agreements that came into force between 1915 and 1939. These conventionalized the principles established at Shanghai in 1909, specifically that: the manufacture, distribution and use of harmful drugs should be limited to medical and scientific need; and that reductions in the cultivation of narcotic plants and the manufacture of drugs was a prerequisite for reducing demand and consumption. Although the accords were not legally binding, signatory countries introduced domestic legislation in line with the thrust of the conventions.

TABLE 4.1 Pre-Second World War drug conventions

Date and place signed	Title of convention	Entry into force
January 1912, The Hague	International Opium Convention	February 1915 and June 1919
February 1925, Geneva	Agreement Concerning the Manufacture of, Internal Trade in, and Use of Prepared Opium	July 1926
February 1925, Geneva	International Opium Convention	September 1928
July 1931, Geneva	Convention for Limiting the Manufacture and Regulating the Distribution of Narcotic Drugs	July 1933
November 1931, Bangkok	Agreement for the Control of Opium Smoking in the Far East	April 1937
June 1936, Geneva	Convention for the Suppression of the Illicit Traffic in Dangerous Drugs	October 1939

International control of the manufacture, distribution and use of drugs was a revolutionary development. There was no previous history of states working co-operatively to control the trade in a commodity (Nadelmann 1990). Devising a control system for drugs was a particular challenge on account of four things: the global scale of the industry; the vested interests of different national players in distinct aspects of the trade; the complexities inherent in trying to regulate consumer behaviour; and finally the dualist nature of drugs. In respect of the latter point, while drugs were recognized as causing social harm, it was also accepted that they were of benefit to society if used judiciously (Steinig 1968). The dilemma was how to construct a framework that could reconcile conflicting interests, ensure an adequate global supply of medical drugs and alter patterns of individual behaviour.

The control framework developed incrementally. Successive conventions built upon previous agreements and eliminated loopholes in the nascent regulatory system. By 1939, a comprehensive system of manufacturing control was in place that regulated the trade in drugs 'from the point at which the raw materials enter the factory to the point at which they finally reach the legitimate consumer'. This was a unique development as it represented a 'planned economy on a world-wide scale' (Renborg 1964).

The International Opium Convention Delegates to the Hague Conference had plenipotentiary powers. This meant they had the authority to commit their governments to any resulting agreement. The resulting International Opium Convention 'raised the obligation to co-operate in the international campaign against the drug evil from a purely moral one to the level of a duty under international law' (May 1950). In line with the principle that medical need was the sole criterion for the manufacture, trade and use of opiates as well as cocaine, the convention set out that national governments should enact 'effective laws or regulations' to control production and distribution. Signatory states were obliged to tighten existing domestic regulations or introduce national legislation if none was in place. The convention further required countries to restrict the ports through which cocaine and opiates were exported, with the aim of ensuring import prohibitions imposed by consumer countries would be respected and enforced by national governments. Recognizing the advances that were being made by the pharmaceutical sector in the development of new derivative drugs, the convention set out that any new cocaine or morphine derivative liable to produce 'ill effects' should automatically be incorporated into national drug laws. This precluded the need for a constant redrafting of the original agreement to incorporate new drugs.

Although the International Opium Convention was a revolutionary document, it was also weak. It did not create mechanisms to oversee the implementation of the agreement or set targets for reducing the volume of drugs manufactured. It was also loosely worded, with parties to the convention required only to 'use their best endeavours' to fulfil their obligations. A particular weakness was that the convention could come into effect only if it was unanimously approved by all country delegations, a provision requested by Germany. But the drift to war created mutual suspicion between states and, in this environment, it was difficult to achieve a unanimous endorsement. Consequently, only China, the Netherlands, the USA, Honduras and Norway ratified the convention (Bewley-Taylor 2001; McAllister 2000).

The League of Nations and drug control The First World War transformed international drug control (McAllister 2000). The conflict led to the destruction of those empires that had been reluctant to ratify the agreement, specifically Germany, Austria Hungary and the Ottoman Empire. Through the Treaty of Versailles in 1919, Britain and other allied countries found a way of bringing the convention into force by conjoining ratification of the Versailles agreement with ratification of the International Opium Convention (Renborg 1964; McAllister 2000). The destruction of the war also generated a spirit of internationalism in the aftermath of the conflict and a search for international institutions capable of maintaining a peaceful global order. This gained organizational form with the creation of the League of Nations in 1919. This institution provided the international community with a centralized body for the administration of the convention.

Article 23(c) of the Covenant of the League of Nations provided the organization with responsibility for overseeing the implementation of international drug agreements. To facilitate this, the League created an Opium Section to provide administrative and executive support to the League Council. The Health Committee of the League, the forerunner of the World Health Organization, also advised the League's Secretariat on drug-related matters. The most important drug control body created during this period was the Advisory Committee on the Traffic in Opium and Other Dangerous Drugs, known as the Opium Advisory Committee (OAC). The Netherlands, Britain, France, India, China, Japan, Siam and Portugal were initially represented on the OAC, with membership later expanded to any country that had an interest in the OAC's work. The OAC created the Opium Control Board to assist it in its duties, with the board assuming responsibility for administering the International Opium Convention.

The Geneva Conventions of 1925 The work of the OAC focused on developing a comprehensive picture of the drug trade in order to determine the scale of the legitimate drug market. It immediately established that the production of opiates, cocaine and derivative drugs was ten times greater than legitimate medical requirements (May 1950). To address this situation, two plenipotentiary conferences were convened in Geneva in 1924 under the auspices of the League of Nations. Forty-one countries attended the conferences and they resulted in two new conventions that built upon the International Opium Convention.

The first convention, the Agreement Concerning the Manufacture of, Internal Trade in, and Use of Prepared Opium, came into force in 1926. It established a fifteen-year timetable for the elimination of recreational opium use in Southeast Asia. The second accord, the Geneva International Opium Convention of 1928, expanded the manufacturing control system by establishing compulsory drug import certificates and drug export authorizations. These were to be administered by national authorities and were required for all drug transactions between countries. The measure was designed to prevent countries importing or exporting drugs beyond medical and scientific requirements. To determine the precise level of legitimate need, parties to the convention were required to provide annual statistics estimating production, manufacture and consumption requirements for opiates, coca, cocaine and, for the first time in drug control, cannabis. This information was to be supplemented by quarterly statistics detailing the volume of plant-based and manufactured drugs imported and exported and estimated figures for opium smoking.

A new drug control organ, the eight-person Permanent Central Opium Board (PCOB) that replaced the Opium Control Board, processed the statistical information. It was an impartial body and because it was created by the Geneva Convention it was independent of the League unlike the OAC and membership was determined by technical competence and no board member could represent a national interest. To ensure that the PCOB could administer the import–export control system effectively, the convention provided it with the authority to request explanations from national governments if they failed to submit statistical information or if stated drug import or export requirements were overshot. The board could also recommend an embargo of drug exports or imports to any country that exported or imported in excess of stated production levels or medical need. This extended to countries that were not party to the convention, universalizing the control system. The PCOB could not directly impose sanctions and was therefore relatively weak but it had a highly effective weapon in the threat of bad publicity and it pursued a high visibility approach that embarrassed states into adhering to their obligations (McAllister 2000; Renborg 1964).

The 1928 convention also increased the number of controlled drugs and it created an open-ended schedule that classified drugs according to their danger to health and relevance to science. The Health Committee of the League had responsibility for determining if a drug should be on the schedule and this introduced uniformity across national control systems.

The 1931 Convention for Limiting the Manufacture and Regulating the Distribution of Narcotic Drugs The Geneva International Opium Convention failed to prevent the seepage of legitimately manufactured drugs into the illegitimate market and drugs were illicitly shipped through non-signatory countries. The OAC determined that, between 1925 and 1929, legitimate demand for opium- and cocaine-based drugs was in the region of 39 tons per year, while 100 tons of opiates had been exported to unknown destinations from licensed factories (Anslinger and Tompkins 1953; Renborg 1964). It was agreed that a system directly limiting the global manufacture of drugs should be imposed but allocating production quotas between countries was problematic. As a result, a system of indirect limitation was introduced through the 1931 Convention for Limiting the Manufacture and Regulating the Distribution of Narcotic Drugs.

The convention set out that the quantity of manufactured drugs required globally was to be fixed in advance. To establish the requisite manufacturing levels a compulsory estimates system was introduced under which all countries had to detail the quantities of drugs required for medical and scientific purposes for the coming year. States were able to revise their estimates but the reason for any change had to be explained. The convention created the four-person Drug Supervisory Board (DSB) to administer the limitation system. The DSB was authorized to draw up its own estimates of individual country needs as a means of checking the information submitted by national governments and it devised estimates for those countries that did not submit their drug requirements. The DSB then sent a statement to each national government showing the annual estimates for each country. No greater quantity of any of the drugs detailed was to be manufactured.

The 1931 convention also strengthened the powers of the PCOB, which was now authorized to directly embargo any country that exported or imported beyond its stated manufacturing volumes or consumption needs. The convention additionally obliged signatory states to create a dedicated national drug enforcement agency to ensure compliance with domestic drug laws. This stemmed from a US proposal recommending that other countries use the American Federal Bureau of Narcotics, created in 1930, as an organizational model to copy.

The 1931 convention made the control system more effective and, in 1933, the OAC claimed that: 'the sources of supply [of drugs] in Western Europe, as a result of the close control now exercised, appear to be rapidly drying up' (Renborg 1964).

1936 Convention for the Suppression of the Illicit Traffic in Dangerous Drugs
The final element of the inter-war drug control system was the 1936 Convention for the Suppression of the Illicit Traffic in Dangerous Drugs. This stemmed from an initiative by the International Police Commission, the forerunner of Interpol. While previous drug conventions had dealt with the legitimate trade in drugs, the 1936 convention focused on the illegitimate trade. It sought to suppress drug trafficking between states through the application of punitive and uniform criminal penalties in all countries. Article 2 of the convention recommended that national anti-trafficking laws should be based on 'imprisonment, or other penalties of deprivation of liberty'. The convention further required signatory states to set up a dedicated agency responsible for monitoring drug traffickers and trafficking trends, in co-ordination with corresponding agencies in other countries.

Evaluating the early drug control system

The inter-war control framework was effective in reducing the production of opiates, cocaine and other drugs. World opium production declined 82 per cent between 1907 and 1934, from 41,624 tons to an estimated 16,653 tons. There was a marked fall in opiate manufacture, and legitimate heroin production fell from 20,000 pounds in 1926 to 2,200 pounds by 1931. Significant progress was also made in reducing the consumption of drugs. In Southeast Asia, there was a 65 per cent fall in opium sales by opium monopolies operated by colonial authorities. In the Netherlands Indies (Indonesia), controls introduced by the Dutch administration led to an 88 per cent fall in opium consumption, which declined from 127 tons in 1918 to 15 tons by 1933 (McCoy 1972).

Beyond reducing drug manufacturing and consumption, the international drug control system also set precedents in international law and as a result it was upheld as a model for international co-operation in other areas, starting with arms control in the early 1930s (McAllister 2000; Nadelmann 1990). The development of the drug control framework was an important step in the direction of states prioritizing the international interest over the separate national interest, and, in implementing the drug conventions, countries surrendered overview of their sovereign affairs to an international body for the first time (Steinig 1968). Through the convention, nation-states also took the unprecedented step of granting judicial authority to an international organ that they were not guaranteed representation on, as was the case with the PCOB, and they also gave this organ the unprecedented right to embargo states that were not party to the conventions (May 1950). International drug control was also groundbreaking as it led to the adoption of uniform penal sanctions across countries and established principles of criminal law on an international basis. A final innovative aspect of drug control was that it marked an attempt by the international community to regulate human behaviour. The model established the concept that the force of law should be used to control what people did to their bodies (McCoy 1972).

The triumph of prohibition? The creation of the international drug control system was a triumph for those Christian lobby groups that had first initiated a global dialogue on the drugs trade in 1909. The framework reflected their main demands and the 'internationalization' of their core values and ideas (Bewley-Taylor 2001). The ability of the USA to bring other countries into the control framework on its terms was remarkable given the powerful economic interest European states had in an unregulated drugs trade. The Netherlands, for example, was the world's leading cocaine producer and the British, French, Portuguese and the Dutch all administered lucrative opium monopolies in their Southeast Asian colonies. Despite this, the Western European states accepted the need for controls. This can be explained through reference to a number of social changes that had an impact on perceptions of the drug trade and drug use within Europe during this period.

The European perspective Drug-related problems in European countries were not as widespread as they were in the USA but they were significant enough for governments to accept that action had to be taken to restrict access to substances that caused harm. This view was in turn influenced by the rise of the European welfare state. Prior to the Second World War, this was at a rudimentary stage; nevertheless, it was important in forging the view that the health and welfare of the individual was the responsibility of government. Doctors also supported drug control as it provided them with monopoly control over the prescription of drugs. The roll-out of European welfare state systems additionally eliminated the need for self-medication, further legitimizing medical and political arguments in favour of controlled drug use (Berridge 2001; Dolin 2001a; de Kort 1995).

Competitive pressures and the need for increased labour productivity also contributed to a shift in attitudes towards drug use. In contrast to the experience during early industrialization, employers began to prohibit drug consumption in the workplace. The increasingly influential trade union movement supported this on health and safety grounds. A similar predisposition towards control developed in colonial areas where drug use had historically been encouraged. White landowners in countries such as Jamaica and South Africa, for example, adopted a hostile attitude towards cannabis smoking, which was seen to reduce labour productivity. Finally, the introduction of national insurance systems to finance the welfare state model contributed to the popular view that individuals should be accountable to other taxpayers for behaviour that was injurious to their health and which required publicly funded treatment.

The Europe–US divide Although the USA catalysed the development of the drug control framework, it never sold prohibition as either a concept or a policy end to other countries. The evolution of the control system was characterized by tension and protracted conflict between the USA and other states. Western European governments did not accept the US view that the cultivation of coca, cannabis and opium poppy could be quickly and easily terminated and the USA failed to achieve limitations on cultivation. Europe was supported by cultivating countries such as Yugoslavia, Iran and Turkey, which refused to sign up to cultivation reduction agreements promoted by America without any guarantee of compensation. The prohibition emphasis on supply-side limitations was consequently problematic for the USA to achieve because it 'required little sacrifice from Americans while demanding fundamental social and institutional change from others' (McAllister 2000: 66). There were additionally security concerns resulting from the fear that low opium stocks would drive up pharmaceutical costs and leave countries vulnerable to medical shortages.

Gradualism also characterized the European approach to illegitimate drug consumption (Dolin 2001a). On the basis that addiction was fundamentally a problem of the will, the USA maintained that non-medical drug use could be terminated through the application of harsh criminal sanctions and a reduction in the supply of drugs. The European countries by contrast took a medicalized approach and emphasized the need for facilities to support people with drug-related problems and the need for gradual reductions in use rather than immediate termination. The danger that the USA claimed was posed by drugs such as cannabis and more particularly heroin was also disputed and the USA faced entrenched resistance to its attempt to effect prohibition of all harmful drugs.

Why the USA prevailed Even though they did not agree with the moral arguments underpinning prohibition, other countries accepted the general direction of US drug policy. There were two main reasons for this. First, the European countries wanted to bring the USA into the emerging system of international organization. The USA initially rejected membership of the League of Nations and it has been suggested that the Western European countries gave the League responsibility for administering the drug conventions in order to pull the USA into the framework of the League (Bewley-Taylor 2001; King 1972; McAllister 2000). After the USA joined the organization in 1924, it was feared that it would pursue its prohibition agenda unilaterally if the League did not support the US policy agenda. The USA signed bilateral policing agreements with twenty-two countries during this period that allowed the USA to extradite and prosecute drug traffickers independently of the international control system (Anslinger and Tompkins 1953). This concerned the Western European states as it undermined the new international organizational arrangements and it went against a trend of multilateral co-operation.

Appeasing the USA came at the cost of alienating other countries from the League, such as the six Latin American states that withdrew from the body between 1936 and 1938 in opposition to the US position. It also led to the creation of a skewed model of drug control that, in contrast to the interests and emphasis of the Europeans, emphasized punishment and suppression over consideration of why people cultivated, produced and used drugs. The influence of the police, the military, politicians and diplomats was institutionalized within this framework while the opinions of doctors, drug users and cultivators were marginalized (Sinha 2001).

The USA exerted significant economic and political pressure on other countries in order to advance its agenda and this is a further explanation for the institutionalization of prohibition. US representatives at the drug conferences and within the control bodies, such as Harry J. Anslinger, director of the FBN, and Herbert May of the PCOB, were forceful individuals and 'their beliefs, morals, ambitions and single-minded determination enabled them to exert exceptional influence over the shape of the international drug control regime' (ibid.). When the American position was rejected, the USA withdrew from proceedings. Ironically, then, the country influenced the evolution of the international drug control framework from outside the system and was not party to the most important founding conventions including the 1928 Geneva convention and the 1936 trafficking convention, on the grounds that they were not rigorous enough (Bewley-Taylor 2001; McAllister 2000; Sinha 2001). The strategies adopted by the USA at the international drug control meetings were heavily influenced by its domestic policy agenda. In this respect, the international arena was used by the American prohibition lobby to push its campaign for strict drug controls in the USA. This underscored a symbiotic relationship between US anti-drug initiatives at the international and domestic level.

Domestic drug control

During the inter-war period, countries honoured their obligations under the international conventions. Examples included the 1919 Dutch Opium Act, the 1929 German Opium Act and the 1920 British Dangerous Drugs Act. Concurrent with this, governments engaged in a concerted campaign to demonize drugs and drug users and this was strongly supported by the print and broadcast media (Levine 2002; Reinarman and Levine 1997). The campaign sought to socialize societies to the view that drugs previously promoted for their health and recreational benefits were evil and dangerous. This legitimized the legislative initiatives and the expenditures that were subsequently channelled into policing private habits. Many of the stereotypes that continue to surround drugs and drug users to this day were developed during this period. They drew heavily on images and claims recycled from the American prohibition lobby. As in the USA, the European anti-drug propaganda emphasized the relationship between a dangerous substance, threatening 'out groups' and criminality. The nation and the integrity of the national group were depicted as embattled by subversive forces seeking to enslave, poison and infiltrate the country. The nature of the 'out group' changed over time and it was determined by the political and social circumstances of individual countries.

The earliest anti-drugs propaganda focused on racial minorities, although as racial communities in Europe were numerically smaller than in the USA, this did not have a strong mobilization appeal (Dolin 2001a; de Kort 1995). In the build-up to the First World War, the nature of the drug threat morphed from racial groups to foreign ideologies and external threats. The German Kaiser began to figure prominently in anti-drugs literature and Germany was accused of attempting to undermine other nations by introducing their civilian population and soldiers to drugs. Bolsheviks and communists replaced Germans as the main drug-threat after the conclusion of the war, before the Germans reappeared, along with the Japanese, in the anti-drugs propaganda of the Second World War period. Popular antipathy towards 'deviant' and bohemian groups such as homosexuals, artists and musicians was also mobilized by national governments in their anti-drugs campaigns and this deepened the relationship between drug use, deviance and immorality in the public consciousness (Speaker 2001).

Drug control emerged as a tool of enormous utility to governments during the political and cultural changes of the inter-war period and the economic turmoil of the Depression. The manner in which the drug control laws were policed, combined with the use of anti-drugs propaganda, allowed states to limit the influence of 'foreign' ideas and regulate social behaviour and interaction. The identification of a dangerous enemy within and outside the national territory assisted in the construction of a sense of national unity. Problematically, this meant that the danger posed by a particular drug was seen to stem from the types of people associated with its use and not the potential harm that the drug itself could cause (Reinarman and Levine 1997).

The gradualist philosophy that characterized the European position in the international drug control bodies did filter through to national-level politics, as with, for example, the 1924 Rolleston Committee in Britain that determined non-therapeutic use of heroin not to be dangerous. European countries were also selective in their enforcement of the drug laws and they did not extend their application to colonial possessions in Southeast Asia. By 1939, state opium monopolies continued to operate in Burma, British Malaya, Netherlands Indies, Siam, French Indo-China, Hong Kong, Macao, Formosa and Kwantung Leased Territory.

US domestic drug control Anti-opium officials in the USA assumed that the international conventions would lead to strict national anti-drugs legislation in the USA. This was because the implementation of international agreements was the responsibility of the federal government. However, this interpretation was not supported by the Supreme Court and, as a result, circuitous legislative routes again had to be taken in order to introduce domestic laws in line with prohibitionist thinking and the obligations of the USA under the international drug conventions.

The anti-drugs legislation that followed was framed as a revenue-raising measure, in line with federal powers to levy taxes. The Harrison Narcotics Tax Act of 1914 and the Marihuana Taxation Act of 1937 imposed punitively high taxes on the non-medical exchange of cocaine and opiates, in the case of the former, and cannabis transactions, including the sale of industrial hemp, in the case of the 1937 measure. The Harrison Act also introduced the prescription of drugs through a taxation framework, with doctors having to register with federal authorities, keep a record of all drugs transactions and pay a prescription tax. Any individual caught in possession of cocaine or opiates without a prescription could consequently be charged, not with a criminal offence, but tax evasion (Musto 1972; Whitebread 1995).

Harry J. Anslinger, the Federal Bureau of Narcotics and domestic legislation The taxation basis of the anti-drugs legislation enabled federal authorities to bypass the state police forces that had vigorously defended against an increase in federal policing responsibilities. Taxation measures were enforced by the US Treasury Department, which created a special Narcotics Division to police the Harrison Act. In 1930, the drug control apparatus was reorganized and a new agency, the Federal Bureau of Narcotics (FBN) was created. For thirty years, Harry J. Anslinger headed the agency. Anslinger and FBN officials assumed a highly pro-active stance in international and domestic drug control matters and worked co-operatively with the US prohibition lobby to advance drug prohibition. In the view of critics, Anslinger's vigorous promotion of drug prohibition and his support for the criminalization of the trade was determined by the institutional interests of the FBN. The incoming Democratic administration considered dismantling the FBN in 1932 and this led Anslinger to defend his 'empire' by exaggerating the drug threat and linking it directly to US national security interests (Bewley-Taylor 2001; Dolin 2001b; King 1972; McAllister 2000).

When Anslinger's initiatives were rejected by the international control apparatus at the League such as enhanced co-operation in trafficking, policing and intelligence matters, he initiated bilateral agreements with individual states. Having convinced a sceptical Democratic Government of the utility of the FBN, Anslinger subsequently talked up the domestic drugs threat in order to secure spending increases and enhanced policing responsibilities for his agency. It is in this context that the campaign against cannabis, traditionally seen as a benign, wild-growing weed, was launched that culminated in the 1937 legislation (Bonnie and Whitebread 1999; Epstein 1977; McAllister 2000; Sinha 2001; Herer 1998).

The stock themes of race, crime and threats to the nation's youth and integrity that characterized the early anti-drugs and the anti-alcohol campaigns were developed during this period (Goode and Ben Yehuda 1994). Among the reams of shockingly racist articles from the period published by the *New York Times* was a piece by Edward Huntington Williams that claimed cocaine made African Americans resistant to bullets. Relaying the experience of the Asheville Chief of Police, Huntington wrote: 'Knowing that he must kill this man or be killed himself, the Chief drew his revolver, placed the muzzle over the negro's heart, and fired [...] but the shot did not even stagger the man. And a second shot that pierced the arm and entered the chest had as little effect in stopping his charge' (*New York Times*, 8 February 1914). In the congressional hearings into the 1914 Harrison Bill, the head of the State Pharmacy Board of Pennsylvania, Christopher Koch, testified that: 'Most of the attacks upon the white women of the south are the direct result of the cocaine-crazed Negro brain' (ibid.).

Until the introduction of Harrison, the primary drugs threat was seen to be African American cocaine use and opiate addiction caused by Chinese dealers. After Harrison and in the build-up to the 1937 Marihuana Tax Act, Mexican migrants emerged as the new drug threat and it was claimed that 'marihuana crazed Mexicans' were committing violent acts as a result of consuming the 'loco weed'. As in the alcohol prohibition and anti-opium campaigns, great stress was placed on the dangers that cannabis presented to American youth. Writing in the *American Magazine* in 1937, Anslinger described the effects of cannabis in his article 'Marijuana: Assassin of Youth': 'The sprawled body of a young girl lay crushed on the sidewalk [...] after a plunge from the fifth story of a Chicago apartment house. Everyone called it suicide, but actually it was murder. The killer was a narcotic known to America as marijuana [...] it is as dangerous as a coiled rattlesnake.'

Alcohol and drug prohibition overlap Those lobby groups that had been at the forefront of the campaign for alcohol prohibition, such as the Anti-Saloon League, were an important source of support for Anslinger, Wright and other officials working to achieve drug prohibition at the international and domestic level. Richmond Pearson Hobson of the Anti-Saloon League formed the International Narcotic Education Association with Wiley in the early 1920s and, as he had done during the alcohol prohibition campaign, he publicized racist, eugenicist, hyperbolic and medically incorrect disinformation about drugs. A reading of his publications and speeches reveals an astonishingly simple substitution of the word 'alcohol' for 'narcotics'. Like alcohol, narcotics were linked to brain disease, racial degeneration, immorality and criminality. Hobson also talked of the 'living dead' who had 'an insane desire to make addicts of others' in publications such as 'The Narcotic Peril and How to Meet It' (Epstein 1977).

The prohibition fervour of the period prevented a considered debate on the legislative measures. The congressional hearing into the Marihuana Tax Bill lasted one hour, the legislation was not debated in the Senate and the expert views of the American Medical Association (AMA) were rejected. The AMA maintained that cannabis was not harmful but, after giving testimony, its representative at the hearing was informed by one congressman: 'Doctor, if you haven't got something better to say than that, we are sick of hearing you' (Whitebread 1995). By contrast, Anslinger's testimony that 'marijuana is an addictive drug which produces in its users insanity, criminality, and death' was influential and widely publicized.

Addiction and crime rates were chronically exaggerated, with Hobson, Anslinger and Wright claiming there were over a million 'heroinists' in the USA alone (Courtwright 1982). This led to increasingly repressive and intrusive policing that was justified by reference to the scale of the drugs threat. As an example of this, the Commissioner of Correction in New York City, Frederic Wallis, claimed: 'All drug addicts are criminals, either actual or potential, and there is no limit to their atrocities', consequently 'no measure is too radical or severe that would prohibit the manufacture and sale of drugs' (cited in Berridge 2001).

There was an emerging problem of drug-related crime after the introduction of the Harrison Act, but officials never linked this to the introduction of the Act itself. Although Harrison did not prohibit the use of opiates, subsequent judicial interpretations of the law made the legislation restrictive. Following the Behrman ruling in 1922, doctors were not allowed to prescribe 'narcotic drugs' to addicts to maintain their addiction (Berridge 2001; Courtwright 1982; Dolin 2001b; Lindesmith 1964, 1968; Speaker 2001; Whitebread 1995). This had four immediate effects. It first created an illicit drug market. Second, morphine and opium users turned to heroin as this was easier to divert from pharmacies and manufacturing facilities. The legislation also influenced a shift away from the sniffing of heroin to intra-muscular injection and mainlining. This was in response to suppliers adulterating and cutting heroin that had previously been available in pure form, in order to increase sales and profit. A final effect of the legislation was to drive up the cost of illicit drugs. For example, the price of heroin increased from $6.50 an ounce before Harrison to $100 an ounce after the legislation was introduced.

These developments contributed to crime in two ways. Individuals were criminals under the new legislation if they produced, distributed or used illegitimate drugs and so, by definition, crime increased. The escalating cost of drugs and the need to obtain supplies also contributed to a rise in crime as users resorted to criminal acts to finance costly, illegitimate drug purchases (Berridge 2001; Courtwright 1982). The drugs legislation also triggered changes to the patterns of drug distribution, with dealers moving into areas where other types of illegal activities such as prostitution took place. As a result, the illicit trade became integrated into wider criminal networks that were involved in pimping and racketeering.

The sustained demand for illicit drugs owed much to the failure of federal authorities to provide rehabilitation and support to users. Immediately after the introduction of Harrison, entrepreneurs connected to the prohibition lobby emerged who offered 'cures' for drug addiction. They included Charles B. Towns whose New York sanatorium offered a five-day course of strychnine to addicts at a cost of $300 per day. These were gradually phased out as a result of pressure from the FBN and prohibition groups while progressive, state-based rehabilitation facilities were closed down after the 1922 Behrman ruling. The potential for crime and illicit markets to flourish under prohibition had been flagged by the Western European countries within the international control apparatus. However, the USA did not interpret these domestic trends as a problem of prohibition per se. Instead, they were seen as a product of lax enforcement that could be countered through more repressive control and policing measures. By the end of the inter-war war period, the division between those countries that supported regulation of the trade and a more gradualist approach and the US prohibition lobby had become profound. When the international community returned to the issue of drug control in the aftermath of the Second World War, it was the US position that prevailed. The reasons for and implications of this for the framework of drug control are discussed in the following chapter.

5 | The post-war international drug control regime

The Second World War catalysed dramatic changes in the framework and strategic orientation of international drug control. In contrast to the pre-war model, the structure that developed after 1945 addressed those issues prioritized by the USA during the inter-war period but which had been rejected by other countries, specifically: the prohibition of opium smoking; restrictions on drug plant cultivation; extension of the control system to cannabis and other drugs; enhanced policing and enforcement; and the application of punitive criminal sentences for those engaged in illicit plant cultivation, drug production, trafficking, transportation, distribution, possession and use (Chatterjee 1988; Bruun et al. 1975). The post-war period consequently marked the instauration and consolidation of a comprehensive international prohibition regime that had its own bureaucratic apparatus, ideology and mechanisms for enforcement (Levine 2002; Nadelmann 1990).

The post-Second World War prohibition model came into existence as the result of new international drug conventions that were signed after 1945 and domestic anti-drugs legislation that was introduced by governments in line with the post-war accords. At the institutional level, change was reflected in the restructuring of those international and domestic drug control bodies that were created during the inter-war period and the introduction of new organs commensurate with the increase in technical, enforcement and administrative responsibilities. The evolution of a comprehensive framework and legislative basis for prohibition ran parallel with the institutionalization of US control of the international control bodies. The USA also continued to pursue drug prohibition unilaterally, and as the country's power and influence expanded after the war, so did its capacity to internationalize its prohibition policy orientation.

Institutionalizing US control The Second World War provided the USA with a unique opportunity to advance its drug prohibition agenda. The war first enabled the USA to cultivate and influence the technical work of the drug control bodies. The Opium Advisory Committee ceased to function after the League of Nations disintegrated during the war. However, the Permanent Central Opium Board and the Drug Supervisory Board existed independently of the League and they continued to process the statistical information submitted by countries.

In 1941, the technical work of the PCOB and the DSB was transferred from Geneva to Washington on the recommendation of Herbert May and Harry J. Anslinger. As funding from the League had been terminated, the two boards were

TABLE 5.1 Post-Second World War drug conventions

Date and place signed	Title of convention	Date of entry into force
December 1946, Lake Success, New York	Protocol amending the Agreements, Conventions and Protocols on Narcotic Drugs concluded at The Hague on 23 January 1912, at Geneva on 11 February 1925 and 19 February 1925 and 13 July 1931, at Bangkok on 27 November 1931, and at Geneva on 26 June 1936	December 1946
November 1948, Paris	Protocol Bringing under International Control Drugs outside the Scope of the Convention of 13 July 1931 for Limiting the Manufacture and Regulating the Distribution of Narcotic Drugs, as amended by the Protocol signed at Lake Success, New York, on 11 December 1946	December 1949
June 1953, New York	Protocol for Limiting and Regulating the Cultivation of the Poppy Plant, the Production of, International and Wholesale Trade in, and Use of, Opium	March 1963
March 1961, New York	Single Convention on Narcotic Drugs	December 1964
February 1971, Vienna	Convention on Psychotropic Substances	August 1976
March 1972, Geneva	Protocol amending the Single Convention on Narcotic Drugs	August 1975
December 1988, Vienna	Convention against Illicit Traffic in Narcotic Drugs and Psychotropic Substances	November 1990

reliant on federal financing and this, combined with their relocation to the USA, led to a 'considerable loss of freedom' (McAllister 2000: 146). Aside from being required to assist the USA in the development of strict, new international anti-drugs policies that included a proposal by Anslinger for an international opium purchasing and selling agency, the boards came under intense pressure to disclose confidential statistical information to US officials relating to national opium stock levels. While the traditional anti-drugs propaganda of the USA had focused on foreign threats introducing American citizens to dangerous drugs, Anslinger's concern during the war was that US access to foreign supplies of opium for medical use would be cut off. This fear was heightened after the German invasion of Yugoslavia in 1941 and, in this context, Anslinger believed the information held by the DSB and PCOB was vital to the security of the USA and allied countries.

To counter the threat of opium being used by the Axis as a weapon of war, Anslinger proposed to stockpile opium from available sources and block supplies to the Axis countries as a means of weakening them in the conflict. Debates on opium security during this period provided the Federal Bureau of Narcotics with a central role in US military and intelligence operations overseas and it forged a tight relationship between drugs, national security and foreign policy that was already implicit in the source-country-focused worldview of the prohibition movement. Underscoring this, Anslinger played an important role in the creation of the Office of Strategic Services (OSS), America's first intelligence agency, established in 1942 and the forerunner of the Central Intelligence Agency (CIA). The emphasis on transnational co-operation in the drug conventions provided enforcement officials from all countries with an institutionalized role in the development of national foreign policies and a presence in overseas diplomatic facilities. However, the level of influence achieved by the FBN and the extent to which anti-drugs efforts and foreign policy were intertwined in the USA was unique (Valentine 2004). The inter-relationship between drugs, security and intelligence also led America and the Soviets to develop research into the use of mind- and mood-altering drugs in conflict and interrogation procedures during the Cold War (Lee and Shlain 1985).

The war also changed the fortunes of international drug control in favour of the USA because it weakened the European countries. This provided the USA with a strategic opening to achieve the prohibition of opium smoking in Southeast Asia. At a meeting held in 1943, representatives from the British, French, Portuguese and Dutch governments guaranteed the USA that opium monopolies would not be re-established in those colonial territories such as Hong Kong, Dutch East Indies, Burma and Malaya that had been invaded by Japan if they were liberated with the help of, or by, the USA. America's offensive military presence in Asia after 1943 additionally served to expand opportunities to impose drug control and prohibition was imposed in those territories that fell under US control. Opium dens and retail outlets were closed down by US troops and, on conclusion of the war, strict anti-drugs legislation was introduced by the American administration in West Germany and Japan. The diplomatic environment also allowed for negotiations with neutral governments, such as Iran and Turkey, and governments in exile, such as the Yugoslavian administration, and this resulted in preliminary agreements on cultivation controls.

The United Nations and drug control

Over fifty countries attended the 1945 San Francisco meeting that led to the founding of the United Nations (UN). Under a protocol signed at Lake Success in 1946, the drug control functions of the League of Nations were transferred to the UN, with primary responsibility for drug-related matters passing to the organization's Economic and Social Council (ECOSOC). At its first meeting, ECOSOC created the Commission on Narcotic Drugs (CND). The commission served as the central drug-policy-making body within the UN. As its role was to advise ECOSOC on drug-related matters and to prepare draft international agreements, it effectively supplanted the defunct Opium Advisory Committee. Administrative support that had previously been provided by the Opium Section was transferred to a new body, the Division of Narcotic Drugs (DND). As the PCOB and DSB existed independently of the League of Nations, they did not need to be replaced. Their 'babylonian captivity' in Washington was ended after their work compiling statistics from national estimates and administering the import/export certification system was transferred back to Geneva (Bruun et al. 1975; McAllister 2000: 140).

Another new institution, the World Health Organization (WHO) assumed the drug control responsibilities formerly executed by the Health Committee of the League of Nations, with the Drug Dependence Expert Committee of the WHO given the task of determining the addictive potential of drugs and their position on the international schedule of controls (Fazey 2003).

Extending the control system: the Paris Protocol of 1948 The Second World War left a complex legacy for the new control bodies. There had been a virtual collapse in the illicit drugs traffic during the war as a result of strict border controls, the expansive theatre of military operations and the requisition of pharmaceutical manufacturing facilities. This limited the transportation routes and drug supplies available for illicit distribution. Any net advantages of the conflict were balanced by problematic legacies. There were stockpiles of medical opium and semi-synthetic drugs that had to be located before they were abused or sold into the illicit market by criminal groups and rebel political organizations in Southeast Asia that were mobilizing independence campaigns. The control regime also had to address the problem of new and addictive synthetic drugs such as methadone and pethidine that had been developed during the war and which fell outside the control schedule established by the 1931 convention. This latter issue prompted the first major multilateral post-war drugs conference.

The 1931 convention addressed only compounds derived from natural raw materials, such as morphine and cocaine, and semi-synthetic derivatives of opium alkaloids, such as heroin. The Paris Protocol of 1948 extended the existing control system to any drug liable to cause harm and addiction, thereby incorporating synthetic drugs into the control framework. The protocol required parties to inform the UN Secretary General of any new drug developed within their territories that had the potential to produce harmful effects, with the CND authorized to place the drug under provisional control pending a final decision by the Drug Dependence Expert Committee (McAllister 2000).

The protocol was contentious and this underscored the extent to which the emerging Cold War between the East and the West and the communist revolution in China created a more complex operating environment for international drug control. Pharmaceutical lobby groups and a number of governments from manufacturing countries argued that the evaluation system led to lengthy delays in the distribution of therapeutically beneficial drugs, while the Soviet Union and Eastern European communist countries considered the reporting requirements of the protocol a violation of national sovereignty.

Controlling cultivation: the 1953 Opium Protocol In 1949, Yugoslavia, India, Iran and Turkey, the world's four largest opium poppy cultivating countries, concluded the Ankara agreement with the assistance of the CND. The accord stemmed from Anslinger's initiative to create an international opium monopoly to supply global licit opium demand, which in 1946 stood at 460 tonnes. Under the plan developed by Anslinger, cultivation targets were to be established based on global medical opium need and cultivation quotas allocated to a restricted number of countries. Opium cultivation was to be prohibited in all states apart from those selected to supply the monopoly, and consumer countries were allowed to choose which official supplier they wanted to purchase from. At Ankara, it was determined that 50 per cent of global opium requirements would be produced by Turkey, 25 per cent by India, 14 per cent by Yugoslavia and 6 per cent by Iran. The remainder was unallocated.

The opium monopoly project was derailed as a result of objections from consumer states. Hostility to the proposal was primarily based on the concern that a monopoly system would increase raw opium prices. It was also argued that cultivation prohibitions in countries not selected to supply the monopoly would be unenforceable, particularly as new methods for extracting morphine base from poppies, so called 'poppy straw', had been developed in Hungary during the war.

The 1953 Opium Protocol was a compromise measure. It extended the import and export controls established for drug manufacturing to opium poppy cultivation; as a result, it was a breakthrough for the USA, which had previously failed to achieve any agreement on cultivation limitations. Under the protocol, cultivating countries were required to detail the amount of opium poppy planted and harvested and volumes of opium exported, used domestically and stockpiled. These reporting requirements were not extended to coca and Andean producer countries maintained their resistance to any restrictions on coca cultivation, which was seen as integral to indigenous life and culture. As with the manufacturing controls, the PCOB was empowered to investigate any anomalies in individual country reports and the protocol extended to coverage of poppy straw. The protocol maintained the principle of an opium monopoly but increased the number of countries authorized to supply the agency from the four detailed in the Ankara agreement to seven, with the inclusion of Bulgaria, Greece and the Soviet Union (Lindt 1953).

The Opium Protocol took nearly a decade to develop but it failed to receive a sufficient number of ratifications for it to come into force. There had been a similar problem with the 1948 protocol on synthetic drugs; by 1956 this had been signed into law by only forty-seven countries, in contrast to the seventy states that were party to the 1931 convention (*Bulletin on Narcotics* 1956). By the time the Opium Protocol finally came into force in 1963, it was a redundant instrument as a result of the 1961 Single Convention.

The 1961 Single Convention In 1961, seventy-three countries attended a UN conference in New York. It was convened to explore a single, anti-drugs convention that would consolidate the nine drug conventions introduced since the Hague conference of 1911. This was a US-sponsored initiative based on a draft convention first presented to the CND in 1948. The American representative on the CND, Herbert May, argued that a single convention was necessary 'not only to simplify the existing international law and administrative machinery concerned with the control of narcotic drugs, but also to make the system of control more flexible and to strengthen it' (May 1955). The resulting 1961 Single Convention consolidated past convention provisions; it introduced controls in new areas; and it revised the existing control apparatus.

Under the Single Convention, the system of licensing, reporting and certifying drugs transactions was extended to include raw plant materials such as cannabis and coca leaves. The convention further required that the consumption of opium, cocaine and cannabis be immediately prohibited. Cultivator countries were required to establish national monopolies to centralize and then phase out cultivation, production and consumption over a twenty-five-year period in the case of coca and fifteen years in the case of opium poppies, culminating in a full international prohibition of the non-medical cultivation and use of these substances by 1989. The 1961 convention introduced a new classification schedule. Those drugs considered to be addictive and 'obsolete' in terms of their scientific and medical value were classified as Schedule I or IV. This applied to the plant-based drugs such as opium poppy, coca and cannabis and their derivatives such as heroin and cocaine. Drugs that were classified as Schedule II or III were considered less dangerous and of some medical value (Bewley-Taylor 2001; Fazey 2003; Sinha 2001).

In terms of enforcement, the Single Convention exhorted signatory states to introduce more punitive domestic criminal laws that punished individuals for engagement in all aspects of the illicit drug trade, including cultivation, manufacture, possession, transportation, sale, import, export or use of controlled drugs for non-medical purposes. According to Article 1 of the agreement, addiction to drugs represented 'a serious evil for the individual [...] fraught with social and economic danger to mankind'. In these circumstances, imprisonment was recommended as the most effective form of punishment for those who violated the drug laws and the convention considered extradition of drug offenders between countries to be 'desirable'.

A final noteworthy aspect of the 1961 convention was that it restructured the international drug control apparatus. The PCOB and the DSB were merged to create a thirteen-person body of independent experts, the International Narcotics Control Board (INCB). The INCB assumed responsibility for the evaluation of national statistical information, the monitoring of the import–export control system and it was also tasked with authorizing narcotic plant cultivation to meet international medical and scientific need (Fazey 2003; Sinha 2001; McAllister 2000). In discharging these duties, the INCB could only recommend and not automatically embargo a country guilty of misreporting statistical and technical information.

PROTOCOL AMENDING THE 1961 SINGLE CONVENTION The powers of the INCB were significantly expanded following an amendment to the 1961 convention that was negotiated in 1972. The body was given responsibility for developing and implementing programmes that prevented the illicit cultivation, production, manufacture, trafficking and use of illicit drugs and to advise countries that needed assistance in addressing these activities within their national territories. The amendment also required that any extradition agreement concluded between two countries should automatically include drug-related offences and, of acute significance, that parties to the 1961 convention should provide 'treatment, education, after-care, rehabilitation and social reintegration' for drug addicts and users. This was the first acknowledgement of demand-side issues in the convention framework and it marked a shift towards detailed consideration of the causes of drug use. Indicative of this, a new agency was added to the UN apparatus in 1971 with the creation of the United Nations Fund for Drug Abuse Control (UNFDAC). This organ was given the task of initiating projects that would strengthen control measures, reduce demand for drugs and reduce the supply of drugs. It also conducted research into drug-related issues. The body emerged from a US initiative and it received $2 million in start-up funding from the federal government.

The 1971 Convention on Psychotropic Substances Although the Single Convention was intended to be 'a convention to end all conventions' (May 1950) and an accord that was flexible enough to adapt to change, two further conventions were introduced in 1971 and 1988. Together with the Single Convention, these three agreements form the basis of the contemporary system of international drugs control.

In July 1971, the international community met to consider how synthetic psychotropic substances including stimulants such as amphetamines, depressants, including barbiturates, and hallucinogens, such as mescalin and lysergic acid diethylamide (LSD), that were not incorporated into the existing regulatory framework but which could be abused and had the potential to be addictive, could be brought into the control system. The resulting Psychotropic Convention introduced a regulatory regime for these drugs that was modelled on the manufacturing and cultivation control system set out in the 1961 convention and it included a schedule of four levels of control that were based, like the Single Convention, on a drug's therapeutic value and abuse potential.

The 1988 Convention against Illicit Traffic in Narcotic Drugs and Psychotropic Substances As in the pre-war drug control system, the final element of the contemporary control model and the last drug convention to come into force related to trafficking. The 1988 Convention against Illicit Traffic that was convened in Vienna sought to ensure full international co-operation and compliance with the campaign to prevent the illicit traffic in drugs. It required states to co-operate and co-ordinate anti-trafficking initiatives with international enforcement bodies and partner agencies in other countries and to introduce strict domestic criminal legislation to prevent money laundering and allow for asset seizure and extradition. The 1988 convention sought to strengthen and harmonize national drug laws and it was groundbreaking in that it set out a number of specific offences that each state was mandated to legislate against. These included the 'intentional possession, purchase or cultivation of drugs for personal consumption'. The convention also introduced controls of chemical precursors required for the production of synthetic and semi-synthetic drugs, with states required to monitor the manufacture and trade in chemicals that could be used in illicit drug production.

While the 1988 convention addressed drug-related criminal activities, it also considered demand-side issues, building on the 1971 Psychotropic Convention. The Comprehensive Multidisciplinary Outline of Future Activities in Drug Abuse Control, which served as the framework for the discussions at Vienna,

TABLE 5.2 The international drug control apparatus

Body	Economic and Social Council	Commission on Narcotic Drugs
Function	Discusses and analyses drug-related issues; initiates drug-related studies; drafts conventions; convenes drug conferences	Analyses drug traffic and trends; advises ECOSOC; prepares draft international drug agreements; provides forum for information exchange
Body	International Narcotics Control Board	United Nations Office on Drugs and Crime
Function	Control organ for the implementation of the drug control treaties; provides advice to the WHO; determines worldwide medical and scientific drug requirements; processes technical and statistical information provided by states; allocates cultivation, production, manufacture, export, import and trade quotas; advises status on anti-drug measures	Co-ordinates UN anti-drug activities; provides secretariat services for the CND and INCB; advises countries on implementation of the drug conventions; executes anti-drugs initiatives in host countries

encouraged states to explore ways of reducing illicit demand and emphasized the need for treatment and rehabilitation programmes (Boister 2001).

Although no new conventions were introduced after the 1988 trafficking convention, the international drug control apparatus was subject to an ongoing process of restructuring. In 1991, the United Nations Drug Control Program (UNDCP) was created to provide more effective co-ordination between the separate and geographically dispersed UN agencies responsible for drug control. The new body absorbed the DND, the INCB and the UNFDAC and derived its authority from the CND. At the same time, membership of the CND was expanded from forty countries to fifty-three, with membership distributed according to the geographical groups that existed within the UN (Fazey 2003). In 1997, the UNDCP was merged with the Centre for International Crime Prevention to form the United Nations Office for Drug Control and Crime Prevention (UNODCCP) and in 2002 this became the UN Office on Drugs and Crime (UNODC).

The post-war model: prohibition victory?

The USA was the driving force behind the succession of conventions that were introduced after the Second World War. With the support of other 'prohibition' states including France, Sweden, Japan, Brazil and China, it succeeded in institutionalizing a universal model of drug control that delineated legitimate and illegitimate drugs and which intensified the campaign against illicit drugs through an emphasis on enforcement, criminalization and punishment. Underscoring the universal nature of the system, by 2005 180 states were party to the 1961 Single Convention, 175 were party to the 1971 Convention on Psychotropic Substances and 170 states had ratified the 1988 Convention against Illicit Traffic.

Domestic legislative responses The post-war shift towards a more punitive system of enforcement was felt in all countries, whether they had ratified the conventions or not. This was particularly the case in the 1960s and 1970s as existing national anti-drugs laws were amended in line with the 1961 and 1971 conventions. Legal changes enacted during this period led to an enhancement of police powers to stop, search, raid, hold without charge and electronically tap suspected traffickers, dealers and drug users. This phase of drug control also saw the introduction of measures such as the death sentence or mandatory life sentence for offences related to trafficking, production and possession, typically without distinction in sentencing in relation to the type of drug or quantities in question.

Restrictive anti-drugs laws were imposed across countries, irrespective of regime type, culture or any other form of distinguishing national characteristic that would ordinarily be expected to generate distinctions in policy structure and application. Aside from the legal obligations that followed from ratification of the conventions, the homogeneity of policy approach, particularly in the consumer countries, stemmed from the utility of strict anti-drugs laws as a mechanism of social control and national security. The 1960s and 1970s were decades of 'youth rebellion', protest movements, revolutionary ideologies, social experimentation and profound East–West tensions. Strict anti-drugs laws, punitive sentencing procedures and harsh enforcement made it possible to suppress and curb dissent. This explains the broad international support for prohibition-based measures and it served to unite systems as diverse as the communist governments of China and the Eastern Bloc, the right-wing authoritarian military regimes in South America, Spain and Portugal and democratically elected governments in Australia, the USA and Scandinavia (Reinarman and Levine 1997). An analysis of Spanish anti-drugs laws during this period illustrates the political advantages of anti-drugs legislation for all governments at this time:

> The law (Law of Social Risk of 1970) was a naked instrument of social control intended to criminalize any form of deviation from the dominant patriarchal, Catholic morality and established a common ground of 'social dangerousness' for homosexuality, pornography, nomadism, begging, prostitution, and even some forms of mental disease. One of its explicit goals was to deal harshly with the new trends of drug experimentation associated with psychedelics, hippies, and alternative lifestyles. Even the new dress codes and hairstyles of rockers, mods, or hippies became suspect. (Gamella and Rodrigo Jiménez 2004)

US drugs laws The USA pioneered punitive national drug control measures and, in doing so, the federal government encroached on the authority of states and judges in areas such as policing, education and criminal sentencing procedures. The Boggs Act of 1951 set this trend and the legislation was also significant for establishing uniform national drug laws within the USA. In addition, the Boggs Act placed cannabis on a par with heroin in terms of its abuse and addiction-forming potential. During the congressional hearings into the Boggs Act, Commissioner Anslinger argued for strict cannabis controls on the grounds that it was a 'gateway drug' that would lead users to try and then become addicted to other drugs. Elaborating on the 'stepping-stone theory', Anslinger argued: 'The danger is this: Over 50 percent of these young addicts started on marihuana smoking. They started there and graduated to heroin; they took the needle when the thrill of marihuana was gone' (Boggs Act Hearings, 1951, p. 206).

This theory supplanted the argument that cannabis caused violence and insanity, a claim that had been used in numerous so-called 'marijuana insanity'-based defences in rape, murder and robbery trials during the 1940s and 1950s in the USA. The 'stepping-stone' argument also emerged after Anslinger was ridiculed for emphasizing the dangers of cannabis through reference to the social problems caused by jazz music and the argument developed as US officials sought to convince other countries of the need to bring cannabis into the schedule of control established in the draft 1961 Single Convention (Whitebread 1995).

In 1970, the Controlled Substances Act (CSA) was introduced by the administration of President Richard Nixon under the rubric of his government's 'war on drugs' launched in 1969. The CSA brought together all previous federal drugs legislation. It was introduced under the right of the federal government to regulate inter-state commerce and it followed a successful judicial appeal in 1969 against taxation-based drug laws such as the 1914 Harrison Act and 1937 Marihuana Tax Act by Timothy Leary, an advocate of hallucinogenic drug use. The CSA, which is the basis of US drugs policy in the current period, established a series of schedules, with cannabis among a number of drugs classified as the most dangerous drugs, or Schedule I narcotics. These cannot be possessed by any individual unless licensed by the federal government. Cocaine, opium and morphine by contrast were classified as Schedule II drugs, on the basis that they had less of an abuse potential.

The CSA was enforced by a new prohibition enforcement agency, the Drug Enforcement Administration (DEA) created in 1973. This followed the termination of the FBN in 1968 for reasons that have never been officially disclosed. It is speculated that the demise of the FBN resulted from its investigation into international trafficking gangs that revealed a high level of collusion between organized criminal groups, the political establishment in Washington, the CIA and the Federal Bureau of Investigation (FBI) (Dale Scott 1996; Valentine 2004). The FBN was replaced by the Bureau of Narcotics and Dangerous Drugs (BNDD), which after a brief existence was supplanted by the DEA.

THE SECOND 'WAR ON DRUGS' During the presidency of Ronald Reagan (1981–89) the federal government aggressively pursed prohibition. Indicative of the new approach was Reagan's declaration in 1982: 'We're rejecting the helpless attitude that drug use is so rampant that we are defenseless to do anything about it. We're taking down the surrender flag that has flown over many drug efforts; we're running up the battle flag' (*New York Times*, 24 June 1982). This marked the beginning of the second 'war on drugs' that has continued under successive Democratic and Republican administrations.

The drugs war was characterized by the adoption of a unilateralist 'source-focused' policy of supply eradication, with a specific focus on South America; the adoption of stricter and broader national anti-drugs laws and a substantial increase in federal funding for enforcement. The Reagan administration introduced a plethora of legislative initiatives that included the 1984 Comprehensive Crime Control Act; the 1986 Anti-Drug Abuse Act; and the 1988 Anti-Drug Abuse Amendment Act. Taken together, the measures that were enacted during the Reagan presidency raised federal penalties for all drug-related offences, they introduced mandatory minimum sentences, they introduced asset seizure without conviction, they established the federal death penalty for drug 'kingpins', and they progressively increased the funding allocation to enforcement bodies (Chase Eldridge 1998). The Reagan period also saw the introduction of the Drug Abuse Resistance Education (DARE) anti-drugs programme in schools (Baum 1996) and in 1986 drug testing of federal employees and contractors under Executive Order 12564. Workplace drug testing was quickly taken up by the private sector and state governments, which were provided with federal assistance in introducing workplace testing through the 1988 Drug Free Workplace Act.

To co-ordinate these anti-drug initiatives, the 1988 National Narcotics Leadership Act created the Office of National Drug Control Policy, with the institution of the 'drug czar' subsequently copied by other countries in the 1990s. Reagan's first drug czar was Carlton Turner and, in a move that critics considered to be in line with Reagan's thinking, he proposed that the death penalty should be introduced for all drug users. This did not gain legislative form.

The legislative momentum continued after Reagan had left office. Subsequent measures included the 1999 Drug Dealer Liability Act that imposed civil liability on drug dealers for the direct or indirect harm caused by the use of the drugs that they distributed. While the federal law was pending Senate approval, thirteen states introduced model Drug Dealer Liability legislation (Reiland 1999). In 2000 the Protecting Our Children from Drugs Act imposed mandatory minimum sentences on drug dealers who involved children under the age of eighteen in the trade or who distributed near schools (Chase Eldridge 1998).

In terms of addressing supply, the post-Reagan period saw the development of three tracks in US source country policy. First, under the drug certification system introduced in the mid-1980s, the federal government could terminate bilateral assistance to any country that was deemed by the State Department not to be co-operating in the drugs war. This was paralleled by the militarization of cultivation eradication and interdiction strategies, with the USA pressing for and financing the deployment of source country military institutions in enforcement activities. Source country strategy was based on a carrot and stick approach. The carrot in this instance was financial support for alternative crops, with the delivery of alternative development projects channelled through the US development agency USAID. The escalation of the US 'war on drugs' and the intensification of efforts to suppress supply and demand led to a sharp increase in federal government expenditures dedicated to anti-drugs initiatives. Between 1981 and 1993, the federal drug budget increased from $1.8 billion to $12.5 billion. The Drug Enforcement Agency's share of these revenues progressively increased from under $200 million to $400 million (Gray 2000). Additional revenue was also made available through the 1984 civil forfeiture law. This allowed enforcement agencies to confiscate drug-related assets and, by the end of the 1980s, this measure alone contributed in the region of $500 million to the Drug

Enforcement Agency, while the Justice Department received an estimated $1.5 billion in illegal assets between 1985 and 1991 (Blumenson and Nilsen 1998).

Rebellion and division within the drug control system

In the 1980s the USA accelerated and enhanced enforcement and repression activities. By contrast, Europe followed a different trajectory. There was a trend of liberalizing drug laws in Western Europe and a questioning of the utility of prohibition-based strategies that criminalized users and focused on supply- as opposed to demand-reduction. Criticism of the operating principles and strategic orientation of international drug control first emerged in Western Europe in the 1970s. The chronology was significant in that critiques of prohibition emerged precisely when the European countries were applying more repressive anti-drugs measures in line with the 1961 Single Convention. Three basic problems with this punitive approach were identified.

First, the emphasis on enforcement and incarceration in the revised national laws of the 1970s led to an exponential increase in imprisonment rates and spending on prisons, policing and legal processes. This not only created an increasing large fiscal burden for the European states, it also became clear that the use of imprisonment failed to reverse a trend of rising drug use. This prompted a reconsideration of the prohibition principle that all controlled drugs were dangerous, a move that was in turn informed by advances in medicine, psychiatry and a growing understanding of the varied 'careers' of drug users. Although many Western European countries made no legal distinction between different types of drugs, it was recognized that substances like cannabis caused minimal to no problems in users and that there was little evidence to support the argument that cannabis itself was a gateway to other drugs. On this basis, countries such as Spain, Italy, Ireland, the Netherlands and Switzerland determined that laws relating to cannabis possession and use should be applied more leniently (Dolin 2001a; EMCDDA 2001; Gatto 1999; Fazey 2003).

The crystallization of a policy distinction between 'hard' drugs that were addiction-forming, like heroin, and 'soft' drugs like cannabis was pioneered in the Netherlands. Following the publication of two influential inquiries into cannabis use, the 1971 Hulsman Report and the 1972 Baan Report, the Dutch government adopted different enforcement practices for soft and hard drugs. While strict controls were maintained over the production, manufacture and trafficking of controlled drugs, the consumption and possession of small amounts of cannabis was dealt with through 'diversions' such as fines, treatment or warnings, rather than incarceration. This made it possible to concentrate enforcement efforts and financial resources on hard drugs that were linked to violence and crime, it allowed for cost savings in the penal system and it was a direct response to criticism that the drug laws of the 1970s, specifically the controls applied to cannabis, led to infringements of civil liberties. In respect of the latter point, there was a growing concern that repressive anti-drugs legislation was disproportionately affecting occasional users of soft drugs and that this damaged the longer-term potential of people convicted of minor drug offences to be reintegrated back into community life.

The utility of incarceration was questioned amid evidence of high rates of recidivism among drug users. Further to this, a surge in heroin use in the 1970s generated strong demand for treatment services. These were, however, limited as a direct result of the international drug conventions and their emphasis on criminalization and imprisonment over treatment and medical approaches to addiction. The European heroin epidemic also had the effect of strengthening the argument for distinguishing enforcement procedures for hard and soft drugs, on the basis that police time and resources needed to be freed up to tackle heroin-related crime and specifically a surge in acquisitive crime by heroin users (EMCDDA 2001; Scheerer 1978).

The development of Western European demand-side policies reflected the culmination of a struggle by these countries against the institutionalization of the US-favoured supply-side focus. As the USA deepened application of its supply-side strategies in the 1980s, the Europeans shifted their policy emphasis towards consideration of demand-side issues and treatment provision. Variations on the Dutch approach were subsequently rolled out across Western Europe. The legislative framework differed across countries but overall there was a trend of non-enforcement of existing legal provisions relating to cannabis possession and use. Spain, Portugal, Italy and Luxembourg fully decriminalized possession and use, which meant that while certain drug-related acts were still illegal, they did not carry a criminal penalty.

Other regional blocs, particularly South American countries that, like the Europeans, had historically questioned the US prohibition model, supported the European drug strategy. However, the development of a more liberal, treatment-oriented approach was strongly criticized by the international drug control bodies, the USA and other prohibition-endorsing countries in the Middle East and Asia. This was despite the fact that the liberalization trend related only to consumption and possession of certain drugs and it did not extend to reconsideration of laws relating to production, manufacturing, trafficking or the cultivation of drug plants. In this respect, the European countries remained within the international control framework and continued to recognize their obligations under the conventions. The policy changes that were introduced came into effect only because the 1961 Single Convention provided a limited amount of space for national strategy development in relation to consumption and treatment (Fazey 2003; de Ruyver et al. 2002).

By the beginning of the twenty-first century and nearly one hundred years after the launch of drug diplomacy, a powerful critique of the drug control model and the underlying principle of prohibition had emerged. Debate gradually extended from consideration of possession and use issues towards consideration of the entire source-focused criminalization approach advocated by the USA and the UN apparatus. In this respect, drug control was at a turning point, with the international community divided over questions of prohibition or regulation, control or liberalization. Arguments in favour of drug liberalization also gained ground, although this was significant at the popular and not the inter-governmental level. There were two basic reasons for this crisis of confidence in the international control model. First, after a century-long campaign to prohibit addictive and harmful drugs, drug consumption, production and plant cultivation were running at an all-time high. Second, it was increasingly felt that prohibition strategies had not only failed, they were also iatrogenic in nature. This meant that the cure, prohibition, was perceived to be worse than the effects of the disease, the illicit drug trade (Gatto 1999). The evidence supporting these two arguments is assessed in the remainder of this book, beginning with an analysis of consumption, cultivation and production trends during the period of drug control.

6 | Trends in drug consumption

The knowledge gap

It is extraordinarily difficult to develop a concise picture of drug use because the collation of statistical information on drug consumption was not traditionally a priority for nation-states or the international drug control apparatus. This reflected the institutionalization of the supply-side approach, which was to the detriment of technical analysis of demand-side issues. The surveys that were carried out in the pre- and immediate post-Second World War period were conducted in the consumer countries of the West and their colonial outposts. They were sketchy, small scale, impressionistic and typically limited to analysis of a specific drug.

Compounding the lack of information on consumption, those states that formed part of the communist bloc during the Cold War did not accept that drug consumption existed within communist countries. With drug use seen as a problem limited to capitalist societies, no national investigations into drug use were conducted and the statistical information that was available was obtained through recourse to unethical practices, such as the reporting of patient history by doctors to state authorities. Information collation in the poorest countries of the world was negligible. Underscoring this, the UN discovered that it had no empirical basis for an African drugs policy when it sought to address a rise in consumption on the continent in 1997 (UNODCCP 1999).

In the 1970s, consumer states began to address the information gap. This was in response to an unprecedented rise in drug use during the first 'wave' of increased consumption that occurred in the mid- to late 1960s in Western Europe and North America. The spread of cannabis, LSD and amphetamine consumption demonstrated the need for adequate data on which to base drug policy, particularly as countries sought to bring domestic legislation into line with the 1961 Single Convention. In subsequent decades, complex survey and information-gathering techniques were developed in order to establish the scale of national drug use and the type of drugs consumed. These were quantitative in approach and they included: national, regional and local-level household surveys; surveys using a targeted sample based on social, racial or demographic groups; emergency room episodes; treatment demand indicators; drug seizure figures; and arrest and imprisonment rates for possession, use and trafficking. The information from the surveys was extrapolated to establish an estimate for national consumption rates, with national data collated by the Commission on Narcotic Drugs at the UN to establish global consumption figures and to determine use trends. However, the international figures compiled by the CND were unreliable as there was no universal system or single methodology for collating national statistical information and countries adopted different approaches for calculating the estimates they submitted (Mansfield and Whetton 1996).

The methodological challenges The utility of the national surveys and the reliability of the figures obtained were also questionable as a result of a host of methodological problems. The most immediate was the challenge of researching an illegal activity. People were reluctant to provide information about their drug consumption habits, particularly in countries with strict anti-drugs regimes. Even if they were prepared to discuss their drug use, they were unlikely to know the precise quantities or purity of the drugs consumed and as a result under- and over-reporting were common. Drug users also had a hierarchy of acceptable drugs and this compounded the problems of researchers. Heroin, for example, was viewed as a particularly unacceptable 'dirty' drug and the taboo around its use is thought to have resulted in significant under-reporting. Additional challenges were locating heavily dependent users, as they tended to be socially marginalized and homeless, and the persistent threat of violence or assault to those surveying a criminal activity (Manski et al. 2001).

The methodological approaches that were used consequently had limitations. The extent to which it was possible to establish figures for national cocaine use from projections based on cocaine seizures was questionable. Rather than serving as a guide to consumption rates, a high level of seizures in a particular country could have been related to the intensification of enforcement efforts or success in identifying a large source of supply. It was also difficult to establish if the drugs seized were intended for the national market or being trafficked through the country where the seizure occurred. The most problematic limitation was that the volume of illicit drugs in circulation in a country could never be known. It was therefore impossible to determine the impact of a drug seizure, or the amount of drugs captured as a percentage of the total amount of drugs on the illicit market.

Drug-related emergency room episodes or treatment demand levels also had limited utility. Once again, the illegality of the drugs involved undermined the reliability of the statistical data obtained. The fear of prosecution meant that an unquantifiable number of people did not present themselves for medical treatment when they suffered drug-related health problems and doctors did not always look for drug-based indicators among patients. The same held true for pathologists and, as a result, drug-related morbidity was difficult to quantify and under-reported. A further problem with the statistical data was that they were influenced by the timeframe set by the survey and, as a result, a survey recording drug use in the past week or month had a different base figure from a survey asking respondents to detail drug use over the previous year or their lifetime. As a result, different surveys by different authorities led to radically different conclusions as to the scale and intensity of drug consumption (Manski et al. 2001; Musto and Sloboda 2003).

Because of the bias towards quantitative research, the data obtained provided national governments with little qualitative information such as how people were initiated into drug use; how they administered drugs; why they chose certain drugs; where they purchased them from; how their drug 'careers' evolved; and why, if the question was relevant, they stopped using. This type of research was being conducted by social scientists in academic and community settings, but in comparison to the resources provided for statistical information gathering, it was vastly underfunded. Drug control institutions, for two inter-related reasons, did not prioritize the development of qualitative approaches. First, the system of reporting and target setting was based on measurable data. This bias meant negligible resources were channelled into qualitative research. Second, qualitative information was seen to legitimize and justify drug use. In this respect, the reason why people consumed certain drugs and how often was deemed an irrelevance because, whatever the motivation, consumption was a criminal act. The neglect of qualitative research was subsequently revealed as a critical limitation when the international community confronted rising levels of drug use during the second and third waves of drug consumption increases in the 1980s and 1990s.

Towards homogeneity In the 1990s there was an improvement in consumption-related information gathering techniques and progress in harmonizing reporting systems. This was pioneered at the regional level by institutions such as the European Monitoring Centre on Drugs and Drug Addiction (EMCDDA) and the South and Central American body, La Comisión Interamericana para el Control del Abuso de Drogas (CICAD, Inter-American Drug Abuse Control Commission) that encouraged the development of uniform regional reporting systems. The 1998 UN Special Session on Drugs further enhanced the profile of demand-focused research. It was acknowledged that enhanced surveying procedures and universalized reporting requirements were necessary if there was to be progress in meeting the UN's goal of a significant reduction in global drug use by 2008.

The 'Extent, Patterns and Trends of Drug Use' section of the annual reports questionnaires submitted by national governments to the CND subsequently required all countries to compile a standard consumption report based on expert opinion, standardized quantitative data and also qualitative research. Increased emphasis was also placed on surveys of drug use in schools, such as those conducted by the European School Survey Project on Alcohol and Other Drugs (EPSAD) and the US Monitoring the Future Survey. The school surveys enabled policy-makers to identify new trends and emerging problems and they provided a basis for preventative intervention and drugs education. However, as with all the surveys, they had limitations, specifically absenteeism and truancy, which typically characterized the behaviour of problem drug-using schoolchildren. A lack of universal access to education in many developing countries also reduced the coverage and the reliability of this type of survey.

The reform of the annual reports questionnaires did allow for the standardization of data collection and presentation. In addition, the UNODC addressed the lack of technical skills and financing for national surveys encountered by developing countries through the Global Assessment Programme on Drug Abuse (GAP). This promoted technical capacity building, regional collaboration and the dissemination of good practice in surveying techniques, with the aim of enhancing the quality of global drug information data and policy responses from all countries.

In the 2000s, regional organizations and the UN continued to explore ways of enhancing the reliability and validity of consumption data and mechanisms for expanding information systems and networks. While progress was made in developing an international consensus on methods and principles of information collection, the fundamental problem remained that, as long as drug use was punished and proscribed, the figures produced could only ever be estimates (Griffiths and McKetin 2003; Manski et al. 2001).

Patterns of controlled drug use

Despite the inordinate problems that surround the determination of a global drug consumption figure, estimates can be established and trends that developed during the period of international drug control can be identified.

Drug control phase 1 Three separate phases of illicit drug consumption can be determined. The first dates from the 1920s to the 1950s and it was dominated by the use of heroin and cannabis. The growth of heroin consumption was attributed to the decline in the availability of other illicit drugs such as morphine, opium and cocaine as domestic and international controls came into effect. Heroin was available in the traditionally large opiate markets of North America and Southeast Asia through diversification from licit channels and trafficking (Anderson and Berridge 2000; Courtwright 1982; McCoy 1972). Those identified with the use of heroin were typically the 'underclass', such as the unemployed, 'hustlers' and prostitutes. There was a collapse in illicit drug supplies during the Second World War and although heroin continued to be available in Southeast Asia, global consumption levels fell to a record low. In the immediate post-war period, the use of cannabis and amphetamines increased, although amphetamines were not subject to control at this point.

Phase 2 In the 1960s there was a dramatic shift in the pattern and nature of drug use. In contrast to the earlier period, drug use during this phase was characterized by an irreversible increase in the number of people consuming drugs; expanding availability and the consumption of different types of drugs; and a more direct relationship between illicit drugs, alternative lifestyles and popular culture. The drugs of choice during the 1960s in the western consumer countries were cannabis, amphetamines, which by this point had been brought into the control system, and LSD. As with amphetamines in the 1950s, LSD was not illegal during this period and the drug was incorporated into the international drug control framework only after the 1971 Convention on Psychotropic Substances came into effect. In the 1970s, heroin consumption increased sharply in North America and Western Europe. It was followed in the 1980s and 1990s by a resurgence of cocaine consumption and a strong rise in the use of amphetamine-type substances (ATSs) such as ecstasy, methamphetamine and LSD (Hartnoll et al. 1989).

Phase three In the late 1990s and 2000s, three inter-related consumption trends were observable. The first was an increase in the use of all controlled drugs, including opiates, heroin, ATSs, cocaine and cannabis. Advances in and the simplification of chemistry, manufacturing and cultivating processes produced a dizzying range of naturally-occurring, synthetic and semi-synthetic drugs. These included: stimulants (uppers), which increase the activity of the central nervous system and produce a feeling of euphoria in users, such as cocaine, amphetamine-type substances and amyl nitrate; depressants (downers), which reduce or inhibit the activity of the central nervous system, such as heroin, Quaaludes, benzodiazepines, tranquillizers, solvents and barbiturates; and hallucinogenic and psychedelic drugs such as psilocybin, LSD, cannabis, ketamine, mescalin, ecstasy (MDMA) and ecstasy-type substances (MDA and MDME), which alter perceptions, emotions and sensory experiences by acting on the neurotransmitter serotonin. New strains of cannabis with varying levels of resin and herb potency were also available.

The increase in drug availability, a trend of falling prices and the variety of illicit drugs obtainable contributed to a trend of users combining different types of drugs to alter their mind and mood, with poly-drug use emerging as the second significant trend in consumption patterns. The final and most important trend of the 1990s and 2000s was the global spread of drug use.

Consumption dynamics in the 2000s

An estimated 200 million people used illegal drugs in the early 2000s (UNODC 2005). This represented 5 per cent of the global population aged between fifteen and sixty-four years old. More people were using illicit drugs in the 2000s than at any previous point in the history of drug control. The development of this 'global habit' (Stares 1996) ran parallel with the deepening of the international control system and the globalization process that was catalysed by the collapse of Soviet communism in the early 1990s. The social and cultural interconnectedness that characterized globalization created a highly favourable environment for the expansion of drug consumption. As the executive director of the UNODC surmised, globalization meant that: 'life styles are shared instantly and internationally', including the culture of drug use (UNODC 2003b: Preface). Interlinked with this, and for reasons explained in the following chapter, globalization led to an increase in the production and trafficking of drugs. This enhanced the availability of controlled substances and reduced their price, in turn expanding access to drugs and the size of the consumer market.

The changing geography of drug use Because of the high mark-up on drugs imported into and sold in the rich, Western European and North American consumer markets, production and trafficking were historically oriented towards supplying these states and the consumption of illicit drugs remained confined to developed countries. This is no longer the case (*The Economist*, 26 July 2001; Griffiths and McKetin 2003; UNODC 2005b). The contemporary surge in drug use was driven by the growth of consumption in three types of 'non-traditional' states. Illicit drug use first increased in the communist and former communist countries of China and the former Soviet bloc. This was despite the introduction of repressive, prohibition-oriented domestic anti-drugs legislation in post-communist countries and the maintenance of a punitive anti-drugs regime in China.

Drug consumption also increased in those countries that cultivated narcotic plants, manufactured controlled drugs and which were positioned along trafficking routes. This included countries such as Afghanistan, Myanmar, Pakistan, Mexico, China, Kenya, Tajikistan and India. Prior to the 1990s, there was little fall-out from the drugs trade in these countries. This changed in the 1990s and 2000s as domestic markets emerged and consumption levels increased (Knickmeyer 2002; Tamayo 2001). Overlapping with the two types of states discussed above, there was a growth in drug consumption across the developing world in general, including South and Central America, Southwest and Southeast Asia and also Africa, where there was a steady rise in illicit drug consumption (Haworth et al. 1982; Klein 1994; Mansfield and Whetton 1996; Nevamdomsky 1981).

The increase in illicit drug use in these new markets was not offset by a fall in drug use in the established consumer markets of the developed world. The trend in Western Europe and North America was one of stabilization or decline of drug use in the early 1990s but, at the end of that decade, drug consumption resumed an upward trend. Although this appeared to have reached a plateau by the early 2000s, no progress was made in reversing existing high levels of illicit consumption. The USA remained the world's largest drug consuming nation. Surveys of last month use in the USA indicated that around 13 million people used drugs in the country out of a population of 260 million. This increased to 25.9 million when drug use over the past year was examined (*The Economist*, 26

July 2001; UNODC 2005b). Western Europe remained the second largest drug consuming area and there was a particularly sharp increase in illicit drug use in Australia in the 1990s after an expansion of heroin and cocaine use in the 1970s and 1980s (UNODC 2005b).

A final aspect of the changing geography of drug use was that consumption ceased to be an urban phenomenon. In countries as diverse as the USA, China, Sweden and Thailand, illicit drug use in rural areas increased, reinforcing a dynamic of diffusion that was the key characteristic of the illicit drug market in the 1990s and 2000s.

The demography of drug consumption The profile of the typical drug user has not radically altered in line with the rise in consumption. Those most likely to use illicit drugs were single, male and aged between eighteen and thirty-five. In developing countries, unemployed men and those with low levels of education and income were over-represented in the drug user community but there was a trend of rising drug consumption among more affluent socio-economic strata (UNODC 2003a: 214). In a reversal of the consumption patterns in the new consumer countries of the developing world, illicit drug consumption in the developed world was historically the preserve of the educated and wealthy. However, from the heroin 'epidemic' of the 1970s onwards this changed as illicit drug consumption diffused downwards to those with fewer economic resources and illicit drug consumption became a classless habit.

There were three other significant demographic trends in drug use observable from the 1990s onwards. The first was the rise of female drug consumption. Women were traditionally a minority group in terms of illicit drug use and in some conservative and religious societies this continued to be the case. In Pakistan, for example, males accounted for an estimated 90 per cent of drug users, while in the Commonwealth of Independent States and South America the figure was 80 per cent. By contrast, in Western Europe females constituted an estimated 40 per cent of illicit drug users, rising to 44 per cent in the USA (ibid.: 213). The increase in female drug consumption was linked to changes in the role and position of women in society and social trends that included women deferring marriage and childbirth.

The second trend was an increase in drug use among young people, specifically those aged between fourteen and eighteen years old. The situation varied between countries and the type of drug used, but overall there was a pattern of increasing juvenile consumption and initiation into drug use at a progressively earlier age. The final trend, although one that had less empirical evidence to support it, was the persistence of consumption as the user aged. This phenomenon was documented in ecstasy and cannabis users and it went against the historically observed pattern of drug use 'maturing out' as a person aged and acquired more social responsibilities (UNODC 2003a, 2005b).

What drugs are being consumed? Before assessing illicit drug use levels in the 2000s, limitations with the available statistical information should be noted. Complex variations existed between and within countries and geographical regions, so there is a danger of over-generalizing when assessing patterns of use. The statistical information produced by international, regional and national drug control agencies and research institutes also differed, so the accuracy of the figures cited is questionable. It is widely assumed, including by the UN itself, that national and global consumption figures are an underestimation of real use levels. As countries such as Thailand, Saudi Arabia and Indonesia retain the death sentence for drug-related offences, under-reporting in these countries was thought to be pronounced. Moreover, despite the technical assistance provided by the UNODC and the GAP, data from the developing world continued to be unreliable. In the case of Africa: 'Monitoring systems [...] are, in general, sparse, and all data currently available have to be treated with a great deal of caution' (UNODC 2003a: 243). The information that was available also tended to be dated, typically appearing two or three years after the original survey work was conducted.

The following analysis is based on the reports of the international drug control bodies at the UN. Although the reliability of the data is questionable, they are useful for providing an indication of the scale and patterns of drug use.

CANNABIS As Table 6.1 indicates, the most widely used drug in the world was cannabis in the form of either herb, meaning the flowers and leaves of the plant, or resin, the secretions from the plant when it is at the flowering stage. Cannabis retained a global appeal and this made it distinct from other illicit drugs.

TABLE 6.1 Global drug use: annual prevalence rate

Controlled drug	Estimated number of users aged 15 to 64	Users as % of global population
Cannabis	160.9	4.0
ATS		
Amphetamines	26.2	0.6
Ecstasy	7.9	0.2
Opiates	15.9	0.4
of which heroin	10.6	0.2
Cocaine	13.7	0.3

Source: UNODC (2005a)

Global cannabis use continued to rise in the contemporary period, increasing from 147.4 million people in the late 1990s to 160.9 million users by 2003–04. The geographical distribution of cannabis use is illustrated in Table 6.2 below.

TABLE 6.2 Annual prevalence of cannabis use

Region	Est. no. of users (millions)		Users as % of population	
	late 1990s	2003–04	late 1990s	2003–04
Europe	31.1	30.4	4.9	5.6
West	20.6	22.9	6.4	7.3
Americas	33.4	36.0	5.7	6.6
North	20.4	28.7	6.6	10.2
South	13.0	8.2	4.7	2.9
Asia	41.6	53.3	1.6	2.2
Oceania	4.4	3.3	18.8	15.8
Africa	36.9	37.0	8.1	8
Global	147.4	160.9	3.5	4

Sources: UNODC (2003a, 2005a)

The majority of cannabis users (53.3 million people) were located in Asia; however, the main area of consumption in terms of cannabis users as a percentage of the total population was Oceania followed by the USA. Papua New Guinea had the highest number of cannabis users in the world, with an annual prevalence rate of 29.5 per cent (UNODC 2003a). In New Zealand and Australia, the figure was 18 per cent and 17.9 per cent respectively although there were indications that cannabis consumption was declining in Australia, with the 2004 National Drug Strategy Household Survey citing an annual cannabis prevalence figure of 11.3 per cent for 2004 (UNODC 2005b). The USA also experienced a stabilization of national cannabis use and a decline in consumption rates among schoolchildren. Among sixteen- to seventeen-year-olds, the National Household Survey on Drug Abuse reported a fall in annual prevalence rates from 50.8 per cent in 1979 to 34.3 per cent by 2004 (ibid.).

Cannabis use levels in Africa were high, with the regional average of 8 per cent shielding individual country prevalence rates that were sharply above the global average. In its 2002 *Global Illicit Drug Trends* Report, the UNODC noted prevalence rates of 21.5 per cent, 18.4 per cent, 16.1 per cent and 14.4 per cent in Ghana, South Africa, Sierra Leone and Nigeria respectively. Cannabis use also increased in Ethiopia and Somalia, Kenya, Uganda and Tanzania. Cannabis-related treatment demand was highest in Africa, where it accounted for 60 per cent of all treatment demand, as opposed to 13 per cent in Europe, 8 per cent in Asia and 23 per cent in the Americas (UNODCCP 1999).

Similarly high per capita consumption rates existed in the Caribbean, with St Vincent recording the highest regional prevalence rate at 18.6 per cent. Cannabis use in Europe was also above the global average, with Britain and Ireland registering the highest levels of cannabis consumption in the region with an annual prevalence rate of 9.4 per cent for both countries. South America and

Eastern Europe had low levels of cannabis use but there were indications that consumption was under-reported (UNODC 2003a: 254). In Asia, cannabis was only the third most widely consumed drug after opiates and ATSs. Even in India, a country with a long history of cannabis cultivation and use, prevalence rates in the late 1990s and early 2000s were below the global average.

AMPHETAMINE-TYPE SUBSTANCES There was a surge in the consumption of ATSs in the mid-1990s. In 2005, it was estimated that 26 million people used this type of drug, with an additional 7.9 million people using ecstasy. Underscoring the rise in the popularity and availability of ATSs, more people used them than the number of heroin and cocaine consumers combined.

TABLE 6.3 Annual prevalence of ATS use

Region	Est. no. of users (millions)		Users as % of population	
	late 1990s	2003–04	late 1990s	2003–04
Oceania	0.6	0.6	2.8	3
Europe	3.3	2.7	0.5	0.5
West	2.4	2.2	0.7	0.7
East	0.9	0.3	0.3	0.2
Americas	4.8	4.3	0.8	0.8
North	2.6	3.0	0.8	1.1
South	2.2	1.4	0.8	0.5
Asia	22.3	16.7	0.9	0.7
Africa	2.4	1.8	0.5	0.4
Global	33.4	26.2	0.8	0.6

Sources: UNODC (2003a, 2005a)

A geographical distinction existed in terms of the type of ATSs consumed. Methamphetamine dominated ATS consumption in Asia and North America, while amphetamine was the primary ATS used in Europe. This pattern was linked to the consolidation of early markets for these drugs and their use in medical practice in the 1930s and 1940s (UNODC 2003b: 15). By 2005, there was no evidence that this geographical division was breaking down but while amphetamine use had stabilized by the early 2000s, there was a consistently upwards trend in methamphetamine consumption.

The highest level of ATS consumption occurred in Asia, which accounted for 16.7 million users. Methamphetamine was the most widely used illicit drug in a large number of East and Southeast Asian countries, with Thailand, the Philippines, the Republic of Korea and Japan experiencing sharp and sustained increases in ATS use from the late 1990s. In Thailand the annual prevalence rate jumped from 0.6 per cent in 1993 to 5.6 per cent in 2001, the highest prevalence rate in the world (UNODC 2005b: 114). The increase in ATS use was paralleled by a surge in ATS-related treatment demand in the region, with more people seeking professional help for problems related to this type of drug than for any other illicit or licit substance. Indicative of this, 92 per cent of all drug treatment demand in the Philippines was for methamphetamine use (UNODC 2003b). There was an important distinction within the Asian methamphetamine market. In Japan, Northeast China, Taiwan, South Korea and the Philippines, high-quality, smokable methamphetamine crystals called Ice were the most widely consumed ATSs. By contrast, in the Southeast Asian countries of Thailand, Laos, Vietnam, Indonesia, Myanmar and also South China, methamphetamine tablets mixed with caffeine and ephedrine known as 'ya baa' were more popular.

While ATS users were concentrated in Asia, the highest rates of ATS consumption in terms of population size were reported in Oceania, with Australia reporting the second highest annual prevalence rate after Thailand. Paralleling trends in North America, where methamphetamine prevalence was also high, the rise in consumption in Australia dated from the late 1990s and it continued to grow strongly in the early 2000s. In the USA methamphetamine use was initially confined to the West Coast, particularly California, but over a five-year period it spread across the country, including the rural interior. Indicative of the high level of contact with and use of the drug, the annual prevalence rate among fifteen- and sixteen-year-olds in the USA during the period 1995 to 2003 was 13.1 per cent (UNODC 2003b: 150). In Western Europe, the use of amphetamines stabilized or declined in the late 1990s after rising throughout the 1980s and early 1990s. A number of Eastern European countries did, however, report a strong increase in use, specifically Estonia, Poland and the Czech Republic.

ECSTASY Ecstasy emerged as a drug of concern for the international and domestic control apparatus in the mid-1980s after its use increased in Western Europe and North America. Its consumption remained concentrated in those two regions and in 2003 they accounted for 80–85 per cent of global ecstasy use.

The distribution of the ecstasy-consuming population began to change as it stabilized in Western Europe and North America but increased in Australia, which at 3.1 per cent had the world's highest annual prevalence rate for ecstasy use in 2003–04. By contrast, the annual prevalence rate for Western Europe and North America was 0.9 per cent and 0.8 per cent respectively (UNODC 2003b). There was a strong increase in ecstasy use in Eastern European and Baltic countries, specifically Poland, Estonia, Lithuania, Latvia and Slovenia and, as with ATS consumption, annual prevalence figures in Eastern Europe began to surpass those of Western Europe.

The ATS 'revolution' and the boom in ecstasy consumption during 1990–2000 largely bypassed Asia, South America, Africa and the Middle East. There were exceptions and countries such as Argentina, Israel, Cameroon and South Africa

TABLE 6.4 Annual prevalence of ecstasy use

Region	Est. no. of users (millions)		Users as % of population	
	late 1990s	2003–04	late 1990s	2003–04
Oceania	0.4	0.6	1.5	3.1
Europe	2.6	3.0	0.4	0.6
West	2.3	2.7	0.6	0.9
East	0.3	0.2	0.1	0.1
Americas	3.8	2.8	0.7	0.5
North	3.6	2.3	1.2	0.8
South	0.2	0.5	0.1	0.2
Asia	0.2	1.3	0.01	0.05
Africa	0.01	0.1	0.002	0.03
Global	7.0	7.9	0.2	0.2

Sources: UNODC (2003a, 2005a)

did report a rise in the use of ecstasy. By the 2000s there were indications that ATS use was spreading, with 77 per cent of African countries and 67 per cent of South American countries reporting an increase in ATS consumption (ibid.: 56). The UNODC concluded that there were insufficient data to substantiate a reported rise in ATS consumption in East and Southeast Asian countries (ibid.: 102). While ATS use was low to negligible, there was a high level of consumption of licit pharmaceutical preparations that contained ATS in these regions, particularly the Middle East, with the use of controlled stimulants such as fenetylline rising in Saudi Arabia, Jordan and Syria.

OPIATES In 2005, the UNODC estimated that 16 million people used opiates, of whom 10.6 million, or 0.3 per cent of the global population, used heroin. At 8.5 million people, Asia had the largest number of opiate users, with the majority concentrated in the southwest and southeast of the region. The Islamic Republic of Iran had the highest number of opiate users in the world, estimated at one million opium and 400,000 heroin users. Pakistan experienced a staggering surge in opiate use in the 1990s, when heroin accounted for half of all drug use, but annual prevalence rates subsequently decreased after rising to 5 per cent in the late 1990s.

Those countries bordering Myanmar, a leading opiate producer, and located along the main trafficking routes out of the country, reported an increase in already high levels of opiate use in the 1990s. In a 1993 survey, the Thai government estimated there were 280,000 opiate users in the country of which 214,000 used heroin, while Vietnam reported 97,000 registered opiate addicts in 1999. The highest level of opiate use was recorded in the People's Democratic Republic of Laos, which had a prevalence rate of 2 per cent throughout the 1990s.

Opiate use spread rapidly in Central Asia in the mid-1990s and it also increased in Afghanistan, a country where there were traditionally low levels of use. In Kazakhstan, the number of registered drug users increased from 70 per 100,000 people in 1992 to 279 per 100,000 people, with over half of those registered using opiates (UNODC 2003a). While the use of opiates in Asia was high and increasing, the total number of users in the region represented 0.3 per cent of the population and this was below the global average.

TABLE 6.5 Annual prevalence of opiate use, 2003–04 (late 1990s in brackets)

Region	Est. no. of opiate users (millions)	Of which heroin users (millions)	Opiate users as % of population	Heroin users as % of population
Europe	4.2 (2.7)	2.9 (1.5)	0.8 (0.4)	0.5 (0.2)
West	1.6	1.5	0.5	0.5
East	2.4	1.2	1.7	0.8
Americas	2.4 (1.4)	1.6 (1.3)	0.4 (0.2)	0.3 (0.2)
North	1.3 (1.1)	1.2	0.5 (0.4)	0.4
South	1.1 (0.3)	0.3	0.4 (0.1)	0.1
Asia	8.5 (8.6)	5.3 (5.7)	0.3 (0.4)	0.2 (0.2)
Oceania	0.09 (0.13)	0.03 (0.6)	0.4 (0.6)	0.2 (0.3)
Africa	0.8 (0.6)	0.8 (0.6)	0.2 (0.1)	0.2 (0.1)
Global	15.9 (13.5)	10.6 (9.2)	0.4 (0.3)	0.3 (0.2)

Source: UNODC (2005a)

The largest opiate-consuming region measured by population size was Europe, which had mixed progress in reducing consumption rates that first started to accelerate in the 1970s. While countries such as Germany, Spain and Portugal experienced a fall in heroin and opiate use in the 1990s, the reverse was the case in Italy and the UK. Britain recorded a three-fold increase in heroin use from 1998 to 2000 and a five-fold increase in the number of heroin-related deaths between 1993 and 2000. The total number of people using heroin in Britain was estimated to be 270,000 people (UNODC 2003a: 118; White 2001).

Any decline in overall consumption figures in the West was offset by a surge in opiate use in Eastern Europe, the Baltic states and specifically Russia, where annual prevalence rates increased from 0.9 per cent in the 2001 *Global Illicit Drugs Survey* to 1.8 per cent in the following year's annual report. This was underpinned by user substitution of 'kompot' poppy straw for heroin and an increase in opiate trafficking from Afghanistan. The Middle East, Southwest Asia and Southern and Eastern Africa also reported increased heroin use while, in Oceania, a sustained fall was recorded between 2000 and 2005 after heroin use had risen strongly throughout the 1990s.

Trends in drug consumption

The pattern of opiate use in the USA was cyclical. During the early 1990s, the consumption of heroin fell back after rising throughout the 1980s. After 1997, however, it began to pick up again. Underscoring this, annual prevalence rates among high-school children increased from 0.6 per cent in 1993 to 1.3 per cent in 2000. The number of hardcore heroin users, defined as those using on at least a weekly basis, increased from 630,000 in 1993 to 977,000 in 2000, out of a total of 1.3 million heroin users (Johnston et al. 2001). Opiate consumption also followed an upward trend in South America in the 2000s after remaining low and stable from the 1970s through to the 1990s. Although national authorities in countries including Mexico, Colombia and Ecuador reported an increase in heroin use, consumption remained low compared to other regions at an annual prevalence rate of less than 0.2 per cent. The singular exception was Argentina, which reported a strong increase in use during the 1990s and an annual prevalence figure of 0.9 per cent (UNODC 2005b).

As in South America, Africa did not traditionally have a high level of opiate use and consumption figures remained low in the 1980s and 1990s. In the 2000s, however, the majority of reports submitted by African countries to the CND detailed rising heroin prevalence, with the island countries of Mauritius and Cape Verde and the Atlantic Coast states experiencing a steady rise in consumption. South Africa, Ghana, Zimbabwe and Tanzania also reported an increase in heroin consumption and opiate treatment demand during the period 2001 to 2004.

COCAINE Cocaine was consumed by 0.3 per cent of the global population in the 2000s, with 70 per cent of consumption concentrated in the Americas. The USA was one of the world's largest cocaine-consuming nations although, as with cannabis, use levels fell back from the high annual prevalence rates of 5 to 7 per cent that were recorded in the 1980s (Adams and Kozel 1985). US school surveys indicated that the drug continued to be popular among younger users, with 5 per cent of twelve- to thirteen-year-olds reporting cocaine use over the previous year (UNODC 2005b). To the south of the USA, cocaine consumption saw an increase in the Caribbean region and in South and Central America during the late 1990s and early 2000s after low levels of use in the 1980s and early 1990s (Jutkowitz and Hongsook Eu 1993). Particularly large increases were reported in Panama, Honduras and Argentina as cocaine use diffused downwards from the elite to poorer groups.

Cocaine use followed an upwards trend in Western Europe from the 1980s onwards and, by the early 2000s, the region accounted for 22 per cent of global cocaine consumption. As with trends in cannabis and heroin consumption, Britain had one of the highest rates of cocaine use in Europe with a prevalence rate of around 2 per cent of the population. Cocaine consumption followed a similar upward trend in Spain and school surveys from these two countries demonstrated a lifetime prevalence rate of 3–4 per cent among those aged sixteen

TABLE 6.6 Annual prevalence of cocaine use

Region	Est. no. of users (millions)		Users as % of population 15–64 years	
	late 1990s	2003–04	late 1990s	2003–04
Europe	3.1	3.4	0.5	0.6
West	2.8	3.2	0.9	1.0
Americas	9.1	8.9	1.5	1.6
North	6.3	6.5	2.0	2.3
South	2.8	2.8	1.0	0.8
Asia	0.2	0.2	0.01	0.01
Oceania	0.2	0.2	0.9	0.9
Africa	0.9	0.9	0.2	0.2
Global	13.4	13.7	0.3	0.3

Sources: UNODC (2003a, 2005a)

and under (UNODC 2003a). Australia experienced a noticeably sharp rise in cocaine use, with prevalence rates tripling in the 1990s.

Cocaine use in Asia, Africa and the former Soviet Union remained negligible but a number of South and West African countries, specifically Ghana, Nigeria and South Africa, reported strong consumption increases in the late 1990s and early 2000s (UNODCCP 1999).

Conclusion The data provide irrefutable evidence that the international drug control system has not only failed to reduce the consumption of addictive and dangerous drugs, it has also presided over a sustained increase in their use. No progress has been made in achieving global abstinence, despite the vast technical, financial and organizational resources dedicated to this end. In the contemporary period, variables such as age, gender, nationality and income level are no longer significant determinants of drug use and, as patterns of drug consumption have been consolidated, it is perhaps more appropriate to talk of established patterns of global drug use rather than emerging trends.

It would appear that the popular interest in experimenting with drugs has never attenuated despite the introduction of criminal sanctions. A resilient connection between consumers and suppliers was maintained throughout a century of control efforts. As the following chapter demonstrates, this was possible because supply-side reduction policies significantly failed to reduce the volume of illicit drugs available.

7 | Trends in cultivation and production

Owing to the formative influence of the US prohibition lobby, international drug control was focused on terminating the supply of drugs from source countries. From the beginnings of international drug control, this was conceptualized as a sine qua non for reductions in illicit consumption. The international control system placed particular emphasis on the elimination of plant-based drugs and semi-synthetic by-products such as opiates, cocaine and cannabis. This reflected the preoccupation with these substances when the USA first initiated drug diplomacy. Throughout the history of international drug control, two different strategies have been used to terminate drug supplies 'at source'. These were cultivation eradication, either forced or negotiated, and alternative development. The aim of alternative development was to encourage cultivators of drug plants to move into the formal economy through initiatives such as crop substitution programmes. Owing to the strength of the prohibition tendency within the international control body and the unilateral pursuit of prohibition by the USA, emphasis was persistently placed on eradication, with alternative development largely marginalized until the 1990s.

Mirroring the record of international drug control in the field of demand reduction, there has been no progress in reducing the supply of illicit drugs. Drug plant cultivation and the manufacture and production of controlled drugs reached record levels by the early 2000s. Just as criminalization and punishment were ineffective in transforming consumption patterns, so repression and eradication failed to have an impact on drug supply.

Supply controls phase 1: opiates, supply reduction and the rise of the Golden Triangle

During the first phase of the control system covering the period from its foundation at the Hague Opium Conference through to the 1950s, major progress was made in reducing the cultivation of the opium poppy through the use of cultivation controls and the introduction of strict reporting requirements by the League of Nations and the United Nations. During the period 1906 to 1934, global opium production fell from 41,600 to 16,600 mt as cultivating countries were brought into the multilateral control framework. The progress made in reducing the supply of opium before the Second World War was continued in the post-war period; by 1970, illicit opium production had fallen back to an estimated 1,094 mt (*Bulletin on Narcotics* 1949; McCoy 1972).

From 1934 through to the early 1970s, opium production in Iran, Afghanistan, India, Turkey – four of the largest opium poppy cultivating and opium producing countries – fell from 1,126 mt in 1934 to 381 mt. However, it was the ending of China's role as the world's largest opium producing country that accounted for the dramatic decline in illicit global opium production (McCoy 1972; McAllister 2000). In contrast to the experience of the four Southwest and Southeast Asian states, China's suppression of cultivation and production did not stem from the country's incorporation into the control framework; it resulted from the communist revolution in the country in 1947. Under Mao Zedong, China embarked on a massive, brutal and highly successful campaign to eradicate opium poppy cultivation, opium production and consumption in 1950. Until the launch of this anti-opium campaign, China had been responsible for 85 per cent of the global opium supply, with cultivation and production flourishing under the nationalist Kuomintang (KMT) administration that seized control of the country after the collapse of the Ming dynasty in 1910 (Yongming 1999).

Despite the advances that were made in reducing the overall supply of illicit opium and opiates, and the ending of cultivation and production in the world's largest opium producing country, the connection between cultivators, producers and consumers was maintained.

The beginnings of the Golden Triangle The Second World War, the decline of Chinese opium production and the displacement of the KMT triggered changes to the geography and distribution of opium cultivation and production in the post-war period. Although this transformation began in the 1950s, it did not result in a large increase in the volume of illicit opiate stocks until the 1970s.

The first important change was the expansion of cultivation and production in the Southeast Asian countries of Thailand, Myanmar, Laos and Vietnam, which until that point had been minor actors in the opium economy. This was a result of the wartime blockade on supplies of Indian opium that were traditionally purchased by the national opium monopolies operating in these countries. Domestic cultivation and production were consequently expanded in order to meet local demand and the fiscal needs of the state. The French administration in Indochina (Laos and North Vietnam) revised its policy of suppressing cultivation by hill tribes such as the Hmong and this led to an increase in opium production in these two countries from 7.4 tons in 1940 to 60.6 tons in 1944 (*Bulletin on Narcotics* 1949; McCoy 1972).

Cultivation and production also rose in Myanmar after the Thai Northern Army annexed the Shan states in the northeast of the country during the war. Like the French in Indochina, the Thai forces encouraged opium production to substitute for the decline in supplies from India and China. Opium production in Myanmar consequently increased from 8 tons in 1936 to an estimated 36 tons by 1942 (McCoy 1991). Mexico also emerged as another 'new' cultivating and producer state during this period, with opium poppy cultivation initiated in the Sierra de la Madre area of the country in the 1930s (Recio 2002).

After the war, illicit cultivation and production in Southeast Asia continued, despite the French administration ending the opium monopoly system in Indochina and Thai forces withdrawing from the Shan Plateau after the capitulation of Japan. KMT elements moved into the Shan states after their expulsion from China and directed cultivation and production, with the revenues raised used to fund anti-communist resistance efforts. The KMT tapped into a large market for illicit opium that had expanded in the post-war period as the international drug control apparatus enforced the suppression of opium smoking and the closure of opium monopolies. The KMT continued to dominate production in the Shan states from bases on the Thai border after their expulsion from the region by Myanmar and Chinese forces in 1961 (Renard 2001; McCoy 1972).

HEROIN MANUFACTURE IN SOUTHEAST ASIA The immediate post-war period also marked the first phase of large-scale illicit heroin manufacture, which contrasted with the pre-war distribution model of diversification from licit supplies. As soon as the control system went into effect in the inter-war period, illicit supply centres emerged. In the 1920s Shanghai was the centre for illicit heroin trafficking. European and North American criminal organizations, such as the Eliopolos syndicate and the New York Jewish gangster network that was led by Yasha Katzenberg and Louis Buchalter, dispatched contacts and built distribution links in the city after heroin exports were prohibited under the Geneva Convention of 1928.

The development of Southeast Asian illicit heroin manufacturing capacity was linked to the KMT. The nationalist forces established heroin refineries in Shanghai and British-controlled Hong Kong at the end of the 1940s for the processing of opium produced in Myanmar and the Thai border area. The KMT worked with Tu Yueh-sheng's Green Gang in the 1930s and 1940s, although the syndicate faced intense and violent competition for control of the trade from ethnic Chinese Chiu Chau networks in Hong Kong (McCoy 1972).

In the late 1960s, the Hong Kong heroin syndicates expanded their operations and established refineries on the Thai–Myanmar border from where they manufactured high-grade No. 4 heroin. There were two large markets for the heroin produced. The first consisted of domestic consumers of opium and morphine, who, like the North American opiate users in the 1930s, turned to heroin. The second consumer market comprised US soldiers in South Vietnam. As the US military presence in Southeast Asia increased in the late 1960s, so did the market for and production of heroin. Opium production was stepped up in the so-called Golden Triangle countries of Laos, Myanmar and Thailand and refining facilities established in all of the main cultivating and producer areas (Booth 1998; Ul Haq 2000; McCoy 1972).

By 1970, Southeast Asia had a self-contained and integrated heroin industry, with opium production in the region totalling 713 mt, in contrast to the 15.5 mt produced at the start of the Second World War. The Golden Triangle countries consequently substituted for production falls in China, accounting for nearly 70 per cent of illicit global opium supply during this period. The supply of heroin to countries outside the region, specifically the US market, was met by illicit Turkish opium that was manufactured into heroin in Marseilles, France. As in Southeast Asia, this was controlled by a large, highly organized criminal gang comprised of Corsican nationals.

The pattern of illicit cultivation, production and supply that had developed in the immediate post-war period underwent significant change in the 1970s. This ran parallel with an increase in unilateral US supply-source eradication efforts during President Nixon's 'war on drugs'.

Diffusion By 1973, Turkey had been taken out of the illicit global opium supply chain as a result of US counter-narcotics efforts that included the provision of $35.7 million in development assistance to the Turkish government. Having previously supplied 7 per cent of illicit opium demand, Turkish production collapsed, falling from 58 mt in 1971 to zero by 1975. Combined with action against the Marseilles heroin laboratories by French authorities, this eliminated the so-called 'French Connection' supply and trafficking route to the USA (McCoy 1972).

The elimination of this supply source did not end the flow of heroin into the USA as Southeast Asian syndicates redirected excess stock to the US market. In response, the Nixon administration stepped up enforcement assistance to the Thai government. Over $12 million was provided to enhance the enforcement and interdiction capacities of Thai customs and drug officials, in addition to training from a team of thirty Drug Enforcement Administration (DEA) agents. This did lead to an increase in seizures of US-bound heroin but as the assistance did not address cultivation, as it had in Turkey, the volume of illicit opium produced remained stable. While large quantities of heroin continued to be available, the direction of the illicit traffic was altered (Ashton 2002; Ul Haq 2000). In the mid-1970s, Southeast Asian heroin previously distributed in the USA was redirected to Europe, while supplies of illicitly manufactured No. 3 Mexican heroin filled the vacuum of supply in the USA. As the focus of US enforcement activities was reoriented to Mexico, demand for and supplies of Southeast Asian heroin increased in the US market.

Supply controls phase 2: supply expansion and the Golden Crescent

Towards the end of the 1970s, there was a second important transformation of cultivation and production patterns. Supplies from Southeast Asia fell back sharply as a result of a major drought from 1978 to 1980 that reduced opium production from 700 mt in 1971 to 160 mt. However, this did not lead to a decline in illicit opium supply as opium poppy cultivation and opium production increased in the traditional Southwest Asian producer states of Iran, Afghanistan and Pakistan.

Production in Southwest Asia had increased steadily throughout the 1970s, rising from an estimated 504 mt in 1971 to 1,400 tons by 1978. There was a pronounced increase in illicit opium production in Afghanistan, where production volumes rose from 100 mt in 1971 to 300 mt by 1982. In 1983, production practically doubled to 575 mt. This meant that Southwest Asian heroin produced in laboratories in Pakistan was available in the European and US markets as Southeast Asian and Mexican supplies declined (Ashton 2002; McCoy 1972; Ul Haq 2000).

There was a surge in illicit global opiate stocks in the 1980s as cultivation increased and production doubled in Southwest Asia, and as the Southeast Asian opium sector recovered from monsoon failure. During the period 1982 to 1989, illicit world opium production surged from 1,500 to 4,100 mt. By the mid-1980s, production levels in Southeast Asia had surpassed those of the Southwest, illustrating a pattern of pendulum swings in production between the two regions. The resurgence of Southeast Asian opium supplies stemmed from a particularly large cultivation and production increase in Myanmar, where the volume of illicit opium produced jumped from 500 mt in 1981 to 2,528 by 1989. As a result of this surge, Myanmar accounted for around 80 per cent of total Southeast Asian production and 62 per cent of global illicit opium supply during this period. Opium poppy cultivation and opium production also rose in Laos, where it increased from 50 mt in 1981 to 378 tons in 1989. Outside Asia, opium production increased in Mexico from an estimated 16 mt in 1982 to 76 mt in 1989 (McCoy 1972).

The contemporary period

SOUTHEAST ASIA As the statistical information in Table 7.1 demonstrates, opium production in Southeast Asia declined in the 1990s after peaking at 2,032 mt in 1991. The most significant contemporary development has been the sharp fall in production in Myanmar, which accounted for 370 mt of illicit opium supply in 2004 in contrast to the 2,528 mt produced at the end of the 1980s. Production levels also fell back as a result of enforcement activities and the introduction of alternative development programmes in Lao PDR, Vietnam and Thailand, with the latter two countries no longer considered significant opium producers by the international control bodies.

Underpinning the fall in production in Southeast Asia was a decline in the total area dedicated to opium poppy cultivation. This fell by one-third between 1998 and 2004. In Lao PDR, the area under cultivation in 2004 was roughly a seventh of the figure reported in 1988, while in Myanmar, the area under cultivation more than halved.

TABLE 7.1 Opium production in Southeast Asia, 1990–2004 (metric tons)

Year	Lao PDR	Myanmar	Thailand	Vietnam	Total
1990	202	1,621	20	90	1,933
1991	196	1,728	23	85	2,032
1992	127	1,660	14	61	1,862
1993	169	1,791	17	21	1,998
1994	120	1,583	3	15	1,721
1995	128	1,664	2	9	1,803
1996	140	1,760	5	9	1,914
1997	147	1,676	4	2	1,829
1998	124	1,303	8	2	1,437
1999	124	895	8	2	1,029
2000	167	1,087	6	n.a.	1,260
2001	134	1,097	6	n.a.	1,237
2002	112	828	9	n.a.	949
2003	120	810	n.a.	n.a.	930
2004	43	370	n.a.	n.a.	413

Sources: UNODC (2003a, 2004a, 2005a)

TABLE 7.2 Opium poppy cultivation in Southeast Asia, 1988–2004 (hectares)

Year	Lao PDR	Myanmar	Thailand	Vietnam	Total
1988	40,400	104,200	2,811	12,000	159,411
1989	42,130	143,000	2,982	14,000	202,112
1990	30,580	150,100	1,782	18,000	200,462
1991	29,625	160,000	3,727	17,000	210,352
1992	19,190	153,700	3,016	12,199	188,105
1993	26,040	165,800	998	4,268	197,106
1994	18,520	146,600	478	3,066	168,664
1995	19,650	154,070	168	1,880	175,768
1996	21,601	163,000	368	1,743	186,712
1997	24,082	155,150	352	340	179,924
1998	26,837	130,300	716	442	158,295
1999	22,543	89,500	702	442	113,187
2000	19,052	108,700	890	n.a.	128,642
2001	17,255	105,000	820	n.a.	123,075
2002	14,000	81,400	750	n.a.	96,150
2003	12,000	62,200	n.a.	n.a.	74,200
2004	6,600	44,200	n.a.	n.a.	50,800

Sources: UNODC (2003a, 2004a, 2005a)

SOUTHWEST ASIA By contrast, the trend in Southwest Asia was one of expanding opium poppy cultivation and an increase in opium production levels. This was accounted for by developments in a single country: Afghanistan. Illicit opium production in the country increased from 1,570 mt in 1990 to 3,276 mt a decade later. In 2004, this had climbed to 4,200 mt, with Afghanistan accounting for 80 per cent of illicit global opium supplies. There was a stunning collapse in production in 2001 after the Taliban regime launched an anti-opium drive that reduced Afghanistan's share of the global supply to 12 per cent. However, as cultivation and production recovered in 2002, so did the country's share of illicit global production, which increased to 76 per cent. As a result of the surge in Afghan opium production and the production declines in Southeast Asia, the Southwest region became the most important and significant opiate production area in the world in the 1990s and 2000s.

TABLE 7.3 Opium production in Southwest Asia, 1990–2004 (metric tons)

Year	Afghanistan	Pakistan	Total
1990	1,570	150	1,720
1991	1,980	160	2,140
1992	1,970	181	2,151
1993	2,330	161	2,491
1994	3,416	128	3,544
1995	2,335	112	2,447
1996	2,248	24	2,272
1997	2,804	24	2,828
1998	2,693	26	2,719
1999	4,565	9	4,574
2000	3,276	8	3,284
2001	185	5	190
2002	3,400	5	3,405
2003	3,600	52	3,652
2004	4,200	40	4,240

Sources: UNODC (2003a, 2004a, 2005a)

As Table 7.4 shows, the area under opium poppy cultivation in Afghanistan increased significantly during the 1990s and 2000s, extending from established growing areas such as Nangahar, Helmand, Uruzgan and Kandahar into all of the country's thirty-four provinces. Consequently, while the area under cultivation in 1990 totalled 41,300 hectares (ha), by 2004 this had increased to 131,000 ha.

Although the area dedicated to opium poppy cultivation was larger in Myanmar than Afghanistan in the 1990s, Afghanistan produced more opium per hectare. This was because the poppies planted in Afghanistan produced higher yields. In 2002, it was estimated that one hectare of opium poppy cultivation in Myanmar produced 10 kilograms of opium. By contrast, in Afghanistan, the yield was 46 kg per hectare. These differences in yield and production ratios were attributed to a number of factors, including: the rate at which the land was used; climatic conditions; and the variety of poppy grown. Moreover, as cultivation in Afghanistan spread across the country, it extended from irrigated agricultural areas to rain-fed fields, a development that significantly increased yields and quality of the poppy and the opium produced.

TABLE 7.4 Opium poppy cultivation in Southwest Asia, 1988–2004 (hectares)

Year	Afghanistan	Pakistan	Total
1988	32,000	6,519	38,519
1989	34,300	7,464	41,764
1990	41,300	7,488	48,788
1991	50,800	7,692	58,762
1992	49,300	9,493	58,793
1993	58,300	7,329	65,629
1994	71,470	5,759	77,229
1995	53,759	5,091	58,850
1996	56,824	873	57,697
1997	58,416	874	59,290
1998	63,674	950	64,624
1999	90,583	284	90,867
2000	82,171	260	82,431
2001	7,606	213	7,819
2002	74,100	622	74,722
2003	80,000	2,500	82,500
2004	131,000	1,500	132,500

Sources: UNODC (2003a, 2004a, 2005a)

A further important trend of the late 1990s and early 2000s was the relocation of Southwest Asian heroin refining. While laboratories in Pakistan continued to play an important role in the manufacture of heroin from Afghan opium, domestic heroin production increased in Afghanistan and, as a result, the country became a self-contained, integrated opiate production unit.

LATIN AMERICA Aside from the rise of Afghanistan as a global supplier of illicit opiates, two Latin American countries, Mexico and Colombia, assumed an increasingly important role in illicit opium supply. The area under opium poppy cultivation in Mexico expanded during the 1980s and this led to an increase in annual production rates from an estimated 17 mt in the 1970s to around 40 mt. The number of heroin manufacturing facilities also increased in the country. In the 1990s, Mexico's opiate trade was eclipsed by the rise of poppy cultivation and opium production in Colombia, where it was introduced by the Cali cartel in 1991. The area under cultivation in both countries expanded throughout the 1990s, with Colombian cultivation surpassing Mexico in 1992.

TABLE 7.5 Opium poppy cultivation in Latin America, 1988–2004 (hectares)

Year	Colombia	Mexico	Total
1988	n.a.	5,001	5,001
1989	n.a.	6,600	6,600
1990	n.a.	5,450	5,450
1991	1,160	3,765	4,925
1992	6,578	3,310	9,888
1993	5,008	3,960	8,968
1994	15,091	5,795	20,886
1995	5,226	5,050	10,276
1996	4,916	5,100	10,016
1997	6,584	4,000	10,584
1998	7,350	5,500	12,850
1999	6,500	3,600	10,100
2000	6,500	1,900	8,400
2001	4,300	4,400	8,700
2002	4,100	2,700	6,800
2003	4,100	4,800	8,900
2004	3,950	n.a.	8,750

Sources: UNODC (2003a, 2004a, 2005a)

Eradication programmes introduced by the Colombian and Mexican administrations that were supported by the US government in the 1990s had a minimal impact on cultivation levels and opium production volumes. In 1991, the countries jointly produced 57 mt of opium. By 2004, this had risen to an estimated 157 mt despite enhanced interdiction and eradication activities. A significant

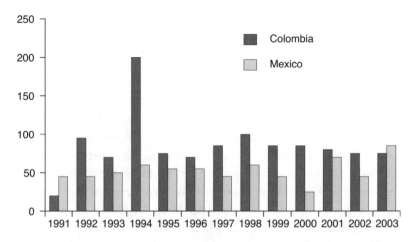

Figure 7.1 Opium production in Latin America, 1991–2003 (metric tons)
Sources: **UNODC (2003a, 2004a, 2005a)**

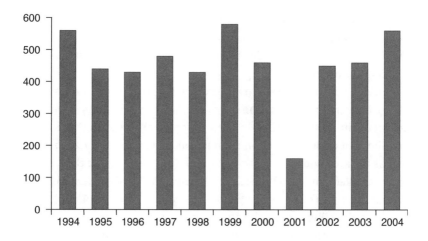

Figure 7.2 Potential global heroin manufacture, 1994–2004 (metric tons)
Sources: **UNODC (2003a, 2004a, 2005a)**

trend in the Latin American opiate producers was that falls in cultivation and production in one of the countries were absorbed by the other. Hence as Mexican opium production declined in the 1990s, it increased in Colombia, with this pattern reversing in the early 2000s.

In line with the global increase in opium poppy cultivation and opium production, the volume of illicit heroin increased during the 1990s and it remained high and stable into the early 2000s. Potential global manufacture in 1990 was estimated to be 376 mt. By 2004 this had risen to 565 mt.

Coca and cocaine

In contrast to the opium poppy, the coca bush can be cultivated only in specific climatic zones. The plant is native to South America and, aside from efforts to transplant it to Southeast Asia at the beginning of the twentieth century, its cultivation remains confined to the Andean region of South America, specifically Peru and Bolivia. Coca is not native to Colombia and the plant was introduced in that country only in the 1980s.

Coca cultivation and cocaine production remained at insignificant levels until the drug was reintroduced into the US market in the 1970s. In contrast to the opium poppy and cannabis plant, the international drugs control apparatus reticently acknowledged the social and cultural functions of coca in Andean societies and as a result of this and the twenty-five-year deadline for eradication set out in the 1961 Single Convention, small-scale legal cultivation was allowed to continue in Bolivia and Peru. As demand for cocaine expanded, illicit cultivation and production increased at an exponential rate, most markedly in the 1980s, a period when US cocaine consumption doubled to 72 tons per year. The rapid increase in cocaine use in the USA and the development of a market for 'crack' cocaine led President Ronald Reagan to launch a 'war on drugs' in the 1980s. US-sponsored supply-side repression measures, combined with changing patterns of demand, led to fluctuations in coca cultivation and cocaine production levels in South America.

In terms of cultivation patterns, Peru lost its position as the largest coca cultivating country to Colombia in 1997, the latter experiencing a persistently upward trend in cultivation levels until enforcement and eradication efforts reduced the area under cultivation from a peak of 163,300 ha in 2000 to 80,000 by 2004. As the area under cultivation in Colombia contracted in the early 2000s, it increased in Peru and also Bolivia, which had significantly reduced cultivation throughout the 1990s to a low of 14,600 ha by 2000. By 2004, Colombia was still the world's leading illicit coca cultivator, supplying 50 per cent of the global total, followed by Peru with 32 per cent and Bolivia on 18 per cent.

TABLE 7.6 South American coca bush cultivation, 1988–2004 (hectares)

Year	Bolivia*	Colombia	Peru	Total
1988	48,900	34,000	110,400	193,300
1989	52,900	42,400	120,400	215,700
1990	50,300	40,100	121,300	211,700
1991	47,900	37,500	120,800	206,200
1992	45,300	37,100	129,100	211,500
1993	47,200	39,700	108,800	195,700
1994	48,100	44,700	108,600	201,400
1995	48,600	50,900	115,300	214,800
1996	48,100	67,200	94,400	209,700
1997	45,800	79,400	68,800	194,000
1998	38,000	101,800	51,00	190,800
1999	21,800	160,100	38,700	220,600
2000	14,600	163,300	43,400	221,300
2001	19,900	144,800	46,200	210,900
2002	21,600	102,000	46,700	170,300
2003	23,600	86,000	44,200	153,800
2004	27,700	80,000	50,300	158,000

* Figures for Bolivia include coca cultivation that is legal under law 1008.
Sources: UNODC (2003a, 2004a, 2005a)

As in Afghanistan, the area under cultivation in these three countries, but most specifically in Colombia, extended from geographically confined areas across the national territory. In the Colombian case, cultivation spread into nineteen of the country's twenty-two states, with declines in established cultivating regions such as Putumayo, Caquetá and Guaviare being followed by an increase in non-traditional cultivating regions such as Antioquia, Nariño and Bolivar.

Paralleling trends in coca cultivation and dry leaf manufacture, cocaine production levels remained high and stable in the 1990s and 2000s. In 1990, potential cocaine manufacture was estimated to be 774 mt. A decade later, this had risen to 879 mt. Colombia assumed the mantle of the world's largest cocaine producer in 1997, when it surpassed Peru. There was a sharp fall in Colombian cocaine production after the launch of the cultivation eradication and counter-insurgency programme, Plan Colombia, in 1999, with production figures dipping to 390 mt by 2004. Although this reduced the global supply of cocaine, production increased in Peru and Bolivia, jumping to a six-year high of 107 mt in the case of Bolivia.

TABLE 7.7 Potential cocaine manufacture, 1988–2004 (metric tons)

Year	Bolivia	Colombia	Peru	Total
1988	148	51	327	527
1989	168	64	373	604
1990	189	92	492	774
1991	220	88	525	833
1992	225	91	550	866
1993	240	119	410	769
1994	255	201	435	891
1995	240	230	460	930
1996	215	300	435	950
1997	200	350	325	875
1998	150	435	240	825
1999	70	680	175	925
2000	43	695	141	879
2001	60	617	150	827
2002	60	580	160	800
2003	79	440	155	674
2004	107	390	190	687

Sources: UNODC (2003a, 2004a, 2005a)

The manufacture and supply of other controlled drugs

Reams of information are available from the UNODC and national drug control bodies in relation to heroin and cocaine, the two controlled drugs that account for the lowest level of global illicit drug consumption. However, there is little information on the cultivation and production of cannabis or the manufacture of ATSs, the two most widely consumed illicit drugs in the world. In the 2005 *World Drug Report*, the UNODC conceded that: 'a lack of adequate data does not enable the UNODC to precisely monitor trends in cannabis and synthetic drug production from year to year' (UNODC 2005a: 10).

There are a number of reasons why cannabis production is more difficult to track than heroin and cocaine. The most significant is the size of the sector.

TABLE 7.8 Distribution of cannabis herb and cannabis resin production

Cannabis herb	% of global supply	Cannabis resin	% of global supply
North America	33	North Africa	42
West, Central and North Africa	19	Near and Middle East/	
South and East Africa	9	Southwest Asia	27
South Asia	9	South Asia	9
South America	8	Central Asia and Trans-	
Central Asia and Transcaucasus	5	caucasus	9
Near and Middle East/Southwest		Southeast Europe	5
Asia	5	Caribbean	3
East and Southeast Asia	4	Other	5
Western and Central Europe	3		
Oceania	2		
Central America and Caribbean	2		
Eastern and Southeastern Europe	1		

Source: UNODC (2005a)

The cannabis plant grows with ease in practically any climate and, underscoring this, the UNODC identified 163 cannabis producer countries out of a total of 197 reporting to the body (ibid.: 82). This demonstrated that production had diversified away from the leading producer countries of the 1960s and 1970s, such as the USA, Morocco, Nepal, India, Lebanon and Afghanistan, although these countries did remain a significant source of supply: Morocco, for example, accounted for an estimated 80 per cent of the cannabis resin market in Western Europe.

The second problem with monitoring cannabis, and reinforcing the dynamic of diffusion in cannabis production, was that indoor cannabis growing increased dramatically in Western Europe, Oceania and North America during the 1990s and 2000s as cheap and simple home-grow and hydroponic kits became available. This contributed to a significant change in the dynamics of cannabis supply, specifically in relation to cannabis herb, with individual consumers in the developed world producing for their own requirements. This import substitution process was most noticeable in the Netherlands, where the UNODC estimated that half of the cannabis in national circulation was domestically produced.

Despite the problems implicit in establishing a global cannabis production figure, the UNODC estimated that in 2003 cannabis herb production may have exceeded 40,000 mt with North America accounting for one-third, or 14,000 mt, of this total. An estimated 28 per cent of production occurred in Africa, which was the second largest producer in the world with 12,000 mt cultivated in countries such as Malawi, Nigeria, Swaziland, Lesotho and South Africa. Production of cannabis resin was in the region of 7,400 mt, of which 31 per cent originated in Morocco. Pakistan (18 per cent), Afghanistan (18 per cent) India (9 per cent), Lebanon (9 per cent), Iran (8 per cent) Albania (8 per cent) and Kazakhstan (7 per cent) were also important resin producer countries (UNODC 2005a: 83).

Amphetamine-type substances Data chronicling illicit ATS production history is sparse and the available statistical estimates are considered unreliable. Information gathering on ATSs is particularly difficult for authorities because, as with cannabis, production is dispersed across many countries. Unlike plant-based drugs, with the exception of 'loft-cannabis', ATS production is also completely 'hidden' from the start to the finish of the manufacturing process. The raw materials for ATS production are precursor chemicals, such as 3,4-mdp-2-P and P-2-P or ephedrine and pseudo-ephedrine that are used in the manufacture of ecstasy (MDMA) and amphetamines.

Although these chemicals are subject to international controls, as laid out in the 1988 trafficking convention, they are widely available from India and China, the largest chemical precursor manufacturing countries, in legitimate pharmaceutical and household products and through diversification from licit chemical supplies. This poses significant problems for governments when estimating production because, unlike hectares under cultivation, manufacturing is not visible. More problematically for control bodies, when controls have been effective in reducing the supply of precursor chemicals, these have been substituted in the ATS production process by other precursors and pre-precursors such as ephedron, fenetylline phenylactic acid and safras oil clandestinely manufactured in former Soviet states such as Russia, the Ukraine and Bulgaria (UNODC 2005a: 101).

Further monitoring problems stem from the fact that the Internet has emerged as an important vehicle for the dissemination of information on how to produce ATSs and this, combined with the availability of the requisite chemicals, again facilitated by the Internet, meant that both amateur and industrial chemists produced unquantifiable amounts of ATSs in garages, warehouses or the 'mom and pop shops', as home-based, kitchen production of methamphetamine in the USA was known.

It was estimated that, in 2003, 332 mt of amphetamine and 90 mt of ecstasy were produced, with the possibility that this figure could be as much as 200 mt higher (ibid.). Production of ATSs, specifically methamphetamine, was concentrated in East and South Asian countries, specifically the Philippines, Myanmar (in the Wa region) and China (ibid.: 31). Thailand was a major ATS producer in the 1990s but, after a series of enforcement operations that led to the seizure of 6.5 mt of methamphetamine in 2002, the government declared that production in the country had been eliminated. There was also a significant reduction in Myanmar although neighbouring producers including the closed and secretive communist regime in North Korea absorbed falls in production in these two countries (UNODC 2003a). All the North American countries of Canada, the USA and Mexico were significant methamphetamine producing countries.

While no European country was a major methamphetamine producer, the region was the centre of amphetamine and ecstasy production. It was estimated that 78 per cent of production of this type of drug took place in the Netherlands, although Belgium, the UK, Poland and the former communist states of Bulgaria, Lithuania and Estonia were important production centres.

PRICE AND PURITY While the economics of the drugs trade is addressed in detail in the following chapter, it should be noted that the main trend in terms of illicit drug prices has been one of decline. Cocaine, heroin, ATSs and cannabis were cheaper to purchase in the 2000s than at any previous point in history. Price spikes did occur but, in general, the trend was downwards. The only major exception was cannabis, which increased in price in a number of developed world markets. The price of illicit drugs remained high in comparison to commodities such as gold, but in terms of the consumer market, they were cheaper than alcohol or cigarettes. Running parallel with the fall in prices, there was a trend for the purity and strength of drugs to increase.

Table 7.9 Price of pure drugs in the USA ($ per gram)

	Cocaine	Crack cocaine	Heroin	Methamphetamine
1981	0.40	0.80	0.11	0.44
2003	0.70	0.70	0.32	0.62

Source: ONDCP (2004).

The traffic in and traffickers of controlled drugs

The distribution routes of controlled drugs and the structure of organizations responsible for trafficking evolved in line with trends in production and demand. In the 1990s and 2000s there was also a high level of innovation and adaptation in response to enforcement activities, technological change and the opportunities opened up by globalization and migration.

The old school The early traffic in controlled drugs was characterized by a south to north flow, with plant-based illicit drugs produced in the developing world trafficked to lucrative markets in the developed world. As Turkey is a bridge between Asia and Europe, the country was traditionally an important connecting point between the cultivation and production areas and consumer markets. Similarly, Mexico served as a key trafficking route from producer countries in

South America to consumers in North America. Industrial and transport hubs such as the port areas of Rotterdam, Marseilles, Antwerp, London, New York, Havana and Hong Kong served as key onward distribution centres once the drugs had been transported by sea, air or freight from cultivation and production areas. They were also used as bases for further refining and manufacturing.

In terms of organizational structure, the cultivation of drug plants and the production and distribution of illicit drugs were controlled by 'warlords' and major cartels that operated in collusion with the state or rogue elements within the state security apparatus. Large and established criminal gangs in the main consumer nations acted as intermediaries between suppliers and consumers and assumed responsibility for distribution of the drugs at the wholesale and retail level. Alternatively, foreign nationals from the producer countries who were resident in the consumer states of the developed world controlled the wholesale and retail end of the supply chain, as was the case with Colombian, Mexican, Moroccan and Chinese groups in Europe and North America. Examples of these drug 'lords' include: Olive Yang, Lo Hsing-han and Khun Sa who controlled the opium and heroin trade out of Myanmar; the Cali and Medellín cartels that dominated the early Colombian cocaine trade; the Arellanos syndicate in Mexico; and Gulbuddin Hekmatyar who directed the Southwest Asian heroin and opium trade out of Afghanistan in the 1980s and 1990s. The main European criminal organizations incorporated into the production, trafficking and distribution chain were Corsican syndicates and the Sicilian mafia (McCoy 1972; Zaitch 2002).

Contemporary structures The dynamic of drug flows and the structure of producer and trafficking organizations in the current period are infinitely more complex. Import substitution, the rise of synthetic drug production and increased levels of consumption in non-traditional areas have meant that the direction of the drugs trade is no longer south to north, but also north to south, south to south and north to north. While the trade in drugs has become more internationalized, contained, intra-regional distribution was increasingly common in the 2000s, and this was demonstrated by the dynamics of the methamphetamine markets of East and Southeast Asia (UNODC 2005a: 103).

The deregulation of transport and the easing of travel restrictions, specifically through the former Soviet communist bloc in the 1990s, facilitated the diversification of trafficking routes. This enabled traffickers to penetrate new markets, adapt to changing demand dynamics and also respond to enforcement efforts in countries such as Pakistan, Iran and Colombia by changing distribution routes. Countries in Central America and the Caribbean, Africa, the Baltic and Balkan regions and Central Asia subsequently assumed a higher level of importance in the distribution chain, marking a diversification away from traditional trafficking staging posts such as Mexico, the Netherlands and Turkey.

This diffusion of routes combined with the diversification of production zones to produce new organizational structures within producer and trafficking organizations. Large-scale, integrated operations controlled by cartels, warlords and mafia groups were displaced by smaller, fragmented organizations that purchased directly from independent cultivators and producers. This organizational evolution followed from the break-up of established trafficking groups and criminal networks by enforcement agencies in the 1980s and 1990s. 'New' criminal organizations supplanted the mafia as intermediaries in the drugs traffic in the 1980s, 1990s and 2000s. But although motorcycle gangs in North America, the Jamaican yardies, Japanese yakuza, Israeli syndicates and the Russian 'mafia' played an important role in trafficking and distribution, organizations based on ethnic and national ties became important players in the global drugs traffic. Once again, the globalization process facilitated this development. Legal and illegal migration in the 1980s and 1990s dispersed populations across the world, with an estimated 120 million people or 2 per cent of the global population living in foreign countries. Relocated nationals served as important points of connection in the increasingly complex and sophisticated chain of trafficking and distribution. While historically it was Chinese, Turkish, Moroccan and Mexican nationals who were associated with distribution activities in Europe and North America, a host of national groups were associated with this type of activity in the 1990s and 2000s, including Nigerians, Kurds, Albanians, Somalis, Pakistanis and Brazilians (Ruggerio and South 1995).

As these groups were based on national and more specifically ethnic identities and alliances, this made it acutely difficult for enforcement agencies to penetrate the trafficking organizations and it made the new organizational structures highly cohesive. As the sources of supply multiplied, competition among trafficking groups and distributors increased and this contributed to escalating drug-related violence from the 1980s onwards. This was in turn fuelled by the increased availability of small arms and light weapons and a growing integration between the traffic in drugs, guns and also people (UNODC 2003a: 21). While the overall picture was one of fragmentation and diffusion of trafficking groups, there was a discernible trend of concentration and trans-nationalization, particularly in ATS distribution, with criminal organizations from different countries working together to allow for economies of scale and a widening of distribution networks.

A further important change to the structure of trafficking groups was that they largely operated in opposition to the state rather than in alliance with it. In the 1980s and 1990s, significant progress was made in disentangling the illicit trade from state authorities in countries like Bolivia, Peru, Thailand, Pakistan, Turkey and Colombia. Aside from fragmenting the trade, this made it more difficult for the activities of trafficking organizations to be controlled and monitored. A final change was the move from bulk to small-scale trafficking. Although large consignments of illicit drugs continued to be trafficked, there was a trend of producers and distributors dispatching smaller volumes. This reduced the financial losses accruing to trafficking groups in the event of a seizure. It was also a response to enhanced enforcement efforts at ports, airports and border crossings.

SEIZURES Record highs were reported for cocaine, heroin, ATS and cannabis seizures in the 2000s. This was linked to improvements in enforcement capacities, enhanced levels of multilateral co-operation and the increase in the volume of drugs in circulation.

The bulk of seizures occurred in producer countries and states that bordered the main cultivator and producer countries. Indicative of this, in the period 2002 to 2003, the highest levels of methamphetamine seizures were in Thailand and the USA. The Netherlands accounted for the highest volume of ecstasy seizures, while Colombia accounted for the largest volume of global cocaine seizures. In terms of heroin, Pakistan and Iran had the highest seizure rates and they accounted for 35 per cent and 17 per cent of global heroin seizures or 34,141 kg and 16,390 kg of heroin. Mexico, Spain and the USA reported the highest volume of cannabis seizures. Given the trends in cultivation, production and price, it can be surmised that although a higher volume of drugs was being intercepted, this had a small to negligible impact on their availability.

Conclusion: the performance of drug control apparatus The statistical data provided by the UN drug control bureaucracy demonstrates that no progress has been made in reducing the cultivation, production or distribution of illicit drugs. Supply remained buoyant after a century of control and regulatory efforts, irrespective of the legal framework put in place by national governments and co-operation between governments in eradication and interdiction activities. Further to this, the dynamics of cultivation and distribution had become infinitely more complex, raising serious questions as to the capacity of the control system to effect any significant reduction in supply levels in the long term. The target of zero cultivation set by the UN for 2008 looks wildly optimistic and hopelessly out of touch with trends in the illicit drug trade.

8 | Accounting for failure: the problem of prohibition

The creation of the international drug control apparatus was a revolutionary development and it stemmed from a unique global consensus. This was the agreement that states should work co-operatively to enforce a prohibition on addictive drugs. An unprecedented number of states surrendered their sovereignty on national drug policy as a means of achieving this end. The control system that evolved led to new forms of multinational co-operation between states and it served as a mechanism for communication with 'pariah' regimes. The complex institutional and legal framework of the control regime held together for nearly a century and demonstrated a capacity to adapt to developments in the illicit drugs trade. But this did not translate into progress in the global campaign to eliminate the trade in and use of substances that can cause addiction. The contemporary trends in consumption, cultivation, production and trafficking raised real concerns as to the effectiveness, utility and capacity of the international drug control system and its ability to address anticipated future challenges.

While individual countries may have successfully reduced the illicit trade in their territory at certain points in time, there has been no overall advance at the international level. Rather than declining, the trade has expanded and become further embedded in the global economy and international society. International drug control has singularly failed to achieve its objective. The reasons for this failure are multiple, but they can be understood through reference to two central factors: the ideology of prohibition that informs the control model, which is explored here; and the policy and strategic orientation of drug control bodies, which are examined in the following chapter.

The limits of prohibition

Drug prohibitionists believe that the state should intervene coercively to prevent individuals from using harmful substances. However, it is impossible to prevent people from voluntarily choosing to use a substance, particularly if they do not accept that it will cause them harm. The retention of the arcane idea that consumption can be controlled by the state explains why international efforts to prevent people from using drugs have not been successful. Prohibition is a utopian objective and it has led the control apparatus to set unrealistic goals that it repeatedly fails to achieve.

Demand for drugs has persisted throughout the history of the international drug prohibition regime. This is despite the threat of harsh punishment, ranging from a long prison sentence to execution for the possession and consumption of controlled substances. If demand persists, it will be met by supply, as was demonstrated by the alcohol prohibition experience in the USA in the 1920s. The supply of drugs is attributed to the high level of profit that can be generated from the provision of illicit substances. For as long as the substance in demand remains illicit, it will be profitable to engage in supply.

The economics of the drug trade

Owing to the clandestine nature of the illicit drug trade, it is impossible to establish an accurate figure for the financial value of the sector. The UN estimated that it was in the region of $300 billion to $500 billion per year. Although the illicit drug market accounted for only 0.9 per cent of global GDP measured at retail level, this was three-quarters of the GDP of all the sub-Saharan African countries combined. Supplying illicit drugs was more profitable than the trade in steel, cars and pharmaceuticals. The drugs market was also more profitable than the trade in other consumable items such as meat, chocolate, wine, wheat, coffee and tea, according to wholesale values in 2003 (UNODC 2005a).

In 2003, the global retail cannabis market was worth an estimated $140 billion a year. The cocaine trade was the second largest economic market, with a value of $70 billion. The retail trade in opiates was worth an estimated $65 billion and for ATSs the figure was $44 billion (ibid.: 132). The most lucrative drug market was North America, which accounted for 60 per cent of amphetamine retail sales ($16.9 billion) in 2003, 52 per cent of ecstasy sales ($8.5 billion) and 62 per cent ($43.6 billion) of cocaine sales. Europe had the largest retail value for opiates at 56 per cent or $37 billion worth of sales. Retail sales of opiates in North America totalled $8.9 billion. This was below Asia, where retail sales were estimated to total $14.4 billion. Asia also had the second largest figure for ATSs at $8.7 billion in retail sales (ibid.: 139). In terms of the impact of these expenditures on the national economies, Oceania had the highest level of drug spending in relation to GDP at 2.6 per cent. For Africa, the figure was 2.1 per cent while in North America, Western Europe and Asia it was estimated that drug expenditures were 1.1 per cent, 0.8 per cent and 0.4 per cent of GDP respectively.

Unlike the price of legal commodities, the cost of controlled drugs is not proportional to input factor costs. It instead reflects the level of risk that is associated with cultivation, production and trafficking. This risk factor is what makes the prohibition of drugs lucrative for suppliers, producers, cultivators, traffickers and a host of other individuals employed in various capacities in the illicit sector. The distribution of profit within the trade also increases in relation to the proximity of the supplier to the consumer. In the case of heroin and cocaine, those furthest away from the consumer are the cultivators of opium poppy and coca. This, and the fact that cultivators can be easily replaced, means that an estimated 80 per cent of profit is realized at the wholesale and retail end of the supply chain, in the wealthy consumer countries of the developed world.

The mark-up on controlled drugs as they proceed through the production and trafficking process is illustrated in Table 8.1 below.

The illicit drug trade is heavily dominated by males. Women are not significant players in the sector and when they do participate this tends to be at the least financially rewarding end of the supply and distribution chain. The main roles played by women in the drugs trade are as cultivators and low-level traffickers. There has been a trend of increased female engagement with the illegal sector, but this has been characterized by an expansion in the number of women at the bottom end of the chain, rather than women assuming leading positions at the lucrative wholesale level. Poverty is the principal reason for female participation in the trade.

TABLE 8.1 Price dynamics in the opiate and cocaine trade (US$ per kg)

Heroin	
Farmgate opium	90
Domestic wholesale	2,870
US wholesale	80,000
US retail	290,000
Cocaine	
Farmgate coca leaves	610
Cocaine base	860
Cocaine hydrochloride for export	1,500
Cocaine hydrochloride US wholesale	25,250
Crack cocaine US retail	50,000
US retail cocaine powder	110,000

Sources: *The Economist* (2001e); UNODC (1998a)

The drugs trade is structured as a vertically integrated industry. It is hierarchical and triangular in shape, with the numbers involved at each stage of the trade diminishing in line with the proximity of the drugs to the consumer countries of North America, Western Europe and Oceania (Bagley 1994; Thoumi 2003).

THE CULTIVATORS Even though the proportion of illicit monies flowing to cultivators in the developing world is low, it is significant enough to make opium poppy and coca cultivation more rewarding than participation in the legal economy. This is because the bulk of cultivation is carried out by socio-economically marginalized farming families on small plots of land (Clawson and Rensselaer 1999; Joyce and Malamud 1997; Smith 1992; UNDCP 2003; UNODC 2003a).

Participation in the illicit economy is a vital source of income in countries with high levels of poverty and where the authority of the state is negligible or has collapsed. In Bolivia, where per capita income was $936 in 2001, one kilo

TABLE 8.2 Farmgate price of coca leaf, 1991–2002 (US$ per kg)

	Peru	Bolivia
1991	1.93	1.32
1992	3.19	1.14
1993	2.43	1.59
1994	3.00	1.36
1995	1.41	1.65
1996	0.75	1.28
1997	0.88	1.72
1998	1.60	1.67
1999	2.29	3.31
2000	2.16	5.86
2001	2.41	5.66
2002	2.48	5.60

Source: UNODC (2004a)

of coca leaves fetched $5.86 (UNDCP 2003; UNODC 2003a). By contrast the sales revenue for coffee, another key Andean crop, was below the cost of production. In Afghanistan, the cultivation of one hectare of opium poppy (producing around 45 kg of opium gum) could earn a farmer $16,100 in 2002. The revenue generated from a hectare of potatoes was $2,000 (Burnett 2003; UNDCP 2002). In Lebanon, a kilo of cannabis sold for $300, while the figure for a kilo of potatoes was 20 cents (MacFarquhar 2001). There was no single legal agricultural commodity that could compete with illegal drug crops in terms of revenue generation for

TABLE 8.3 Farmgate price of opium, 1990–2000 (US$ per kg)

	Afghanistan	Pakistan	Lao PDR	Myanmar	Colombia
1990	35	45	106	242	2,360
1991	35	78	139	165	2,264
1992	35	77	127	116	1,369
1993	36	67	90	119	591
1994	36	69	143	173	587
1995	36	65	243	269	540
1996	50	120	265	208	585
1997	70	109	157	124	432
1998	62	125	63	64	370
1999	58	83	63	128	198
2000	30	110	46	142	340

Source: UNODC (2003a)

people living in rural areas in poor countries, and this was particularly the case for farmers living in remote and inhospitable areas.

This pointed to a second advantage of engagement in illicit cultivation. While the price of legal crops fluctuated in the international economy as a result of changing patterns of consumer demand and global competition among agricultural producers, the farmgate value of illegal crops remained constant and high, as demonstrated in Table 8.2. The illicit sector also benefited from the existence of established transportation and distribution routes from even the most inaccessible cultivation areas and, in contrast to legal produce, there was a guaranteed market for illicit drug crops.

Combining the sales revenues that went to cultivators, middlemen and other participants at the production end of the process, an estimated 5 to 10 per cent of total drugs sales remained in the producer country. Even though this was a small percentage of the wealth generated by the sector, it had significant effects on producer countries.

The macroeconomic impact of drug revenues In the late 1980s, it was estimated that $700 million or 15 per cent of annual GDP in Bolivia was generated by revenue from cocaine sales. In Peru, where per capita GDP in 2001 was $2,051, the figure was thought to be in the region of 2 to 11 per cent of GDP. In Colombia, where per capita GDP was $1,915, the flow of drug-related money into the country was estimated to be $3.75 to $5 billion per year in the 1990s, or between 3 and 13 per cent of GDP. This was double the earnings from coffee production and just below the income generated by the country's oil sector (Kawell 2002; Thoumi 2003). Data from Pakistan, where average per capita GDP was $415, put the revenue from the opiate trade in that country at around 4 per cent of GDP in the early 1990s (UNODC 1998a). In Afghanistan, opium sales were thought to have contributed $1.5 billion to the national economy in 2003.

Participation in the drug trade consequently has significant benefits in poor countries. First, it generates employment. In Bolivia 120,000 to 460,000 people were employed in the coca economy, which was around 16 per cent of the labour force. In Peru and Colombia, the illicit drugs economy accounted for a lower but none the less significant level of employment, estimated to be between 2.5 and 4.5 per cent of the labour force in Peru and 3 per cent in Colombia, around 300,000 people (Kawell 2002). In the opium producing regions, employment generation and dependency on the illicit sector was also high. In Afghanistan and Myanmar, the livelihood of an estimated 3.3 million people in both countries was dependent on the opium economy (Jelsma and Kramer 2005; UNODC 2003a). Even in the cannabis cultivating states, there was a high level of dependency on the drugs sector, with 96,600 families reliant on cannabis production in Morocco (Mansfield and Whetton 1996). The illicit drugs trade also had backward linkages into the economy through money-laundering activities and this generated further employment in sectors such as construction and the services industries (Thoumi 2003).

The significance of the drugs trade for employment generation increased in the 1980s and 1990s as a result of neoliberal economic policy implementation in the Andean cultivator states and conflict and instability in the opium producing countries of Myanmar and Afghanistan. In Bolivia, Peru and Colombia, poverty and unemployment increased after state assets were privatized and public spending cut in line with economic stabilization and structural adjustment measures. This led people previously employed in the formal economy to move into the illicit sector as a means of survival. The drugs trade therefore cushioned the Andean countries from the full impact of neoliberal economic policies by absorbing unemployed workers and providing sustainable incomes (Hargreaves 1992; Kawell 2002; Livingstone 2002; Painter 1994). In Myanmar, economic mismanagement by the ruling military junta, combined with the international community's use of sanctions as a mechanism to pressure for liberalization of the political system, increased the economic importance of the opium sector in that country. This was also the case in Pakistan and Afghanistan after the international community sanctioned the two countries in the 1990s. The importance of the opium economy in Afghanistan increased dramatically in the 1980s and 1990s owing to the destruction and instability caused by the civil conflict between the Taliban and the Northern Alliance. As formal institutions and the economy had disintegrated, opium assumed the status of a quasi-currency. It was used as a form of savings, collateral, insurance and payment (UNODC 2004c). As political instability continued during and after the US-led invasion, Operation Enduring Freedom, in 2001, the role of opium as a source of liquidity was consolidated. The laundering of drug money also provided access to informal credit for poor people who were excluded from formal lending because no effective banking system existed or because they were considered a lending risk (Keh 1998; Thoumi 2003).

The dysfunctional nature of drug money The benefits of 'narco-dollar' inflows were offset by their distorting effect on the national economy, and for this reason drug 'wealth' had negative ramifications for economic development. As the revenues were controlled by criminal organizations and not the state, they could not be directed by the national government into identified areas of social need or productive investment. Moreover, as the drug revenues could not be taxed, the state received no direct financial benefit from the trade (Painter 1994; Thoumi 2003). Illicit drug revenues also complicated macroeconomic management and reduced the ability of central banks and finance ministries to control the money circulating in the economy. This in turn made it difficult to set interest rates and control the currency.

In those countries which had a high inflow of illicit drug revenues, such as

Bolivia, there was an additional problem of Dutch disease. The high volume of dollars circulating in the national economy inflated the value of the domestic currency and this crowded out legal exports and made them uncompetitive. The end result was a higher level of dependence on drug export revenues. The practice of laundering illicit revenues through land purchases also served to inflate the value of land and this exacerbated existing inequalities in the cultivating countries. For example, in Colombia, land purchases by the Medellín cartel in the late 1980s increased prices from US$ 500 per hectare to US$ 2,000 per hectare (Tullis 1995). The existence of the illicit trade and the presence of drug-related violence and criminality also undermined development and growth opportunities because it negatively affected investor perceptions of the country. This offset the intended benefits of trade liberalization and it contributed to problems of capital flight as wealthy nationals placed their financial assets abroad amid concerns over government corruption and extortion by criminal organizations.

THE CHAIN OF POVERTY AND PROFIT As illicit drugs were trafficked from producer states, their value progressively increased. The profit made from trafficking one kilo of heroin from the north of Afghanistan into Karachi, Pakistan, was $2,643. For neighbouring Tehran in Iran, it was $3,091. The most lucrative cross-border movement out of Afghanistan was into Turkmenistan, with a $6,960 profit made from trafficking (UNDCP 2002). As with cultivation, trafficking served as an important means of revenue generation for people living in poor countries. In Turkmenistan, for example, the average per capita income in 2001 was just $1,097. In Kyrgyzstan, which formed an increasingly important trafficking route for Afghan-produced opiates, annual per capita income was just $308. The rise in poverty in these Central Asian countries was linked to the collapse of the old Soviet command economy and the transfer of financial subsidies from Moscow. In Albania, a key crossing point for illicit drugs traffic from Central Asia and Turkey into the consumer countries of Europe, a quarter of the population lived below the poverty line, unemployment was 15 per cent of the economically active population and just one in six homes had running water (*The Economist* 2004).

Poverty and inequality also characterized those countries that formed part of the cocaine trafficking routes out of South America. Central America, Mexico and the Caribbean countries all experienced economic adjustment, contraction and rising levels of unemployment in the late 1980s and 1990s and this increased the benefits associated with participation in the illicit drugs trade. Underscoring the importance of trafficking and distribution activities as a source of income in these countries, there was a noticeable trend of increased female participation in the drugs trade in Central Asia, the Caribbean and South and Central America.

As in the cultivating states, the opportunities for wealth and job creation presented by the presence of the trade in trafficking countries had counter-balancing negative effects. These included: a rise in drug-related violence between trafficking groups; an increase in all forms of criminality, with the traffic in drugs integrated with the traffic in guns and people; and a rise in money-laundering activities (*The Economist* 2003a). This in turn contributed to a criminalization of the economy that was seen to be particularly severe in those countries that liberalized their financial and economic systems in line with neoliberal policy recommendations (Keh 1998; Varese 2001).

In contrast to the cocaine and heroin supply chains, the profit that could be obtained from ATS production was far higher. This was due to the proximity of producer to supplier and low input costs. Consequently: 'A $50 investment at the supermarket can produce $3,000-worth of methamphetamine' (*The Economist* 1999).

THE DILEMMA OF PROHIBITION Illicit drugs can never be eliminated because of the supply and demand dynamic that has persisted throughout the history of drug control. As was demonstrated during the alcohol prohibition period, enhanced enforcement in the context of sustained demand served to disperse, displace and fragment supply sources and distribution routes, in turn making them harder to monitor and eliminate. Indicative of this, federal government spending in the USA on anti-drugs initiatives directed by the Office of National Drug Control Policy rose from $1 billion in 1981 to $17.1 billion in 1999 (ONDCP 1998a). During this period, it was estimated that drug consumption in the USA increased three-fold while the price of drugs halved and their purity doubled. This 'balloon effect', whereby squeezing the trade in one area led it to pop up in another, characterized every element of the illicit drugs sector (Bagley 1994; *The Economist* 2002a). Reducing cultivation in one area led it to relocate. Closing down one trafficking route and improving interdiction capacities in one region led new trafficking routes to emerge elsewhere.

The central dilemma for prohibition was that success in reducing supply created a shortage. Shortage in turn led to an increase in prices. The increase in price was an incentive for further cultivation and production. As an example of this dynamic, the campaign to eliminate opium cultivation by the Taliban regime in Afghanistan in 2000 led the farmgate value of opium to rise from $35 per kilo before the ban to $350 per kilo as the ban took effect. There were also negative knock-on effects in consumer countries of the reduction in the supply of heroin from Afghanistan. First, some heroin users changed to other illicit drugs such as cocaine and amphetamines. Second, there was an increase in drug-related crime as some heroin users had to find funds to cover the inflated costs of the drug. Finally, the incidence of injecting heroin increased. This was a result of the decline in the purity of the drug, a factor that was in turn related to the heroin shortage. Distributors responded to a reduction in supplies and a rise in price by increasing levels of adulteration and consequently the profit made on heroin sales (Topp et al. 2003). It can consequently be concluded that success in reducing supply from source countries has the counter-productive effect of increasing crime and illness among drug users in the consumer countries and displacing cultivation in producer states.

Founding myths Prohibition was institutionalized during the first decades of the twentieth century. This was a period when racist and Social Darwinist ideas flourished, medical understanding of addiction and dependency was limited and individual freedoms considered secondary to the authority of the nation and state. Many of the arguments that were originally put forward to legitimize prohibition – such as the claims that drugs produce addiction; that demand was caused by supply; that drug users were criminals; and that cannabis was a stepping-stone to other drugs – were subsequently shown to be wrong or a consequence of prohibition.

CONSUMPTION It is now recognized that addiction-causing substances do not cause addiction and dependency in all users. The majority of people who use controlled drugs act rationally to minimize the risks of their drug use (Chase Eldredge 1998; *The Economist* 2001d). Rather than the substance forcing users into a life of addiction and depravity, users have learnt how to control the substance, in effect 'taming' drugs that were considered dangerous (Becker 1963; Cohen 1999; Decorte 2000; Harding and Zinberg 1977). The vast majority of people who use a controlled drug do so only once. Those who continue to use tend to consume infrequently, they usually stop after a relatively brief 'career', they buy their drugs from people they know and trust and they have rituals around use that minimize the negative physiological and psychological impact of drug consumption. There is no evidence that limitless supply would dramatically alter this pattern of controlled drug use (Cohen 1999; Jutkowitz and Hongsook Eu 1993).

A complex of factors influence consumption and these are very difficult, if not impossible, to legislate against. These include: cultural trends and generational change; socio-economic conditions; availability; peer group influence; and the price of drugs. These different motivations for use make it hard to determine definitively the demand dynamics of a particular drug. For example, an increase in the consumption of heroin may be attributable to a rise in supply. However, rising use can also be linked to cultural trends. As a consumer commodity, heroin has demonstrated a remarkable capacity to 'reinvent itself and add new layers to its myth' (Ashton 2002: 13). Having been widely portrayed as the drug used by 'wasters' during a renewed surge in its use in the 1980s, heroin was reborn in the 1990s as the drug of choice for a diverse group of people that included models, artists and musicians. This dramatic reversal in the portrayal of heroin was epitomized by the rise of so-called 'heroin chic'.

ADDICTION Only a small minority of people who use drugs become addicted to them and, even then, drug-related problems are found in relation to the consumption of certain types of drug, specifically heroin and crack cocaine. Aside from the type of drug used, addiction has been linked to a number of other factors that include: a genetic predisposition to addiction and dependency; personality types, with depressed, isolated and attention-seeking people variously seen as vulnerable to addictive behaviour; and life structure. In respect of this last point, structured lives, defined as family and work commitments, militate against the development of problem use and addiction. People who were socially and economically marginalized and who lack daily routines are by contrast more vulnerable to problem drug use (Cohen 1999; Nakken 1996; Peele and Brodski 1975; Peele 1985, 1989; Schaler 2000).

PRICE Price is a more complicated aspect of demand dynamics. There is evidence that a sharp increase in price can lead to a reduction in consumption and this has informed the drug control policies of international and national enforcement agencies. The logic of supply-side activities such as interdiction is that this will create a shortage of drugs and trigger a rise in price. If the price rise is sufficiently high, this will act as an entry barrier to new users and it will force established users to terminate their drug consumption (Becker et al. 1991; Moore 1977; ONDCP 2004). However, the evidence demonstrates that this applies only to a limited number of drugs and most specifically cannabis. The price elasticity of heroin and cocaine has been shown to be limited as demand tended to persist despite a cost increase. This inelasticity in the price of 'hard' drugs was linked to two factors. First, addiction had the effect of driving people to continue purchasing drugs, whatever their cost. This was particularly the case with heroin. A second reason was that occasional users of drugs like cocaine were prepared to pay a higher price because consumption formed part of established patterns of 'recreation'. As drug use among this group of people was infrequent, they were prepared to pay a higher rate for their leisure activity and as a result, high prices did not act as a barrier to entry (DiNado 1993; Stolzenberg and D'Alessio 2003).

CRIME Crime and drug use have been linked since the beginnings of international drug control. The two continue to be seen as inter-related by the general public and this in turn has led 'moral entrepreneurs' such as politicians, the media and religious leaders to press for or introduce stronger enforcement measures (Becker 1963; Inciardi 1986; Tonry and Wilson 2000). In most countries, users of controlled drugs are by definition criminals, so the argument that drugs and crime are linked is tautological. However, the idea that all drug users commit crime in order to finance their drug use is applicable only to a tiny minority of drug users and even then it tends to be found in users of certain types of drugs such as crack cocaine or heroin (Stolzenberg and D'Alessio 2003). Even within this minority group, it is difficult to establish if the individual was already a criminal or whether the use of drugs led the individual into criminal activities.

Drug use was also historically linked to crime through the argument that people committed acts of murder, rape and violence under the influence of drugs. This idea, which was popularized during the 1930s and gained ground as a result of particularly horrifying acts of drug-induced savagery, was found only in a statistically insignificant number of controlled drug users. Even in these cases, it was difficult to determine if drug use precipitated some form of psychotic event or illness, or whether the individual was already predisposed to mental health problems that were triggered by drug use. This issue has been the subject of intense academic and scientific dispute, specifically in relation to cannabis (Degenhardt, Hall and Lynskey 2003; Castle and Murray 2004; Veen et al. 2004).

While the relationship between crime and individual drug users was the subject of ongoing debate, the link between drugs and violent crime was explicit. It was evidenced in the conflict within and between different drug distribution networks and it was exacerbated by a rise in the use of guns and other forms of weaponry. The inter-relationship between drugs and crime at this macro-systemic level was overt in cultivating and producer countries, such as Colombia and Mexico, and by the 1990s it was prevalent in all countries where there were significant trafficking and distribution activities. However this drug–crime nexus was a direct result of the control system. It was because controlled drugs were illicit and lucrative that criminal gangs were integrated into the trade and because the trade was profitable and covert, market share was defended from rivals and enforcement agencies through the use of violence (Dowdney 2004; Tonry and Wilson 2000; Zimring and Hawkins 1999).

GATEWAY DRUGS The argument that cannabis was a 'gateway' to even more dangerous and addictive substances, a claim that justified the incorporation of cannabis into the 1961 Single Convention and the application of punitive legal sanctions against those cultivating, distributing or using cannabis, has been shown to be spurious. The empirical basis for this assessment is a reading of the consumption figures. An estimated 161 million people used cannabis in 2003, while the combined number using ATSs, opiates and cocaine was 78 million. This left a shortfall of 83 million people. While users of 'hard' drugs like cocaine and heroin were likely to use cannabis, not all cannabis users went on to use hard drugs (Runciman 1999; Baan Commission Report 1972; Morral et al. 2002).

The Baan Commission Report published in the Netherlands concluded that if cannabis were a stepping-stone to other drugs, this was a result of the control system. In this respect, people wishing to obtain cannabis would have to acquire it from dealers who were typically engaged in the distribution of other controlled drugs. Consequently, it was the act of purchasing cannabis and the contact made with criminal dealers that brought the cannabis user into touch with drugs like cocaine, heroin and ATSs. In order to prevent this, the Dutch state intervened to disentangle the 'soft' and 'hard' drug markets through the mechanism of the coffee-shops. Through the tightly regulated coffee-shop system, cannabis users can buy small amounts of the drug without having to come into contact with hard drugs (Abraham 1999; Levine 2002). While cannabis was not a stepping-stone to other illegal drugs, cigarette smoking and alcohol consumption in schoolchildren was found to be an important indicator of future cannabis use (Kandel 2002; Morral et al. 2002).

Conclusion The conceptualization of drugs and drug users within prohibition thinking was naive and simplistic. The founding myths of drug control were also misinformed and scientifically wrong. However, the images and assumptions about drugs and drug users implicit in prohibition thinking continue to inform the guiding principles and policies of the control model. It is intensely problematic for the international and national drug control apparatus to acknowledge and respond to changes in public and scientific understanding of drugs, the drug trade and drug users as this would require a fundamental overhaul of the control system, guiding principles and organizational structure. Moreover, prohibitionist thinking continues to be influential and that in turn limits interest in restructuring or adapting the control model or the thrust of existing policy.

In the 1990s and 2000s, there was a move in some countries and regional organizations to adjust drug policy in line with the altered dynamics of the illicit trade and in response to changed understanding of drug consumption patterns. This was reflected in the trend of liberalization of drug control measures, specifically in relation to cannabis, and a stronger emphasis on demand-side policies such as harm reduction in European and South American countries. These modifications to drug control policy were rejected by the international control apparatus and prohibition-oriented countries such as the USA, on the grounds that they violated the drug control conventions. This pointed to a final reason why the ideology of prohibition impeded effective control of addiction-causing substances. Prohibition is a fundamentalist ideology. It does not allow for compromise and it interprets failure as a product of lax enforcement. This prevented the drug control apparatus from adopting 'lessons learned' from failed initiatives. In maintaining prohibition as the central guiding principle of drug control, the control system was locked into a set of policies that aimed to achieve an unrealizable objective.

9 | Accounting for failure 2: institutions and policy

The manner in which the international drug control system operates does not address or compensate for the contradictory and counter-productive results of pursuing prohibition. The entire structure and orientation of the control system is towards repression, criminalization and suppression of supply-side activities, as it has been since the foundation of international drug control at the beginning of the twentieth century. There has not been any pragmatic adjustment in the conceptualization of the 'drug problem' and, as a result, the control system has proved incapable of addressing the effects of prohibition strategies at policy level. In organizational terms, the UN control apparatus was sclerotic, inflexible and subject to the institutionalized dominance of prohibition-oriented countries. Consequently, the work of the drug control institutions was unbalanced and ineffective. This can be evidenced through analysis of three issues: alternative development programmes; education and research; and treatment provision.

Alternative development

The experience of alternative development strategies is a cogent example of why the drug control system has failed. As has been discussed, drugs are lucrative to cultivate, produce and distribute because they are prohibited. Yet the international control system has not devised policies that address or reduce the incentives for supply-side participation. On the contrary, the policy onus in source countries continued to be focused on eradication rather than alternative development. In those cases where alternative development initiatives have been introduced, these have been inadequately funded and, as a result, failed to reduce the incentives for supply-side participation.

Cultivating countries sought compensation for the eradication of drug crops since the initiation of the international control system. In the 1920s and 1930s, Mexican, Turkish and Iranian authorities pressed the international community for financial recompense for reductions in drug crop cultivation (McAllister 2000). This was rejected on the grounds that these countries had a 'moral' duty and a responsibility under international law to terminate cultivation. This position reflected the institutionalized dominance of the consumer countries. Although the drug 'problem' was recognized as trans-national in character, there was a profound reluctance among consumer states to spread the financial cost of ending the trade. Despite the supply-side focus of the control model, no assistance was provided to the poorer cultivator states and they carried a disproportionately heavy socio-economic and political burden in imposing the control regime. As these states lacked both the physical and financial capacity to comply with cultivation restrictions and eradication targets, little progress was made in reducing drug supply.

No significant effort was made to address the problems faced by the cultivating countries until the 1970s. During this decade, the King of Thailand, Bhumibol Adulyadej, pioneered crop substitution programmes through the Royal Highland Development Project. This sought to reduce the incentives for illicit crop cultivation through the provision of financial and technical support for alternative legal agricultures. By the 1980s, the project had evolved into a programme of integrated rural development that was characterized by the provision of educational facilities, training, credit and infrastructure in order to reduce the marginalization and isolation of cultivating regions. The project also served as a mechanism for integrating the ethnically diverse hill tribes that cultivated opium poppy in the northern border region into the Thai state structure. The project was also informed by the government's campaign against the Communist Party of Thailand, which had a strong organizational presence in the highland areas (Buergin 2000; Renard 2001).

The Royal Highland Development Project continued into the 1990s and 2000s, during which time it focused on enhancing the mechanisms for community participation and decision-making in the crop reduction process. Over a thirty-year period, the project was successful in reducing illicit cultivation, which fell from an estimated 17,920 ha in the mid-1960s to 330 ha by 2000 (Buergin 2000; Renard 2002). The Thai alternative development model had its limitations and there was criticism that it led to deforestation and the repression of minority ethnic groups. But it also provided important 'lessons learnt' and examples of best practice for sustainable cultivation reduction. These were not assimilated by the international control bodies.

The UN and alternative development (AD) The aim of AD is to eliminate the cultivation of drug crops through the introduction of rural development programmes that reduce poverty and provide economic alternatives for cultivators. The history of AD within the international drug control apparatus was one of trial and error (Mansfield 1999). In the first stage of AD development during the 1970s, emphasis was placed on crop substitution projects that were co-ordinated by the UN drug control apparatus and national governments in cultivating countries. Under these AD projects, farmers were provided with seeds that would allow them to produce legitimate crops such as bananas, apples, potatoes and flowers. These early AD initiatives did not reduce cultivation levels for four basic reasons. First, the legal crops that substituted for coca or opium poppy did not generate sufficient sales revenue to maintain cultivator households. Second, the cultivators lacked the skills necessary to work with new crops and in new agricultural sectors such as livestock. Climate and terrain also made it difficult to substitute opium poppy and coca for other crops. Finally, there was no market for the legal agricultural goods produced.

The project failures of the 1970s led to the development of a new approach in the 1980s that did incorporate lessons from previous AD experiences. Crop substitution was absorbed into broader rural development programmes that provided training for farmers in new agricultural techniques; road building for the transportation of products; and assistance with marketing. However, these projects had only a limited effect on cultivation levels and they did not arrest the trend of cultivation displacement. This was despite investments of $180 million in the Bolivian AD programme of 1983 and an investment of $190 million in AD projects in Peru during the period 1987 to 1996 (Bagley and Tokatlian 1992; Clawson and Rensselaer 1999; UNDCP 2001: 11).

A key factor accounting for the limited success of AD during this period was that it was insufficiently integrated into national development projects. As long as the country remained poor, people continued to be pulled into cultivation. This dilemma was exacerbated by the process of economic globalization and the adoption of neoliberal policies in countries such as Peru, Bolivia and Colombia. The economic contraction that was associated with the introduction of stabilization and structural adjustment measures limited the domestic market for the legal agricultural products while the liberalization of trade led to an influx of cheap, imported agricultural goods that undercut the alternative agricultures. Competition from other agricultural suppliers in the international market also drove down the price of legal produce and this further undermined the credibility of AD.

There was also a problem of appropriateness and sustainability in AD programming. As an example of this, the US government implemented an agricultural loan project with Lebanon as part of a drug cultivation reduction scheme in the Bekaa Valley. Over 3,000 dairy cows were exported to Lebanese farmers. There was no supplementary provision of veterinary surgeons, training in livestock handling or marketing techniques and the Lebanese government had to import cattle feed (Abdelnour 2001).

UNGASS and the 2008 target By the 1990s, regional development assistance was recognized as a crucial component of AD. This led to a higher level of interaction between the drug control bodies and international financial institutions. 'Debt for drugs' swaps and trade agreements that privileged cultivator countries, such as the Andean Trade Preferences Act introduced by the US government in 1990, created a securer national economic environment for AD initiatives. At the operational level, there was a strong emphasis on building community agreement and participation into AD projects and development of institutional capacity at the local, regional and national level. This allowed cultivators to identify their own needs, in contrast to the experience of top-down delivery in earlier crop substitution projects. There was also strong emphasis on gender mainstreaming in AD in recognition of the central role of women in the cultivation process and in line with the UNDCP emphasis on the gender component of anti-drugs initiatives articulated by the body in 1990 (UNDCP 2000, 2002; Mansfield 1999).

At the 1998 UN General Assembly Special Session on drugs (UNGASS), AD was identified as an important tool for the achievement of the UN goal of zero cultivation of opium poppy and coca by 2008. The UNGASS conference and the resulting Political Declaration and Action Plan on International Cooperation on the Eradication of Illicit Drug Crops and on Alternative Development called for a more balanced approach between eradication, interdiction and AD and international financial support for AD projects (TNI 2002). Although AD emerged as a central component of drug control strategies after 1998, by the early 2000s it was evident that there were severe limitations to the type of AD policies that were being put in place.

SEQUENCING Despite the revision and reorientation of AD strategies, significant problems with the application of AD persisted. A serious challenge related to the sequencing of AD with illicit crop eradication programmes. The success of the Thai AD programme was linked to its pragmatism. Eradication was introduced only when alternatives for cultivators existed. The Thai authorities accepted household use of opium by cultivating groups such as the Meo, Hmong and Karen and cultivation for domestic use was tolerated (Mansfield 1999; Renard 2001). By contrast, in the AD projects implemented in Colombia, Bolivia and Myanmar in the 2000s, eradication commenced before, or was introduced alongside, the implementation of AD. This undermined the credibility and effectiveness of the AD programmes. In Colombia, where 200,000 people were dependent on employment in the coca economy, the spraying of coca crops in areas like Putamayo was initiated before a comprehensive package of alternative development projects had been introduced. This reduced cultivators' trust in state authorities and AD project managers. It additionally led to political violence between cultivators and officials responsible for eradication. This was also the experience in Bolivia, where conflict over the eradication component of Plan Dignity escalated into a major political crisis.

In Myanmar, the launch of eradication activities before the consolidation of AD led to a humanitarian crisis in 2003 as 250,000 families living at subsistence level in the Wa cultivating regions lost their livelihoods. The UN was consequently placed in the position of having to provide humanitarian assistance and food aid while at the same time calling for the cause of the problem, forced eradication of opium poppy, to be stepped up (TNI 2003). In an implicit acknowledgement of the grave political and humanitarian costs of forced eradication, political authorities in Afghanistan did not press ahead with eradication of opium poppy plantations after the 2001 US-led invasion.

Alternative development projects require an estimated three to five years to be effective in providing sustainable, legal livelihoods for drug cultivators. Critics of the AD strategies implemented in the 2000s argued that in order to reach the eradication targets set out for 2008 by UNGASS, there was a rush to eradicate. This left insufficient time for AD to become embedded in rural and national economies (ibid.).

The debate over sequencing eradication and AD led to conflict between development agencies, the UN, European donor governments and the USA. Crop eradication in Bolivia and Colombia in the 2000s was supported by financial assistance from the USA and enforced through the threat of de-certification and sanctions for non-compliance in the 'war on drugs'. Eradication consequently proceeded while AD projects funded by development agencies such as the German GTZ were at an early stage. Violence, migration out of eradication areas and the forced relocation of cultivators reduced the effectiveness and legitimacy of AD, leading critics, including GTZ, to conclude that it was counter-productive to use simultaneously the 'carrot' of AD and the 'stick' of eradication (ibid.). The problem lay in the fact that while AD was recognized by UNGASS as an important tool for cultivation reduction, it was only one part of a three-pronged strategy that also included eradication and interdiction. In failing to prioritize AD over the two other elements of drug control, the utility of AD was undermined.

FUNDING Financial support for AD remained at risible levels in the 2000s and this raised questions about the sustainability of the projects introduced and the commitment of the control apparatus to the principles underpinning AD. Indicative of this, the funds dedicated to AD by the British government in Afghanistan during the reconstruction of that country after the US-led invasion of 2002 was $30 million. By contrast, $150 million was provided for the training of Afghan security forces (Burnett 2003). In Plan Colombia, 70 per cent of the $1.3 billion funds received from the US government were ring-fenced by the US Congress for capacity building within the Colombian armed forces and crop eradication programmes. Although the Colombian government had stressed the need for $2 billion for AD in its original Plan Colombia, the USA provided just $120 million of additional spending, while the European Union contributed $280 million (Livingstone 2002).

Of the $900 million that was pledged by US, European and other donors for the AD component of the Bolivian Plan Dignity, only $53 million was delivered by the UNDCP. A meeting scheduled for November 1999 to reassess AD funding commitments was cancelled due to a lack of interest. A further common line of criticism in relation to the financing of AD is that the funding provided was not distributed in a transparent or efficient manner.

THE SECURITY DILEMMA The mismatch in the funding that was provided for

AD and security sector reform (SSR) underscored a further dilemma for the drug control bodies. On the one hand, SSR and drug and border control capacity building was necessary for the prevention of trafficking activities and drug production. This was particularly the case in weak states experiencing or emerging from conflict. However, conditions of insecurity that security sector reform was intended to address were perpetuated by those groups that profited from the illicit trade, such as the right-wing paramilitary group, the Autodefensas Unidas de Colombia (AUC, United Self-Defence Forces of Colombia) and the notorious warlords of Afghanistan. Hence, in prioritizing SSR over AD, the international drug control apparatus became locked in a cycle of militarization and defence spending to counter the threat posed by drug-financed rebel groups.

The disparity in spending between those projects that could reduce the incentives for engaging in drug-related activities, such as AD, and those that enhanced the capacity of security forces was also evident in the trafficking states of Central Asia, the Caribbean and East Africa. In these regions there was substantial donor assistance for projects that strengthened national security and the integrity of territorial borders but significantly fewer resources provided for economic development assistance. Without addressing problems of poverty, unemployment and under-employment in these areas, little progress could be made in reducing the incentives to supply.

The price of enforcement Just as prohibition was lucrative for suppliers of controlled drugs, it also became highly profitable for those agencies responsible for upholding it. Enforcement and interdiction activities generated employment opportunities in the police, customs, prison, military, legal and intelligence services. This was particularly the case in and after the 1980s as levels of consumption and production rose, the international drug control conventions tightened criminal sanctions and set ambitious drug interdiction targets and the US government adopted a more unilateralist and militarized approach in anti-drugs policy. For example, in the USA the number of people employed in the justice system increased from 1.27 million people in 1982 to 2.2 million by 2001. During this period, the federal prison budget increased 1,350 per cent from $220 million in 1986 to $3.19 billion by 1997 (Bauer and Owens 2004; Gray 2001).

This confluence of factors made drug prohibition a financially rewarding industry for suppliers of the 'tools' of enforcement. In the 1980s, this supply role was increasingly assumed by the private sector, as national governments privatized services such as prison management and construction, and outsourced responsibilities previously performed by the military and police to contractors (Singer 2004). This was particularly the case in the USA. For example, contracts awarded by the US government to American firms as part of Plan Colombia included a $234 million agreement with the Texas-based corporation Textron to supply the Colombian armed forces with eighteen Blackhawk helicopters and a $120 million contract with Sikorsky Corporation for the upgrading of forty-two Colombian Huey surveillance helicopters. Contracts were also awarded for the flying and maintenance of the coca crop spraying planes and training of Colombian personnel. These were distributed across the private sector but the largest beneficiary was DynCorp, the largest defence contractor in the USA. The company had been awarded an estimated $600 million in federal government contract work in South America since 1997 (Centre for International Policy's Colombia Project n.d.; Livingstone 2002). DynCorp was also awarded a $50 million contract by the US State Department to lead opium poppy eradication efforts in Afghanistan in 2002.

There were consequently a number of vested financial interests in the drug control model and drugs themselves became an increasingly 'useful enemy' (Bruun et al. 1975). The spending on this type of enforcement activity was to the detriment of funding for projects like AD that had the potential to change significantly the supply dynamics of source countries.

Research: a hostile environment

The international control system faced acute problems in determining the scale and nature of the drug 'threat'. Because of the hidden nature of the illicit drug trade, there were no reliable indicators of progress in reducing the level of cultivation, production, trafficking or consumption (Reuter and Greenfield 2001). Complicating this situation further, drug data were subject to contrasting interpretation and political manipulation (Musto and Sloboda 2003). For example, there were significant discrepancies in the cultivation reduction figures for Peru during the US-sponsored coca eradication project:

> From the mid-1980s to the mid-1990s, the figures on coca acreage [...] cited in reports by the United Nations and the Peruvian Ministry of Agriculture, and a respected private consulting firm all showed a steady rise. The State Department's figures, on the other hand, showed the amount of acreage to be flat or declining. The divergence was so great by 1994 that the U.N. estimate was nearly twice that of the estimate contained in the I.N.C.S. Report. (Galen Carpenter 2003: 97)

There were similar disparities in the figures produced by the USA and other agencies in relation to US-sponsored reduction programmes under Plan Colombia and the Bolivian Plan Dignity.

The functioning of the drug control apparatus did not facilitate improvements to general understanding of the drug trade and, by default, the drug control bodies' knowledge of their own task. Research commissioned and funded by international and domestic drug control apparatus was skewed towards quantitative and medical analysis and the research agenda was manipulated and constrained. In this respect, there was a significant allocation of resources towards projects that legitimized prohibition thinking and strategies. This in turn exacerbated the gap between the control apparatus and the realities of the drug trade 'on the ground'. A cogent example of the politicization of drug research was provided by the 'Ricaurte error'.

THE POLITICS OF ECSTASY In 1999, the head of the US National Institute on Drug Abuse (NIDA) Alan Leshner presented a series of slides showing scans of two brains. One of the brains was damaged. The image of the damaged brain formed the centrepiece of the federal government's ecstasy awareness campaign. It was popularized through the public advertisement 'This is your brain on drugs', showing an egg frying in a pan of hot oil. It was based on the work of medical researcher George Ricaurte of Johns Hopkins University School of Medical Science.

Further work on ecstasy by Ricaurte's team appeared in the October 2002 issue of the journal *Science*. In 'Severe Dopaminergic Neurotoxicity in Primates after a Common Recreational Dose Regimen of MDMA ("Ecstasy")', Ricaurte claimed that, following tests on ten primates, it could be concluded that one tablet of ecstasy could damage the functioning of the brain and create symptoms of Parkinson's disease in users. The findings created alarm within the medical and scientific professions, national governments and among the general public. They also created a favourable climate for the introduction of legislative restrictions on outdoor 'rave' parties, where ecstasy was commonly taken. In the USA, the congressional and public debate on the 2002 Reducing Americans' Vulnerability to Ecstasy Act (RAVE) was dominated by Ricaurte's research and the measure passed without significant objection. One year later, and after RAVE had come into force, Ricaurte retracted the paper. The ten primates in the original experiment had been injected with a high dosage of methamphetamine, not MDMA. This was blamed on a labelling error.

The Ricaurte error outraged the scientific and medical community (Earth Erowid 2003; Pearson 2004; Revill 2003; Walgate 2003). It appeared to demonstrate an ongoing and close inter-relationship between the politics of prohibition and sensationalist pseudo-science that dated back to early prohibition campaigners such as Richmond Hobson. There was intense scepticism towards *Science*'s motives for publishing Ricaurte's paper, particularly as publication coincided with the hearings into the RAVE Act. Critics argued that *Science* failed to conduct an adequate peer review of the article and much attention was paid to the role played by Alan Leshner in the Ricaurte affair (Pearson 2004). As head of the NIDA, Leshner had responsibility for the campaign to prohibit ecstasy use. Leshner was also the executive publisher of *Science*, a combination of roles that eroded the checks and balances necessary to prevent science being used for political ends.

The Ricaurte experience also drew attention to the fact that the distribution of funding for research on drugs was biased towards investigations that explored the physiological and psychological impact of drug use on humans, largely through experiments on animals. This was to the detriment of qualitative research that examined the drug careers of users and the patterns and causes of consumption. That the bulk of spending was focused on medical research was particularly unfortunate given the low level of overall funding made available for research into drugs. In the UK, for example, annual spending on all drug research was between £2.5 and £3 million. This represented 0.2 per cent of the £1.4 billion allocated to anti-drug policy. In the view of the British Royal Colleges of Psychiatrists and Physicians: 'Research is the most under-funded component of the UK's response to drugs.' The UK Police Foundation was 'forcibly struck by the lack of research and the weakness of the information base about drug use in the United Kingdom' (Joseph Rowntree Foundation 2005). The proportion of funding distributed to research in the USA was traditionally higher, at nearly $1 billion in the early 2000s, but this still represented only 4 per cent of total budget spending on drugs. Moreover, in the USA, the research funding allocation was channelled through the NIDA.

The NIDA had been established by the US government in 1974. The mission statement of the institute, which was funded through congressional appropriations, was 'to lead the Nation in bringing the power of science to bear on drug abuse and addiction'. Critics argued that NIDA bowed 'to the political agenda of its paymasters' (Pearson 2004) and, as a result, did not fund research that went against the thrust of prohibition, such as investigations into harm reduction or the medical use of cannabis. By contrast, work that legitimized prohibition and repressive controls, such as that conducted by Ricaurte and the so-called 'crack baby' phenomenon of pre-natal crack cocaine exposure that was also found to be flawed, received official support, was heavily publicized and insulated from peer scrutiny. In this respect, the 'reefer madness' and drug hysteria of the 1930s continued to echo through the history of drug control, with media myth and moral entrepreneurs supplanting medical reality and fact (Levine and Reinarman 1997).

SIDELINING EXPERTISE Throughout its history, the drug control model failed to provide the funding necessary for the development of empirically-based drug policy. Even though a high proportion of the revenues that were made available were directed towards medical research into the effects of drug use, by the early 2000s, the medical and scientific community was still no closer to establishing the 'truth' about the impact of drug use on the mental and physical health of the individual.

Not only did the drug control apparatus fail to develop a cohesive and informative research agenda, reports by expert committees that went against prohibition thinking were sidelined or suppressed. Table 9.1 lists some of the most important expert reports on drugs that were produced and subsequently marginalized.

TABLE 9.1 Expert drug reports

Report*	Country	Date
Indian Hemp Drugs Commission Report	UK	1894
Departmental Committee on Morphine and Heroin Addiction, Report (Rolleston Report)	UK	1926
Panama Canal Zone Military Investigation	USA	1929
LaGuardia Committee Report	USA	1944
Interdepartmental Committee, Drug Addiction (First Brain Report)	UK	1961
Drug Addiction: Crime or Disease? Joint Committee of the American Bar Association and the American Medical Association on Narcotic Drugs, Interim and Final Reports	USA	1961
Interdepartmental Committee, Drug Addiction, Second Report (Second Brain Report)	UK	1965
Advisory Committee on Drug Dependence, Cannabis (Wootton Report)	UK	1968
Canadian Government Commission of Inquiry into the Non-Medical Use of Drugs (Le Dain Report)	Canada	1970
Dealing with Drug Abuse: A Report to the Ford Foundation by the Drug Abuse Survey Project	USA	1972
Marihuana: A Signal of Misunderstanding. National Commission on Marihuana and Drug Abuse	USA	1972
Drug Use in America: A Problem in Perspective, National Commission on Marihuana and Drug Abuse	USA	1973
The Nation's Toughest Drug Law: Evaluating the New York Experience, by the Joint Committee on New York Drug Law Evaluation, of the Association of the Bar of the City of New York	USA	1977
An Analysis of Marihuana Policy. National Research Council of the National Academy of Science	USA	1982
A Wiser Course: Ending Drug Prohibition. A Report of the Special Committee on Drugs and the Law of the Association of the Bar of the City of New York	USA	1994
Legislative Options for Cannabis	Australia	1994

* All these reports can be read online: <www.druglibrary.org/schaffer/Library/studies/studies.htm>.

It was even alleged that research by the World Health Organization into the effects of cocaine and cannabis use, conducted in 1995 and 1998 respectively, was suppressed by the international drug control bodies as a result of strong pressure from the USA (Anderson 1998; Arthur 1998; Berger 1998; Jelsma 2003;

New Scientist 1998; Radford 1998; O'Coffin 1998; Taylor Martin 2001). On the 1995 study on cocaine, Neil Boyer, a US representative at the UN drug control apparatus, stated: 'The United States government has been surprised to note that the (study) seemed to make a case for the positive uses of cocaine [...] If W.H.O. activities [...] failed to reinforce proven drug control approaches, funds for the relevant programs should be curtailed' (Taylor Martin 2001).

Demand-side neglect

One of the most cogent and often repeated criticisms of the drug control model is that demand-side issues have been neglected. The prohibitionist view that reductions in consumption can be achieved through the elimination of supply has been institutionalized by the drug control bodies. As a result, the distribution of funding in the international 'drug war' has been channelled into eradication and interdiction activities. The resources that have been dedicated to demand-side issues have focused on law enforcement and criminal justice, to the detriment of education and treatment provision. This is despite the evidence that treatment provision is more effective, in terms of cost and recidivism rates, than incarceration and supply reduction in limiting drug use and problem drug use (Caulkins et al. 1997; Chase Eldredge 1998; Gray 2001).

Addicts and dependent users were conceptualized as criminals within prohibition thinking; where treatment provision did exist, it emphasized immediate termination of use and abstinence. The success rate of this type of programming was limited and it was painful and difficult for addicts to follow. Alternative treatments that emphasized gradual reductions in drug use and the substitution of illicit substances for synthetic equivalents were criticized by drug control authorities for violating the drug conventions and perpetuating user dependency (Berridge 2001).

In the 1970s and 1980s, the reform-oriented countries in Western Europe, Oceania and South America began to experiment with new forms of treatment provision. This was in response to the clear limitations of criminalization strategies. The approaches developed sought to respond directly to the needs of the problem drug user, rather than imposing top-down solutions that failed to recognize the diversity of the user experience. The most common treatment projects that have been introduced combined counselling, detoxification and substitution therapy delivered in a range of treatment settings including the drug user's home, clinics, in-patient and out-patient services. These were delivered by diverse agencies such as national health services and non-governmental organizations and they were both long-term and short-term in approach. But while there was progress in identifying and responding to the needs of problem drug users, there continued to be a chronic under-funding of treatment provision. The distribution of funding between supply- and demand-side programmes continued to be skewed towards the former, both at the international and national level. While an estimated 70 per cent of all funding for anti-drug initiatives was channelled into eradication, interdiction and enforcement, just 30 per cent was made available for demand-side reduction initiatives. Consequently, there was also insufficient funding available to address unemployment and social marginalization, the key drivers of problem drug use.

EDUCATION Supporters and opponents of the current drug control model concur that education should be an essential component of consumption reduction strategies. Targeting the consumers of the future in the school setting is seen to be one of the most effective methods of containing drug experimentation, drug use and drug-related harm. However, there are major differences in the approaches that have been followed. Prohibition-oriented countries such as the USA and Sweden emphasized abstinence and the dangers of drugs in drug education provision. An example of this was the US federally funded programme, the Drug Abuse Resistance Education (DARE). Established in 1983, this was a seventeen-hour-long drug curriculum that was delivered in schools by police officers. Prohibition-focused education emphasized moral and community responsibility and the need to 'just say no'. Critics argued that this type of intervention was ineffective and counter-productive.

The key problems associated with abstinence-focused education projects were, first, that they failed to provide clear and scientifically correct information about drugs. In presenting all controlled drugs including cannabis as dangerous, the information provided went against the experience and knowledge of most students. Second, the emphasis on the dangers of drugs increased their allure and the symbolism of drug use as an anti-establishment act. Third, the education programmes were not targeted. In this respect, they did not reflect or incorporate known indicators of potential drug abuse, such as parental or peer group influence. Fourth, there were no in-built mechanisms for evaluating their impact over time. As a result, they were not cost-effective and prohibition-focused education had no overall impact on levels of drug consumption. Finally, they were criticized as a tool for political and religious proselytizing rather than being a vehicle for an informed analysis of drugs (Beck 1998; Becker 1992; Brown et al. 1998; Douglass Fyr 1993; Fountain et al. 1999; Leverenz 2004). By contrast, liberal drug education programmes in countries such as the Netherlands and Switzerland were informed by the idea that the harm caused by drugs could be minimized by providing students with information about the science of drugs and safe drug use. In this respect, the role of educators was not to inculcate drugs education with moral or political values but to provide students with practical information that would reduce the risk of using drugs. This type of approach was condemned by the international drug control bodies and prohibition-oriented countries for promoting and condoning drug use.

By way of a conclusion: institutional crisis and decline

A final factor accounting for the failure of the international campaign to prohibit drug use was the performance of the international drug control institutions themselves. It has been argued that the international apparatus was rigid, anachronistic, self-serving and controlled by the USA. The influence of the USA was seen to be exercised through all of the main drug control bodies, including the CND and the UNDCP, but most significantly through the INCB, which had responsibility for interpreting and policing adherence to the conventions (Bewley-Taylor 2001; Fazey 2003). This institutionalized control enabled the USA and other prohibition-oriented countries such as Sweden, Japan and Nigeria to deflect pressure for change to the drug control regime. The dependency of the UN drug control apparatus on donors compounded the inability of the apparatus to revolutionize its working practices or to refocus policy. Moreover, as donors typically tied financial contributions to the drug control bodies to specific projects, the UNDCP could not be pro-active in redefining drug strategy (Fazey 2003). In addition, mechanisms for debate, policy evaluation and review within the UN were limited and this further impeded the reform of UN and drug control approaches.

Underscoring the limitations imposed on debate within the multinational forum, the INCB issued a paper in 1995 that stated: 'The international community has expressed a desire not to reopen all debates but to build on those commonly defined strategies and broad principles and to seek ways to further strengthen measures for drug control [...] Any doubt, hesitation, or unjustified review of the validity of goals will only undermine our commitment' (INCB 1995a). The approach of the prohibition lobby within the UN led them to be characterized as a 'drug prohibition church' that treated the drug conventions like 'religious texts' with heretical countries that pressed for modernization of the control regime marginalized (Bewley-Taylor 2003b; Cohen 2003b; Fazey 2003; Wodak 2003).

There were further institutional constraints on reform and renewal. According to Fazey, staffing structures within the UN impeded critical reflection on international policy and strategy. Because many of those employed by the UN were not on permanent contracts, there was a reluctance to critique policy and reports 'from within' or go against the mainstream of UN thinking as this could result in redundancy. The same constraints applied to specialists contracted to work on consultancy projects. Individuals known to be 'difficult to manage' because they did not concur with UN drug control approaches were either taken off projects or not considered for them (Fazey 2003: 163). There was also the threat of redeployment to crisis countries for permanent UN staff and this ameliorated any temptation to criticize working practices. The UNODCP was also embroiled in a number of scandals related to nepotism, corruption, cronyism, procedural irregularities and the bullying of staff. In a letter of resignation to the director of the UNODC, Antonio María Costa, a senior UNODC employee, wrote: 'I do not have the stomach to be promoting a fight against organized crime and corruption around the world when I am working in an office that tolerates administrative and in some cases criminal violations.' Mr Costa's predecessor, Pino Arlacchi, left the agency after he was accused of mismanaging the body's funds and violating procedural regulations (Catýn 2003).

There were also practical organizational limitations to the work of the international drug control apparatus. The key drug agencies were geographically dispersed across Geneva, Vienna and New York and this reduced collaboration and institutional cohesion. The cultural diversity of the UN also created problems in terms of working languages in the drafting and development of legislation and legal treaties. Finally, there was a mismatch between generalists, that is to say UN civil servants, and specialists with competency in the drugs field. As generalists tended to occupy senior administrative positions, this led to the downgrading of specialist knowledge within the control system (Fazey 2003: 160).

As a result of institutional paralysis and ideological dogmatism within the static UN control apparatus, the control system was unable or unwilling to respond to the well-documented problems caused by prohibition-based strategies. There was no reorientation of funding into alternative development programmes, the emphasis on repression and criminalization was retained, research into the dynamics of the drugs trade was controlled and politicized and the supply-side focus maintained. Substances that were known to be harmful and addictive, such as tobacco and alcohol, were freely available, while those that were not addiction-inducing and known to be useful in medical practice and psychotherapy, such as LSD and cannabis, were prohibited (Abramson 1967; Cashman 1966; Holland 2001; Grinspoon and Balakar 1979; Solomon 1966).

The failure of the international control system to eliminate the trade in drugs was a direct result of the existence, ideology, structure and programmatic orientation of the international prohibition regime itself. In persisting with and accelerating the application of control measures and in continuing to set unrealizable objectives, the system began to do more harm than good.

There was a further important reason why drug control failed. As is discussed in the following chapter, respect for the international drug control treaties and the principle of drug prohibition was pragmatically sidelined when the pursuit of this end went against the commercial or political interests of a country. This was particularly the case for the USA due to the tight inter-relationship between drugs policy and foreign policy. While on the one hand the USA vigorously promoted and defended prohibition both domestically and at the global level, it also conspired with the illicit drugs trade when it was in the 'national interest'.

10 | The political impact of drugs and drug control

Drug-related activities such as production and trafficking require a territorial base from which to operate. Geography, climate and agricultural tradition historically dictated that a limited number of easily identifiable countries would be the source of plant-based drugs such as heroin and cocaine. By default, countries such as Panama and Pakistan that bordered producer states were also identifiable as potential trafficking routes for illicit drugs and semi-processed raw materials. The historical experience of these traditional source and trafficking countries was one of penetration and corruption of state institutions by the illicit drugs trade. This had profoundly negative consequences for political stability and governability in these countries.

The contemporary trends identified in Chapters 6 and 7, such as the rise in the synthetic drug market and the fragmentation and dissipation of the illicit sector, have blurred the traditional distinction between source, trafficking and consumer countries. It has consequently become more difficult to identify those countries that are at risk from penetration by the illicit drugs trade and the political influence of drug revenues. While geographical proximity to drug supply source was historically the determinant of drug corruption, the strength and legitimacy of the nation-state emerged as the key variable influencing drug penetration of political systems in the 2000s. Geography remained an important influence in terms of where criminal organizations, trafficking groups and money launderers chose to begin or locate their activities, but as globalization opened up a new range of locations, the strength of the state determined whether or not the illicit trade flourished within a nation's territory.

The strong rise in drug consumption and related distribution activities from the 1980s onwards also demonstrated that the capacity of the state to maintain a viable and legitimate presence in local communities determined the extent to which drug-related activities developed and consolidated at the local level. This was the case in both wealthy democratic states in North America and Europe and weak states in the developing world.

The importance of state presence
The community level Drug-related activities in a community have a damaging impact on residents of the area. The experience of cities as diverse as Rio de Janeiro in Brazil, Los Angeles in the USA, Manchester in the UK, Nuevo Laredo in Mexico and Narino in Colombia showed that the arrival of the illicit trade was accompanied by violence and, increasingly, gun-related violence. This link

between the trade and social violence is a direct result of the informality of the sector. Business transactions, such as market takeovers and enforcement of contracts, are reliant on the use or threat of force. The intensity of the violence is influenced by the scale of the trade in a given locality, the value of the market, the existence of competitors and the type and origin of the drug.

Drug-related violence triggers a sequence of events that culminate in the isolation or *ghettoization* of the affected community (Harrell 1992). Residents who are financially able to relocate move out of the area and this marks the beginning of a wider process of decapitalization and disinvestment as shops, bars, clubs and service and manufacturing sectors withdraw from the area owing to security concerns. As drug-related activities expand, this is usually paralleled by a rise in other criminal activities such as racketeering. This further increases the pressure on enterprises and service providers to move out of the community. In extreme cases, the risk and fear of violence leads to the cancellation of basic public services such as transportation (Chase Eldridge 1998; Gray 2001).

As formal economic opportunities in the affected community decline, un-employment and poverty increase. In this context, the drug trade becomes an important source of employment, wealth creation and social organization in the form of gangs. Membership of a drug gang provides young unemployed males with protection, prestige, money and a sense of identity. The growth of these gang cultures fuels the violence that is associated with the illicit drugs trade (Bing 1992; Morris and Hopkins 2003; Moore and Garcia 1979).

In the slums or *favelas* of Rio, which have replaced Los Angeles as a case study of drug-related ghettoization, an estimated 10,000 people were involved in drug-related activities in the 1990s and 2000s. Underscoring the associa-tion between drug-related activities and violence, more people under the age of eighteen years were killed in the *favelas* than the number of minors killed in the Israel–Palestine conflict. Between 1987 and 2001, 467 minors were killed as a result of gun-related violence in the Israel–Palestine conflict. In Rio, the figure was 3,937 (Silva Iulianelli et al. 2004).

Drug-related violence is never contained within the gangs or criminal organ-izations. Innocent members of the community, including children, are frequently caught in the cross-fire. There is also a perceptible trend of sexual and physical violence against women in those communities where the trade becomes consoli-dated, as the influence and wealth that flows from the trade inverts structures of authority and norms of respect. These impacts are felt in all countries, regardless of economic development levels, if the illicit trade is present.

The creation of 'narco-communities' dominated by drug gangs exacerbates existing problems of poverty and unemployment and it isolates people within their own communities. Drug-related violence additionally leads to the closure of public spaces such as parks and avenues for public interaction, thereby con-tributing to the atomization of citizens. The manner in which the trade operates inhibits community interaction and communal resolution of problems. Active citizenship and community engagement is replaced by fear, suspicion and distrust. The experience in cities such as Los Angeles, Rio and Nuevo Laredo also showed that those who criticized the trade or pressured for police action were threatened or murdered.

Understanding the state (non-)response It would be expected that the presence of drug-related activities in a community would provoke a preventative or defensive intervention on the part of the state through law enforcement agencies both to protect its citizens and in line with its responsibilities under the international drug conventions. There are two problems with the assumption that the state will act. First, it may not have the capacity or motivation to intervene. For example, a large number of countries in the developing world do not have the financial capacity to present or maintain a state presence in marginal areas. This is particularly the case in countries such as Colombia, Thailand and Pakistan where the state territory incorporates difficult and inhospitable terrain.

Even if the state does have the institutional and financial capacity to extend its presence across the national territory, the government may decide not to move pro-actively to address problems of community-level *narcoization*. Neglect and inactivity can be attributed to a number of factors. In the case of Los Angeles and other cities with large black populations in majority white countries, it was linked to institutionalized racism. In this interpretation, a national or local administration may determine that the problem is confined to a specific ethnic community and choose not to act. There are also economic reasons. Neoliberal policies such as public spending cuts and the privatization of welfare provision have led to a squeezing of local services in those countries where these types of free market policies have been implemented. This created marginalized and vulnerable communities that lacked a proper state presence and which were neglected in terms of housing and education provision.

A second problem with the assumption that the state can act to prevent local-level *narcoization* is that state institutions such as the police have been shown to be susceptible to drug-related corruption. In order to protect their activities, criminal organizations purchase the support or compliance of the police. This was the case during the era of alcohol prohibition in the USA and it has been a pervasive feature of the contemporary drug control model. Drug-related corruption of enforcement officials has occurred in all countries at some point in time, regardless of the level of economic or institutional development. It is a particularly insidious and institutionally corrosive practice because, unlike other forms of police corruption, officers involved in drug-related corruption were also likely to commission other crimes, such as stealing drugs or money from dealers and providing false testimony about drug operations. The main motivations for drug-related corruption included: profit; fear, pressure and threats to officers and their families; and a sense of vigilante justice on the part of officers (US General Accounting Office 1998). This susceptibility to corruption meant that even if the state had a presence in drug-affected communities, this did not necessarily translate into action against the trade.

National level of influence While the illicit drug trade gained an increased presence at the local level in cities across the world, it penetrated national-level politics in only a limited number of countries. These included the main cultivating states of Colombia, Bolivia, Peru, Afghanistan and Myanmar, and neighbouring trafficking states such as Pakistan, Panama and Thailand. As the sources of illicit supply become increasingly diversified and trafficking activities extend into new countries and geographical regions, it can be expected that more states will be susceptible to *narcoization*, particularly countries in the Caribbean, Central America and Central Asia (Clutterbuck 1995).

The term 'narco-state' refers to those countries where criminal organizations connected to the drug trade acquire an institutionalized presence in the state. In order to protect their interests, major drug syndicates and organizations have looked to elements of the state for collaboration and protection. These links between criminal groups and public officials are nurtured and utilized to ensure that the assets, trading networks and individuals associated with the illicit drug organizations are not negatively affected by legislation, interdiction or enforcement efforts. Those institutions that are the key targets of narco-corruption are the security sector, specifically: the police, military and customs agencies; the judiciary; the government; and politicians. Drug traffickers have also run for elected office in order to institutionalize their influence and acquire immunity from prosecution for extra-parliamentary activities. The problems experienced by narco-states are the same as those experienced by narco-communities at the local level but national in scale. They include the spread of impunity and corruption, a rise in drug-related violence and the suppression of critics of the drug trade. Narco-states are the antithesis of democracy: freedom of speech is negated, political choice is restricted, rights of association are contained by the threat of violence and the rule of law is eroded.

States that are fragile and lacking in popular legitimacy are particularly vulnerable to drug corruption or penetration. If concepts of public service are weak, public officials can be easily corrupted by drug money. The susceptibility of politicians to bribery and corruption is particularly pronounced in political systems where mechanisms for democratic accountability, political renewal and constituency representation are precarious. There has to be, then, an existing problem of state and democratic weakness that can be exploited by the drug trade (Andreas 1998; Jordan 1999). Once the illicit trade has established itself within the national territory and institutional framework, it exacerbates the state's pre-existing legitimacy crisis. This is because corruption of the political system and institutional framework erodes the moral and political legitimacy and capacity of the state. As drug corruption typically benefits the wealthiest and most powerful, this fuels social and political divisions between the rich elite and the poor majority (Warren 2004).

Drug-related interests are intensely difficult to rein back once they have been consolidated. Reform initiatives are contained by defensive violence on the part of criminal organizations, as demonstrated by the experience of Colombia in the 1980s. The administrations of President Belisario Betancur (1982–86) and Virgilio Barco Vargas (1986–90) sought to suppress the activities of the large drug cartels with initiatives that included the extradition of key Colombian traffickers to the USA. The cartels initially sought to dissuade the government from its pro-active enforcement policy. The Medellín cartel offered to repay the country's national debt in 1984 in exchange for an end to extraditions and the formalization of its economic interests. When inducement and persuasion failed, the cartel launched a 'total war' against the state in 1989. Three presidential candidates for the 1990 election were assassinated, as were scores of police, journalists and over 200 judges and court officials (Bergquist et al. 2001).

Drugs and conflict In states where the legitimacy crisis is so great that it provokes armed rebellion against the national government, the presence of the illegal drug trade can sustain and exacerbate armed conflict, specifically if control of the trade is in the hands of the rebel group. This is because illicit drugs, like diamonds, gemstones and timber, are a lootable commodity (Addison et al. 2001; Ballentine and Sherman 2003; Collier and Hoeffler 1999; Klare 2001; Le Billon 2001, 2003; Renner and Prugh 2002; Ross 2003). Once the trade in illicit drugs is controlled or taxed by rebel groups, it provides the financial resources necessary to sustain or step up a conflict, with the revenues used for the purchase of weaponry and the recruitment and payment of rebel members.

In Peru, the Maoist Sendero Luminoso (Shining Path) organization that launched a violent assault against the political system in 1982 (McClintock 1998; Poole and Renique 1992; Scott Palmer 1992) charged cocaine and coca paste traffickers $3,000 to $7,000 per flight out of the Huallaga Valley (Steinitz 2002). The organization's drug-related revenues in the late 1980s were estimated to be in the region of $15–100 million or 60 per cent of their total funds. The civil conflict between the Maoists and the Peruvian armed forces was brought to an end in 1992 with the capture of Sendero's leader, Abimael Guzman. Between 60,000 and 100,000 people are thought to have died in the conflict.

In Colombia, taxation of the drug trade financed the operations of the left-wing Fuerzas Armada Revolucionarios de Colombia (FARC) in the second half of its protracted, forty-year-long conflict with the Colombian state (Safford and Palacios 2002). This was particularly the case in the late 1980s as domestic coca and cocaine production surged. Figures from the late 1990s demonstrated that the FARC charged $16 per kilo of coca paste and $53 for every kilo of cocaine produced in territory controlled by the organization. Transhipment of chemical precursors along river routes were taxed at 20 per cent and the tax levied for the protection of flights out of FARC territory was $2,631 for a domestic flight and $5,263 for international flights (Steinitz 2002). Right-wing paramilitaries grouped in the Autodefensas Unidas de Colombia (AUC) also exploited the financial opportunities presented by the drugs trade to fund their conflict with the FARC. Paramilitary groups loyal to powerful landowners and political figures had a long and established history in Colombia and they were a root cause of the intense, triangular political conflict between the left, the right and the state. The AUC itself emerged from a death squad created by the Medellín cartel in 1981 called Muerte a Secuestadores (Death to Kidnappers), which was formed after the kidnapping of a cartel member's sister. The AUC continued its 'anti-communist' operations against the FARC after the break-up of the Medellín cartel in the early 1990s. The leader of the AUC, Carlos Castano, claimed in 2000 that 70 per cent of the organization's funding was derived from taxes on the drug trade. In contrast to the FARC, whose central leadership maintained that the organization's involvement in the drugs trade was limited to taxation despite evidence to the contrary (Human Rights Watch 2002), the AUC was also heavily involved in the production and trafficking of cocaine (Buscaglia and Ratliff 2001).

In Myanmar, Afghanistan and Central Asia, opium poppy cultivation and heroin trafficking financed the anti-state campaigns of the United Wa State Army, the Mujaheddin and the Northern Alliance and the Islamic Movement of Uzbekistan in the 1980s and 1990s (Chouvy 2003; Fishel 1995; ICG 2001; Leader and Wiencek 2000; Makarenko 2002). After the Taliban seized power in Afghanistan in 1996 it continued to tax opium poppies while adopting a harsh and repressive stance towards those engaged in the production or consumption of cannabis. It was estimated that the Taliban received between $20 and $40 million per year from the poppy tax out of total annual revenues of an estimated $100 million earned from the smuggling of contraband (ICG 2001; Rashid 2001).

The instability of wartime conditions increases the benefits associated with participation in the drug trade and it provides a propitious environment for the expansion of the sector across the national territory. Conflict distracts the national government and the security sector from enforcement and interdiction activities. As a result, small-scale drug production and trafficking activities can expand unhindered into larger operations. Second, the deterioration of state service provision during conflict increases the reliance of the local population on employment and revenue generation opportunities in the illicit sector (UNODC 2001: 156). This was the experience of Tajikistan, which emerged as a centre for opiate trafficking after its civil conflict between 1992 and 1997, which led to the death of over 60,000 people (*The Economist* 2003, 2002b; ICG 2001). In conditions of conflict, violence and poverty, it is acutely difficult for either the state or the rebel group to suppress cultivation and production, even if they were inclined to do so, as this would produce protest and further violence. The end result is a vicious cycle of state illegitimacy, civil conflict and the growth of the drugs trade, with wartime conditions then fuelling the growth of drug production which in turn sustains rebel activity and conflict. The cycle of violence can be broken only if there are political mechanisms that allow for resolution of the underlying conflict but, even then, rebel groups flushed with drug revenues may choose to continue their anti-state campaign. Hence, while grievance may be the catalyst of the original conflict, it can be displaced by greed if the financial benefits of perpetuating the conflict outweigh the benefits of negotiating peace (Kay 1999; Rangel Suarez 2000).

Anti-drug responses: more harm than good?

While the presence of the drug trade within the national territory or local community has a politically destabilizing impact, anti-drug responses by the state can have equally deleterious ramifications for political stability and democracy. There are two reasons for this. First, anti-drug responses have become militarized. This has negative implications for human rights, institutional accountability and civilian oversight of the armed forces. Second, anti-drugs strategies and legislation are punitive and unjustly applied. The stepping up of criminal sanctions and enforcement activities after the 1980s compounded the harm already caused by existing legislative approaches, with deleterious ramifications for liberty, freedom and social justice.

The militarization of anti-drug initiatives Militarization of drug strategies refers to two things. It first means the use of military-grade weaponry, combat strategies and military rules of engagement by national police and enforcement agencies. As violence is expected from criminal organizations, enforcement agencies have responded by increasing their own capacity for violence. Militarization also refers to the incorporation of the armed forces into anti-drug operations. The trend of militarization, specifically the deployment of the armed forces, was a central feature of anti-drugs strategies in the 1980s. The adoption of militarized anti-drugs strategies is linked to four inter-related factors.

Militarization emerged as a response to the failure of traditional law enforcement approaches. In consumer, but more specifically the producer and trafficking countries, national police forces proved themselves vulnerable to drug-related corruption and too inefficient, underfunded and disorganized to suppress the growth of drug-related activities in the 1970s and 1980s. In this context, the armed forces were perceived by domestic governments, the USA and the international drug control apparatus as the only institution capable of engaging and repressing well armed, organizationally coherent and geographically spread traffickers, cultivators and producers. Second, countries are under intense pressure to meet the UN goal of significant reductions in cultivation, production and trafficking by 2008. The need to meet this target led to the promotion and adoption of increasingly sophisticated and ruthless anti-drug strategies and techniques such as 'shoot to kill' policies.

Militarization also developed as a logical outgrowth of drug strategies that are conceptualized as a 'war'. Under the rubric of its 'war on drugs' the USA was instrumental in pressing for the deployment of the South American armed forces in anti-drug operations, particularly in Bolivia and Colombia, and the bulk of its financial assistance to producer and trafficking countries concentrated on military capacity building. The USA was specifically positioned to impose militarized responses to the drugs trade on South American countries because of the region's geographic location within the US sphere of influence. European donors and the UN drug control bureaucracy reinforced this militarized approach pioneered by the USA by focusing financial support to weak states in Central Asia, Africa and the Caribbean on security sector reform and capacity building.

Finally, the 'war on terrorism' contributed to the militarization of control efforts. After the Al Qaeda attacks on the USA in 2001, America developed new concepts of domestic, hemispheric and international security. In the Americas, this was characterized by the 'securitization' of on-going problems such as poverty, environmental degradation, drug production and political instability (Chillier and Freeman 2005). These were subsequently conceptualized as security threats, as outlined in the 2003 Declaration on Security in the Americas that was adopted by the Organization of American States. This strategy of securitization to combat the ill-defined and nebulous concept of 'terror' post-11 September looked to the armed forces to defend the state against threats that had previously been understood as products of economic underdevelopment. This widening of the concept of security meant that the armed forces in South, Central American and Caribbean countries acquired new domestic and intra-regional mission responsibilities, including a larger role in anti-drug operations.

The impact of militarized drug wars Militarized responses to the drugs trade have not succeeded in reducing levels of production or trafficking. However, they have accelerated the pace of fragmentation and displacement in the illicit sector. As a result, it is as counter-productive as all other repression-based strategies. While there was an increase in interdiction and eradication activities in countries such as Thailand and Colombia, both of which reported production and cultivation reductions after the deployment of the armed forces in the 1990s, drug-related activities increased in neighbouring countries. Not only did the militarization of anti-drug strategies fail to deliver tangible benefits, they exacerbated existing problems of social and political violence, popular alienation and state illegitimacy.

Countering drug-related violence with the political violence of the state increased the vulnerability of innocent citizens to injury and death, with adults and children caught in the cross-fire between security forces and criminal organizations. The altered rules of engagement, with law enforcement perceived as combat duties, in addition to weak civilian oversight of the security sector, led to the systematic violation of basic human rights, including the right to life. In Thailand, Peru, Colombia and Bolivia, there were reports of 'shoot to kill' policies, arbitrary detention, disappearances and torture in anti-drug operations. Militarized responses were also seen to fuel internal displacement in countries like Colombia that already had an existing internal refugee problem as a result of the civil conflict. In the Bolivian case, there was sustained violence and conflict in coca cultivating areas in the Chapare region as the security forces stepped up eradication efforts in the late 1990s. Over two hundred people were killed in a succession of protests against forced crop eradication over the period 1999 to 2002 (Kohl and Farthing 2001). In Brazil, the number of deaths resulting from 'resistance to arrest' during the adoption of a militarized response to drug trafficking in that country increased 236 per cent between 1997 and 2003. The number of people 'disappeared' by the security forces was over 15,000. Those killed by security forces had an average of 4.3 bullet wounds, the majority of which were to the head: 'Summary executions seem to be the preferred method of the police in Rio' (Silva Iulianelli et al. 2004). The capacity of the security forces to act with apparent impunity was enhanced by national governments in these countries as legislation enhancing the autonomy of the security forces was introduced to provide the military with flexibility in the execution of anti-drug missions (*The Economist* 2001a, 2001c, 2001f; ICG 2003 on Colombia). Further to this, because of the civil conflict in countries such as Colombia, anti-drugs and 'anti-terror' operations were intertwined by the armed forces and, as a result, a more coercive approach was followed in interdiction activities.

Victims of police and military repression encountered major obstacles in seeking accountability and compensation for abuses committed. This was attributed to the closed juridical procedures within the armed forces and the weakness of institutionalized mechanisms for civilian oversight and control. The US strategy of funding and training paramilitary organizations operating outside the command and control structure of the armed forces, such as the Bolivian Expeditionary Task Force, also delimited mechanisms of accountability and oversight (Amnesty International 2001).

A DEMOCRATIC SOLUTION? Aside from its impact on human rights, the militarization of drug control had negative ramifications for democracy and democratic consolidation in South America, Southeast Asia and the Central Asian countries. The militarization strategy first enhanced the autonomy of the armed forces and, by default, reduced civilian oversight of the military. This was a particularly deleterious development in countries such as Thailand, Bolivia and Colombia, where the military had a long and bloody history of involvement in government and political affairs. The incorporation of the armed forces into domestic law enforcement during the 1980s and 1990s consequently countered a positive global trend of demilitarization and democratization. Civilian authority in the South American country context was further eroded as a result of the integration of military forces from the region into US hemispheric security projects and strategic operations. This meant that the South, Central and Caribbean military were locked into US-defined missions and strategies, rather than nationally directed activities, further distancing them from the control of elected civilian governments (Griffith 1997; NACLA 2001; Pion Berlin 2001; Youngers and Rosin 2004).

The incorporation of the military into domestic political affairs through the 'war on drugs' was also negative for democracy as it legitimized the deployment of the military in other areas of law enforcement, such as the maintenance of social order and, interlinked with this, the suppression of protest movements. In Bolivia, for example, the military was deployed against anti-government protesters in 2003 and clashes in the capital, La Paz, led to the death of thirty-two protesters. This pointed to a third, profoundly undemocratic, element of drug control strategies. Because of the overarching role of the USA in defining anti-drug responses in the region, domestic debate on drug reduction strategies in these countries was contained. This was acutely problematic given that indigenous groups in countries like Peru and, more specifically, Bolivia had historically pressed for coca cultivation to be formalized. Despite this, the powerful Bolivian coca movement that first emerged in the 1980s was not party to negotiations between the USA and the Bolivian government. When the *cocaleros* mobilized protests against militarized anti-drug strategies, they were criticized for their 'anti-democratic' and 'terrorist' actions. The *cocalero* organizations in Bolivia were part of a wider indigenous protest movement that mobilized against neoliberal policies, the privatization of water and gas services and racial discrimination by the white minority elite that was supported by the USA and which had political control of the country. The *cocaleros* defended the cultivation and use of the coca plant and pressed for coca and cocaine to be decoupled in anti-drug strategies. From this perspective, coca was an integral and harmless element of indigenous culture and lifestyle, the plant becoming dangerous and illegal only as a result of US demand-side failures. This view made the *cocaleros*, and their leader Evo Morales, the centre of a campaign against perceived US control of the country (Vann Cott 2003).

In the national election of 2002, Morales came within 0.02 per cent of winning the presidency. On the eve of the election, the US ambassador Manuel Rocha stated: 'I want to remind the Bolivian electorate that if they vote for those who want Bolivia to return to exporting cocaine, that will seriously jeopardize any future aid to Bolivia from the United States' (ibid.). The Bolivian case demonstrated that the militarization of anti-drug responses had implications for democracy and political choice. Because drugs were conceptualized as a security threat, so were those groups opposed to drug policy. This in turn legitimized the suppression of challenges to the political and economic status quo. This was also the case in Colombia, where the 'war on drugs' and the 'war on terror' became increasingly blurred with the state campaign against rebel groups.

Militarization consequently encouraged the consolidation of authoritarian political tendencies, with the 'war on drugs' serving as a mechanism for the suppression of anti-US sentiment and demands for meaningful political and economic reform. In the Central Asian countries of Kazakhstan, Tajikistan, Uzbekistan and Kyrgyzstan, the militarization of anti-drug strategies also led to the violation of civil, political and constitutional rights (Human Rights Watch 2003). In this region, the 'war on drugs' was: 'used for political ends [...] to crack down on political opposition, target particular religious and ethnic groups, limit civil liberties, and to tighten political control' (Lubin 2001).

The militarization of anti-drugs strategies is not only bad for democracy, human rights and control efforts in general; it also has negative effects on the military. Deployment on anti-drug operations, which are rightly a matter for national policing, distracts the armed forces from defensive duties and leaves them vulnerable to corruption by drug-money. It was in recognition of this that the Colombian military resisted deployment in anti-drug operations until the introduction of Plan Colombia in 2000. Similarly, in Afghanistan, the US-led coalition forces did not see drug eradication as part of their mission (Gertz 2002).

SUMMARY: THE APPROPRIATENESS OF MILITARIZATION There were then a number of critical problems with the militarized anti-drug strategies being promoted by the USA, the UN and European donor countries in the 1990s and 2000s. Militarization first distracted attention and finances from those socio-economic problems that allowed illicit drugs to become embedded within a society or community in the first place. Second, intensifying repression undermined democracy, accountability and political stability without any concomitant reduction in drug supply. Militarization also facilitated and legitimized authoritarian government and political responses and it was an obstacle to the negotiation of existing conflicts.

The experience of Central and Southeast Asia and South America raised serious questions as to the appropriateness of western anti-drug strategies. The utility of providing financial support to countries with weak democratic systems and a history of human rights abuses for the purpose of repressive police and military activities was questionable. Further to this, the contemporary approach threatened to weaken further the legitimacy of fragile states, in turn making them more vulnerable to rebellion and narco-penetration. In its 2000 World Drug

Report, the UN stated: 'Progress in reducing illicit crop cultivation depends on the political environment in which central governments and local communities interact' (UNODCCP 2000). A central lesson that has not been learned from recent experience is that militarization creates an unpropitious environment for state and civil society interaction and consequently any progress in reducing cultivation, production and trafficking.

The drug war in consumer countries While the USA pressed for the deployment of the military in domestic anti-drug operations in South America, it did not follow the same strategy domestically. However, domestic enforcement agencies adopted militarized anti-drug strategies, as did consumer countries in Western Europe and Oceania. This militarization of law enforcement ran parallel with the application of increasingly severe penalties against engagement in the drug trade. The logic of this policy course was that prohibition was failing because it was not being pursued aggressively enough. As with developments in the producer states, this acceleration of the 'drug war' had deleterious implications for human rights.

The policy of criminalizing the drug trade was already criticized as inhumane before repression activities were stepped up in the 1980s. In the period since, it has become clear that the manner in which the legal system operates and drug laws are applied causes profound social harm. First, drug laws and drug policies were seen unfairly to target the weakest and most vulnerable people. In this respect, the overwhelming majority of people incarcerated for drug-related offences were individuals convicted for possession, low-level street distribution or mules. Arresting and incarcerating such people had no overall effect on the drug trade because these individuals were marginal to its operations. Moreover, the majority of drug offenders were non-violent, had no previous record and the largest number were convicted for cannabis-related offences. By contrast, less than 5 to 10 per cent of people incarcerated on drug charges were important traffickers or 'drug kingpins'. Leading figures in the trade also had the opportunity to reduce their sentences through plea bargaining or turning state witness.

In respect of sentencing procedures, there was particular concern at the severity of the prison terms imposed on offenders. Critics in different countries across the world argued that mandatory minimum sentences led to the imposition of unduly long sentences for drug-related offences and that these sentences were disproportionate in comparison to other crimes such as murder, manslaughter and rape. Drug laws were also seen to be unfairly applied, with minority and socially 'dangerous' groups sentenced to longer terms. In the USA, the problem of discriminatory practices in sentencing procedures was seen to be particularly severe. Although only 12 per cent of US drug users were African American, black people comprised 45 per cent of prisoners in federal institutions convicted of

The political impact

drug-related offences and 60 per cent of inmates in state prisons (Human Rights Watch 2000). Further to this, legislation was applied in an 'exclusivist' manner that did not allow motivations for the offence to be taken into consideration. An example of problems caused by this approach is shown by a case study of female drug traffickers.

In 2002, prisons in the UK were reported to be 'flooded' with Jamaican mules who accounted for 15 per cent of all female prisoners (Gillan 2003; Rose 2003; Thompson 2002). The average sentence imposed on these women was ten years for the importation of an average 900 grams. The majority of these women were young, single parents and poor. A study of Colombian female mules imprisoned in the UK found that over 90 per cent of the sample group interviewed were between twenty and thirty years of age, like the Jamaican women a large number were also single parents, and they were also poor (Dorado 2002). A majority of the women imprisoned were not aware of the sentences imposed for trafficking and they expected to return home within two or three days of dropping off the trafficked drugs. Their children were typically left with friends. Arrest and imprisonment led to children being made homeless and displaced from the female parent.

This had devastating social consequences for those affected and it was seen to be unjust and ineffective as it had no effect on trafficking rates. Further to this, the bulk of drugs trafficked into the UK came through cross-channel routes, with mules accounting for less than 10 per cent of the total volume of illegal drugs brought into the UK. Finally, and as an illustration of the skewed distribution of resources in the 'drug war', it cost the British government £25 million to incarcerate an estimated 437 foreign nationals accused of drug-related offences. By contrast the total economic aid provided by the British Department for International Development to Jamaica was £5 million (Rethinking. org 2003).

Despite the severity of the punishments imposed on drug offenders, including capital punishment in the USA and a number of Southeast Asian and Muslim countries, the trade continued to grow. It was therefore clear that punishment had no deterrent effect. Moreover, because there was no 'victim' who could involve the police in the trade, anti-drugs agencies resorted to activities that violated basic rights and civil liberties in order to secure convictions, including wire tapping, armed raids without warrants and arbitrary arrests. This led to a backlash against national drug laws and anti-drug strategies in the 1980s and 1990s as well as to the production of a body of literature assessing the extent to which the manner of executing the 'drug war' contradicted the constitution and federal legislation (Chase Eldridge 1998; Gray 2001; Lynch 2000; Wisotsky 1990).

United States: the heart of the problem

The most ardent supporter of the failed policy of militarizing the 'war on drugs' has been the USA. Critics of the strategy argue that America has promoted the 'war on drugs' not as a strategy for reducing the trade but as a vehicle allowing it to defend its economic and political interests in, and control over, other countries. In this respect, US drug policy is an integral instrument of US foreign policy. As the following section demonstrates, US foreign policy objectives have traditionally been prioritized over and above progress in reducing the illicit trade, even in those countries where the US presence was initially premised on anti-drug operations. In using drug policy as an element of foreign policy, the USA has played a wholly counter-productive role in international drug control and the dominance of the country emerges as a key reason for the failure of drug control.

The USA initiated and remained at the forefront of international efforts to prohibit the trade in illicit drugs. At the same time, the country was one of the most unco-operative actors within the multilateral drug control framework. There has always been a significant overlap between US foreign policy, national security policy and drug control policy. As a result, drug control was frequently subsumed into or used as a mechanism for achieving other foreign or security-related ends. Moreover, the goal of drug prohibition was covertly jettisoned when anti-drugs activities clashed with or undermined competing security or foreign policy priorities. A fundamental contradiction consequently existed at the heart of US drugs policy. The US government maintained a double-discourse on drugs, publicly demanding measures to end the illicit trade while at the same time being complicit with it.

Mechanisms of pressure Throughout the history of the international drug control system, the USA sought to institutionalize its own policy priorities and approaches. The subsequent internationalization of domestic US drug prohibition (Bewley-Taylor 2001), with its emphasis on strict supply-side controls and harsh criminal sanctions, was achieved through coercive diplomacy. Countries were pressured by US officials at the UN and international drug conferences to support the US position. This US leverage was based on the financial and military dominance of the country. During the Cold War, the USA was constrained in terms of the pressure that it could apply to those countries that formed part of the Soviet bloc. With the ending of the Cold War and the emergence of a unipolar world order, these constraints were removed.

If pressure and persuasion failed within the UN bodies and the USA found that it could not develop an international consensus on its proposals, representatives from the country would boycott or walk out of meetings. The USA frequently threatened to halt funding for and co-operation with the international drug control institutions and to pursue its ends unilaterally if these were not met through the multilateral UN apparatus. The USA also developed a number of unilateral mechanisms that it applied to those countries it did not perceive as complying with the international drug conventions or co-operating in drug control efforts. This included the annual drug certification system introduced in 1985. The certification system was based on an analysis of the drug policy record of individual countries conducted by the US State Department in conjunction with the Bureau for International Narcotics and Law Enforcement Affairs and US embassies. If it was found that a country was not co-operating with US anti-drug agencies and had not made progress in reducing the cultivation, production or trafficking of drugs, then the US president could deny them certification. This rendered decertified countries ineligible for various forms of US foreign and financial aid.

The US government and drug control apparatus credited the 'narcotics certification law' with inducing reform and co-operation on drug-related issues in 'major' production and trafficking countries such as Mexico, Colombia and Thailand, all of which were decertified and then recertified as control efforts were stepped up. However, the certification system was controversial and it continued to be criticized despite a modification of certification procedures in 2002 (Bureau for International Narcotics and Law Enforcement Affairs 2003). A primary complaint was that the USA exploited the financial vulnerability of individual countries through the certification system and, by denying aid, compounded the difficulties of enforcing drug control. The measure was also counterproductive. The loss of US financial assistance negatively affected the national economies of decertified states, in turn increasing the financial importance of the illicit drug trade.

Certification was additionally criticized because it undermined multilateral drug control efforts and a sense of 'shared responsibility' for eliminating the trade (Amatangelo 2001). There were also claims that the certification system was a way of displacing responsibility for the trade, diverting attention away from demand-side failures in consumer states such as the USA, the world's largest drug-consuming nation, to poorer supply-side countries (Galen Carpenter 2003). A final criticism was that certification was used as a tool for punishing politically 'deviant' states, while pro-US countries were certified even if they had a poor enforcement record.

The use of the certification process to achieve political and drug-related objectives was most keenly exercised in South America. The region was particularly vulnerable to unilateral US anti-drugs initiatives on account of two things: it was a major source of US drug supply; and it had been identified as within the US sphere of influence since the Monroe Doctrine of 1832. These two factors legitimized constant US intervention in and pressure on South American countries, and because they were so heavily integrated with the USA, the certification system was a particularly potent weapon. Indicative of this, exports to the USA from Peru, Bolivia, Colombia and Mexico were 24 per cent, 21 per cent, 38 per cent and 85 per cent respectively. As decertification led to the imposition of trade tariffs and embargoes, the process was highly effective in enforcing compliance with US policy precisely because it was economically devastating when applied to the South American states (ibid.).

Complicity and corruption The US government and its agencies have been complicit with the illegal drugs trade and this has chronically undermined efforts to eliminate the supply of controlled drugs. Drug producers and traffickers have been used as allies or proxies by the US government in political and economic conflicts and they have been protected from arrest or prosecution as a means of repayment for their co-operation (Dale Scott 1996, 1998, 2003). Further to this, trafficking and other drug-related activities were encouraged or condoned by the CIA and the US government as they provided the finances necessary for anti-communist activities by proxy forces. The use of drug proxies was a key element of the US strategy to contain and roll back communism during the Cold War and it operated in South and Central America, Southwest Asia, Southeast Asia and Europe.

Although the US government was emphatic that there could be no compromise with the 'evil' of narcotic drugs, a compromise did begin during the Second World War and was institutionalized through an agreement made in 1954, between the Central Intelligence Agency and the US Department of Justice. Under this accord, the CIA was able to determine unilaterally which cases should be forwarded to the Justice Department for prosecution or criminal investigation. If the CIA determined that collaboration with a particular asset was essential to national security, details did not have to be submitted to the Justice Department, even if it had a high level of involvement in the drugs trade. This was despite the introduction of a congressional resolution, also in 1954, that made the reporting of such crimes mandatory. As such the CIA's definition of national security took precedence over the rule of law (Dale Scott 2003). This agreement was repealed in 1975 when it came to light during the Rockefeller Commission's investigation into CIA activities. It was subsequently restored in 1982 when the CIA reached a secret memorandum of understanding with the Justice Department that exempted officials in the intelligence services from their obligation to report drug-related activities on the part of assets or agents.

US policy-making during the Cold War was consequently characterized by 'deep' or 'para politics'. These terms are used to describe 'sinister and unacknowledged influences' such as criminal groups like the Mafia within US policy-making circles (ibid.). However, the benefits derived from these tactical alliances were balanced by the high costs associated with legitimizing criminal partners and, by definition, criminal practices. Deep politics made the USA vulnerable to 'blowback', the term used to describe the negative and unintended consequences of these criminal relations. Blowback in the USA came in the form of higher levels of cocaine and opiate availability, a development that also impacted on other countries. Of crucial importance, US use of drug proxies has repeatedly occurred when the drug trade or a trade in a specific drug was in decline. Consequently, a key factor in accounting for continued and high levels of supply was the US role in stimulating it.

Examples of proxies used by the USA include the mafia during the Second World War. Salvatore 'Lucky' Luciano, who had developed mafia interests in heroin after the repeal of alcohol prohibition in 1933, was released from prison by the USA after he helped US intelligence develop contacts with Don Calogero Vizzini, the head of the Sicilian mafia. This ensured that the mafia provided political and logistical support for General Patton's troops when they landed in Sicily in 1943. In releasing Luciano, the US freed 'the greatest criminal talent of his generation to rebuild the heroin trade' (McCoy 1972: 23). Corsican and Sicilian mafia connections were subsequently utilized by the USA to counter the growth of left-wing organisztions in Sicily, Italy and France in the immediate post-war period.

In the 1950s and 1960s, the CIA formed strategic alliances with the Chinese nationalist forces, the KMT and Hmong tribesman in Myanmar, Thailand and Laos to contain the expansion of communism in Southeast Asia. These groups were heavily involved in opium production and trafficking activities and this was condoned by the CIA and the US government because it financed the anti-communist efforts. Logistical support was also provided to the illicit trade by US agencies. Although the damaging implications of employing 'drug proxies' were revealed in the heroin boom and 'blowback' of the 1970s, the strategy was not dropped. Those involved in the 'parapolitics' framework of US policy re-engaged in the tactic of supporting illicit drug-funded anti-communist and anti-Islamicist movements in Afghanistan in the 1970s, 1980s and 1990s. This contributed to the displacement of the Golden Triangle as the centre for opiate production and its replacement by the Golden Crescent of Pakistan and Afghanistan by the early 1980s (Cooely 1999; Makarenko 2002).

One of the most notorious and well publicized cases of the US government's use of drug proxies was Ronald Reagan's campaign against the Sandinista government of Nicaragua. The Sandinistas had gained power in 1979 after a revolt against the US-backed dictator Somoza. Former members of Somoza's National Guard were trained and recruited by the CIA and mobilized as an 'anti-communist' resistance movement called the Contras. Operating from bases in neighbouring Honduras, the Contras were financed and armed through a complex network of drug trafficking organizations spread across Bolivia, Panama and Colombia. 'Blowback' in this instance came in the large increase in cocaine and crack cocaine shipments to the USA and the accompanying rise in consumption and cocaine-related violence in the USA and also Europe.

The relationship between drug trafficking, Contra activities and the US government was exposed in 1986, despite a campaign of 'perception management' by the Reagan administration and vigorous efforts to repress and discredit media investigation of US foreign policy in Central America (Claridge and Diehl 2002; Webb 1999). Senior members of the US administration were implicated in the Contra scandal, including Colonel Oliver North, Elliot Abrams and John Poindexter. President Reagan provided testimony to the Tower Commission investigation into the Contra affair but claimed to have no knowledge of Contra operations.

Despite the political damage caused to the international and domestic reputation of the USA by the use of drug-funded proxy forces, US intelligence services continued to work closely with known traffickers in all geographic regions in order to protect higher national security interests. While pursuing this foreign policy course, the USA simultaneously pressed for the use of increasingly violent strategies as a means of suppressing the drug trade.

Full circle: more harm than good?

The international community faces significant challenges in disentangling the illicit drug and conflict nexus. To reiterate a common theme running throughout this book, it is only because drugs like cocaine and heroin are illegal that it is lucrative to engage in their production and distribution. It is therefore to be expected that as long as these substances remain illegal, they will be an important cash generator for rebel groups and a source of political instability and state failure. Moreover, drug prohibition poses a particular problem in terms of strategies for reforming war economies. While illegally exploited commodities such as diamonds or timber can be brought under a national regulatory framework, this is not possible with illicit drugs. As there is no mechanism for integrating this source of rebel finance into the formal economy, illicit drugs will remain an important income stream.

The drugs and conflict dilemma cannot be resolved under the current control system and this is a particular concern given the increase in intra-state conflicts and the rise in the number of conflict-prone countries since the end of the Cold War. To date, the existing academic literature has focused on the relationship between illegal drugs and existing conflicts. There is, however, a real danger that illicit drug revenues will increasingly be used by political and economic 'entrepreneurs' to launch rather than simply sustain conflict, with new and more rebel groups becoming integrated into the illicit trade (Collier and Hoeffler 2001; Fearon and Laitin 2003).

The only effective counter to drug penetration is the creation of strong, viable democratic states supported by economic development assistance. However, in the 2000s, democracy was conceptualized and promoted in a minimal form, with an emphasis on elections and procedures rather than on justice, integrity

The political impact

and political legitimacy. The rush to democratize and stabilize conflict-prone countries such as post-Taliban Afghanistan led to the promotion of hollow democracies that were as vulnerable to drug-related corruption as authoritarian systems (Makarenko 2002). Further to this, the international community maintained a double discourse on drugs, on the one hand simplistically linking terrorist and anti-state activities to the illicit trade, while at the same time working with or covertly condoning the trade if it was controlled by pro-western interests. The political costs of acting against the trade were deemed higher than allowing it to operate. Such was the case in Afghanistan and Colombia, which remained the world's largest producers of opiates and cocaine even when they were controlled by western powers.

11 | HIV/AIDS and intravenous drug use

The following two chapters explore a crucial policy dilemma facing the international community and the drug control system. This is the spread of HIV/AIDS among injecting drug users. The rise of HIV infection among this sector of the population is a case study in the harmful effects of the current drug control model. The drivers of this new HIV 'epidemic' will be examined in this chapter. Chapter 12 explores the limitations that have been imposed on effective policy responses to the contemporary HIV crisis by the international prohibition regime.

The epidemiology of HIV/AIDS

According to the Joint United Nations Commission on HIV/AIDS (UNAIDS), 37.8 million people were living with HIV/AIDS in 2003. Of this total 2.1 million were children under the age of fifteen. In the same year, there were 4.7 million new infections and 2.9 million AIDS-related deaths, bringing the total number of AIDS deaths from 1981 to 2003 to 20 million people.

TABLE 11.1 Regional statistics for HIV and AIDS, end of 2003

Region	Adults and children living with HIV/AIDS (millions)	Adult (15–49 years) infection rate (%)	Deaths of adults and children (millions)
Sub-Saharan Africa	25.0	7.5	2.2
East Asia	0.9	0.1	0.04
Oceania	0.03	0.2	0.0007
South and Southeast Asia	6.5	0.6	0.46
Eastern Europe and Central Asia	1.3	0.6	0.049
Western Europe	0.58	0.3	0.006
North Africa and Middle East	0.48	0.2	0.024
North America	1.00	0.6	0.016
Caribbean	0.43	2.3	0.035
Latin America	1.6	0.6	0.084
Global total	37.8	1.1	2.9

Sources: UNAIDS (2004a, 2004b, 2004c)

There are four main routes of transmission for the virus: penetrative sex between men and between men and women, intravenous drug use and blood or organ tissue transplants. Intravenous drug use with contaminated needles is one of the most efficient ways of transmitting HIV. It injects the virus directly into the bloodstream and it is the primary mode of infection in between 5 and 10 per cent of worldwide HIV/AIDS cases (Archibald et al. 2003). In the twenty years since the virus was first identified, the epidemiology of HIV/AIDS infection has changed substantially. During the initial phase of the virus in the early 1980s, male homosexual sex and intravenous drug use were the activities most commonly linked to HIV transmission and infection. In the current period, heterosexual transmission is the predominant means of infection. The geography of AIDS has also changed significantly. During the first wave of HIV/AIDS infection, the majority of infections occurred in Western Europe and North America. Today, Africa has the highest number of people living with the virus and the highest cumulative number of AIDS-related deaths. Within this picture of a constantly evolving epidemic, diverse regional, national and even localized patterns of transmission and infection exist.

There are deeply worrying trends in the current epidemiology of the virus. First, areas that were previously considered marginal to the epidemic have seen a surge in HIV/AIDS. This is particularly the case in those countries that were formerly part of the Soviet Union. In the early 2000s, states in the Baltic region, the Commonwealth of Independent States and Central Asia experienced the highest growth in rates of HIV/AIDS infection. As a result of the rapid and unanticipated development of the epidemic in this region, earlier statistical projections of HIV/AIDS figures have been overshot. The HIV/AIDS statistics for 2003 were, for example, 50 per cent higher than was initially predicted by the World Health Organization a decade earlier (Vickerman and Watts 2003). A second aspect of current HIV/AIDS trends is that the primary means of transmission in these 'new' areas of infection is intravenous drug use (IDU). Related to this, the third epidemiological trend was an increase in IDU-related HIV/AIDS in parts of Asia and South America. As a result of these trends, IDU re-emerged as a significant driver of HIV/AIDS infection in the 2000s.

The rise of the post-Soviet drug problem

In the 1990s and 2000s, there was a strong increase in the use, production and trafficking of controlled drugs, specifically heroin, in the countries of the former Soviet Union. After decades of insulation from the drug trade, drug use first began to increase in the 1980s. This has been linked to the Soviet invasion of Afghanistan in 1979. The occupation of Afghanistan exposed Soviet soldiers to heroin, in a parallel of the experience of US military forces in Vietnam in the late 1960s and early 1970s. It has been suggested that US-backed Islamic resistance deliberately targeted the Soviets with cheap opiates as a means of undermining their military capabilities. On return to the Soviet Union, soldiers who had used heroin in Afghanistan sought out domestic supplies of the drug. However, owing to the tight border and security restrictions that operated during the Cold War, it was difficult to obtain heroin produced in Southwest or Southeast

Asia. Demand was subsequently met by a rise in the domestic production of heroin from poppy straw.

While there are no figures for domestic rates of controlled drug consumption during the communist period, data on addiction illustrate a trend of rising drug use. The number of officially registered drug addicts in the Soviet Union increased from 32,254 in 1984 to 67,622 by 1990. Within the Russian Federation itself, the number of registered addicts doubled during this period, rising from 14,324 to 28,312 (Butler 2003). Addiction rates accelerated after the collapse of the communist system in the early 1990s. By 2000, there were 271,268 registered addicts in the Russian Federation alone, the majority of whom were addicted to heroin.

TABLE 11.2 Registered drug addicts in Russia, 1991–2000

Year	Number of registered drug addicts
1991	31,482
1992	32,692
1993	38,759
1994	47,901
1995	65,164
1996	88,976
1997	121,752
1998	161,553
1999	210,521
2000	271,268

Source: UN Drugs Control Programme

Of crucial importance, an estimated 90 per cent of heroin users administered the drug intravenously, with the total number of injecting drug users in the country thought to be between 1.6 and 1.8 million people. The official UN figures of drug use in the region were thought to underestimate the scale of drug use. Non-governmental and philanthropic organizations put the number of injecting drug users in the Russian Federation at 4 million out of a population of 143 million. In the Ukraine, it was estimated that there were one million injecting drug users out of a total population of 47 million people (Lowndes et al. 2003). Drug consumption and intravenous drug use also accelerated in the Baltic states of Estonia and Latvia and the Central Asian countries of Tajikistan, Uzbekistan, Kazakhstan and Kyrgyzstan, where it was thought that between 1 and 2 per cent of the population injected drugs (UNAIDS 2004b).

The rise of IDU Injecting was preferred as the mode of drug administration over smoking or snorting for three inter-related reasons. First, it creates an immediate high; second, it makes heroin cheaper to use because the drug can be administered in smaller quantities; and third, if the quality of the heroin is low, injecting has a stronger physiological effect on the user. Not only did the majority of drug users inject their drugs, they also shared needles and injecting equipment. A survey of the Russian city of Togliatti found that the average life of a needle was twenty-two users (Lowndes et al. 2002; Frost et al. 2000; Rhodes et al. 2002a). A sample of users in Moscow found that 75 per cent had shared injecting equipment and, in a survey of sixty-one Russian cities, between 40 and 70 per cent of drug users reported shared needles (Wall 2003). In Moldova, an estimated 80 per cent of users shared injecting equipment, while in Tajikistan the figure was 95 per cent (UNAIDS 2004b).

This risky behaviour was attributed to a number of factors, the most immediate being ignorance about the dangers of injecting with used needles and syringes. The lack of understanding around the HIV virus and how it was transmitted was a widespread problem in the region and it was not limited to the injecting drug community. A survey of sexual behaviour conducted in St Petersburg found that a high proportion of respondents believed the virus could be transmitted through kissing and also the sharing of cigarettes (Amirkhanian et al. 2001). Popular ignorance was exacerbated by national governments that had limited experience of dealing with HIV/AIDS and operated within a conservative and authoritarian political and cultural context. State administrations from Ukraine to Tajikistan, Russia to Latvia were reluctant to address or discuss the issue and this compounded public ignorance and vulnerability to exposure. The situation has improved somewhat in the 2000s; however, throughout the 1990s, no head of state in the former Soviet countries publicly acknowledged the issue of HIV/AIDS, a stance that paralleled the information blackout on the subject that characterized the initial approach of the Chinese government.

There were two other factors that were used to account for the sharing of injecting equipment. One of these was the problems encountered by drug users in obtaining clean and sterile syringes and needles. Legal restrictions on the dispensing of injecting equipment, the high price and a lack of access to pharmacies in particularly remote places all increased the likelihood of equipment sharing. Equipment was also shared because of cultural factors, such as the ritual of users affirming trust towards each other by sharing equipment. Anecdotal evidence from the Baltic and Eastern European states also identified a practice of users mixing fresh blood with heroin in order to absorb toxins prevalent in home-manufactured opiates.

From IDU to HIV In 2001 UNAIDS/WHO reported that the HIV/AIDS epidemic was growing faster in the former Soviet states than in any other part of the world. By 2003, an estimated 1.5 million people in Eastern Europe and the Central Asian republics were infected with HIV, with 230,000 people infected in 2003 alone. In the Russian Federation, 1.5 million people between the age of fifteen and forty-nine were estimated to be HIV positive. The number officially registered as HIV positive was 230,000, triple the figure recorded in 2000 (Open Society Institute 2003). In the Ukraine, reported HIV infection rose from 20,000 in 1996 to 52,000 in 2002. The virus subsequently spread into neighbouring states, such as Lithuania, where reported cases of infection were concentrated in areas bordering the Russian town of Kaliningrad; Latvia, Lithuania, Georgia and Belarus all had escalating levels of HIV infection. In the five Central Asian states that sit between Afghanistan and Russia, a sharp increase in infections was reported after 2001. In Uzbekistan, only fifty-one cases of HIV/AIDS were recorded between 1987 and 1998. By 2003, this had increased to 2,534, of which 63 per cent were IDU related. In Kazakhstan, there were 4,174 reported HIV cases in 2004 and 168 cases of AIDS. In Kyrgyzstan the figure was comparatively low, with 364 cases of HIV reported in 2003. Within the Russian Federation itself, HIV infection extended out from established areas of incidence into Siberia, the Urals and the Volga region, which had the highest rates of prevalence by the late 1990s (Dehne and Kobyshcha 2000; Dehne 2001; Rhodes et al. 1999). In all of these former Soviet countries, intravenous drug use was the dominant mode of infection.

TABLE 11.3 HIV infection caused by IDU

Country	Number of reported HIV infections	% of HIV infections caused by IDU
Belarus	–	76
Kazakhstan	–	80
Kyrgyzstan	364	83
Latvia	–	72
Russian Federation	230,000 (2003)	76
Tajikistan	–	73
Ukraine	52,000 (2002)	72
Uzbekistan	2,534 (2003)	–

Source: UNAIDS (2004b)

In contrast to the USA and Western Europe, where HIV infection was concentrated in the sector of the population over the age of thirty, in the Russian Federation, Kazakhstan and Kyrgyzstan, over 70 per cent of those infected with the virus are under the age of thirty (UNAIDS 2004b). In Belarus, 60 per cent of infections were among the fifteen to twenty-four age group, while in Ukraine, 25 per cent of people with HIV were under the age of twenty.

Causes of drug use in the post-Soviet states

GEOPOLITICS The boom in drug use in the former Soviet states can be explained through reference to a number of overlapping causes. The primary reason was a large increase in the availability of cheap heroin. This was in turn linked to three factors: the collapse of border integrity; a rise in trafficking through the region and a strong increase in opiate production in Afghanistan. In geographical terms, the former Soviet states are a bridging point between the wealthy drug consumer countries of Western Europe and the Golden Crescent cultivator and producer states of Afghanistan and Pakistan. Turkmenistan, Uzbekistan and Tajikistan, all former Soviet states, share a border with Afghanistan, while the Baltic states of Ukraine, Latvia and Estonia link the Central Asian region to the European markets.

During the Cold War, the borders of the Soviet Union were tightly patrolled by the Soviet military. After the Soviet empire disintegrated, the majority of states assumed independence and responsibility for their own border security. However, this proved to be a serious challenge for the newly autonomous states. Aside from lacking the technical capacity to police the national territory, these countries did not have the financial resources to secure their borders. Turkmenistan, Tajikistan, Uzbekistan, Kazakhstan and Kyrgyzstan were all classified by the UN as low income or least developed counties. This was an acutely problematic situation given that the first three countries border Afghanistan. These weaknesses were exploited by trafficking organizations, which re-oriented the opiate distribution routes away from Pakistan, Iran and Turkey and through the Central Asian region.

Political factors served to increase the vulnerability of the region to trafficking. The authoritarian and corrupt nature of the majority of post-Soviet states created a viable framework for drug-related activities. The absence of accountability, democracy and the rule of law inhibited effective enforcement activities and it generated a propitious environment within which the drugs trade could embed itself. Although the bulk of the heroin trafficked through the region was destined for lucrative western markets, increased volumes remained within the new transit countries, where autonomous drugs markets developed. In Turkmenistan, for example, an estimated 30 per cent of the 80 tons of heroin that entered the country was distributed to domestic consumers (International Crisis Group 2003).

ECONOMIC VARIABLES The collapse of the command economy and COMECON regional trading system and the termination of economic and trade subsidies from Moscow created severe fiscal problems for the independent states and economic hardship among their populations. In a number of former Soviet countries, the increase in poverty and hardship was exacerbated by the transition to neoliberal economic systems, with the shift away from state intervention, subsidies and planning leading to an increase in unemployment and a chronic decline of welfare state systems. These economic conditions had the effect of bringing more people into the drugs trade as consumers, traffickers or distributors. In Tajikistan, where the average income is $700 per year, illiteracy rose by 30 per cent in the 1990s and three-quarters of those aged fifteen to eighteen years were not in the education system, and an estimated 30 per cent of the population had links to the drugs trade (Malinowska-Sempruch 2002).

While the increased availability of controlled drugs created new opportunities for acquiring and using them, this does not explain why people opted to consume them. Economic factors and sociological explanations have been used to explain this development. 'Transition trauma' has emerged as an influential explanation. This refers to the loss of certainty, structure and routine that characterized Soviet life and the disorientation and insecurity that followed the collapse of the communist system. Within the radically altered economic, social and political landscape of post-communism, engagement in risky behaviour such as drug and alcohol use became an escape valve for those pessimistic about the future and alienated from the rapidly changing societies within which they lived (Burrows and Alexander 2001; Grund 2001; Lowndes et al. 2003; Wall 2003). There was also a breakdown of family and community structures and this removed the traditional cultural constraints that had formerly limited risky behaviours. The fact that heroin was even cheaper than vodka in many former Soviet countries increased the attractiveness of drugs to the alienated and socially marginalized, such as street children, of whom there were estimated to be 2 million in the Russian Federation alone (UNICEF 2003).

The collapse of communism not only generated dislocation and disorientation, it also led to a reduction of state control and the surveillance of the population that had been an important feature of these political systems. These changes created freedom of movement and activity, thereby increasing the opportunity for people to acquire and engage in drug use.

IDU-related sub-epidemics: the global picture

The transmission of HIV through the sharing of needles was not a public health issue confined to former Soviet countries. On all continents apart from Africa, it was a sustained problem, although one that tended to be confined to specific geographical areas. A particularly important trend discernible in the 2000s was the overlap between drug cultivation areas, trafficking routes, injecting drug use and HIV. This was evident in the former Soviet countries and a number of states in Asia and South America.

ASIA China experienced a rapid growth of HIV/AIDS after the virus was first detected in the country in 1985. From 1999 to 2003, the annual rate of increase in infections was 30 per cent, culminating in an estimated national infection rate of 840,000 people in 2003. Of this total, 60 to 70 per cent was attributed to injecting drug use and blood/tissue transplants. A large number of organ, tissue and blood donors were injecting drug users, with the revenue obtained used for drug purchases. While heterosexual transmission predominated in the east of the country, in the south and southwest, injecting drug use drove the spread of the virus (Zhang et al. 1999). UNAIDS reported HIV prevalence rates of between 20 and 80 per cent among intravenous drug users in traditional opium cultivation areas such as Guangdong, Yunnan and Xinjiang.

Myanmar also experienced a 'generalized' epidemic in the 2000s with prevalence rates of between 1 and 2 per cent of the population, despite the country's low population levels and limited urbanization. While an estimated 65 per cent of the 330,000 infections reported in 2003 were linked to heterosexual sex, injecting drug use was the primary source of infection in urban settings, such as Mandalay, with intravenous drug use accounting for a quarter of national HIV infection statistics. Similarly in India, where the first AIDS-related death was recorded in 1986, the preponderant means of virus transmission was heterosexual sex, particularly in the southern states. Despite the prevalence of heterosexual transmission, injecting drug use was of rising significance and regionally concentrated pockets of infection driven by IDU emerged in Manipur, Nagaland and Mizoram in the northeast of the country and close to the border of Myanmar (Dorabjee and Samson 2000). Manipur had the highest rate of HIV/AIDS infection in India, and in Manipur City, the level of HIV infection among injecting drug users increased from 61 per cent in 1994 to 85 per cent by 1998. There was also evidence that drug injecting and HIV transmission were shifting into major cities, such as Delhi, Chennai and Mumbai (Panda et al. 2001). In Vietnam, the initial spread of HIV/AIDS in the 1990s was linked to injecting drug use, although by 2000, unprotected heterosexual sex became the primary mode of infection. Despite enormous success in reducing IDU-related infections, mini-epidemics persisted and in Ho Chi Minh City an estimated 80 per cent of injecting drug users were HIV positive (UNAIDS/WHO 2002).

SOUTH AMERICA In South and Central America and the Caribbean, 2 million people were infected with the HIV virus in the early 2000s. As in Asia, sexual activity was the primary means of virus transmission; however, HIV infection through injecting drug use predominated in Uruguay, Brazil and Argentina. Brazil accounted for nearly 40 per cent of all HIV/AIDS cases in the region with injecting drug use identified as being responsible for the spread of the virus in urban centres in the south of the country, such as Santos (Bastos et al. 2002). In Argentina, 40 per cent of new infections in 2002 were linked to intravenous drug use. In Uruguay, injecting drug use was the mode of transmission for 28 per cent of new infections in 2002, with the prevalence rate of HIV among the country's injecting drug population estimated to be 9.5 per cent. These three countries were founder members of the regional trade organization Mercosur (the Common Market of the South). Established in 1991, the launch of Mercosur led to a lifting of restrictions on the movement of goods and people.

As with the collapse of the Iron Curtain, this provided new opportunities for drugs traffickers.

THE DEVELOPED WORLD In the 1990s HIV infection related to injecting drug use declined in North America and Western Europe, after emerging as a predominant means of transmission in the 1980s. However, although figures for IDU-related HIV stabilized, injecting drug use continued to be a significant driver of the virus. In 2002, injecting drug use accounted for a tenth of all new infections in Europe and it was the predominant mode of transmission in Scotland and Portugal. In Canada and the USA, a quarter of new infections were IDU-related, rising to over 50 per cent in concentrated pockets of infection in urban centres such as New York and Ottawa.

From IDUs to broader infection

In comparison to the situation in sub-Saharan Africa, where 25 million adults and children were infected with HIV, the situation in other regions, including the former communist countries, was on a small scale. There was, however, a consensus that the incidence of IDU-related HIV would escalate and that this in turn could trigger a large and generalized epidemic (Wall 2003).

Epidemiologists initially assumed that pockets of infection among specific groups, such as injecting drug users, could be contained within that specific community. However, the experience of the 1990s and 2000s demonstrated two things. First, that the virus could spread rapidly through a group of injecting drug users. HIV rates among IDUs in Chiang Rai and Bangkok (Thailand), Manipur (India), Mytkyina, Mandalay and Yangon (Myanmar), and Ruili (China) increased to over 40 per cent within the first year of detection (Saidel et al. 2003). From an infected user group, the virus could then quickly 'jump' to non-injectors and spread into the wider community. The likelihood of the virus jumping was determined by the presence of 'bridges'. Individuals act as bridges when they interact with both high- and low-risk groups. If no bridging population exists, the virus was contained within the existing group of infected people. This was rarely the case.

Building bridges Injecting drug users acted as a bridge to the non-injecting community in two ways. The most significant was unprotected sex with a married or regular partner. In the USA, it was estimated that nine out of ten cases of heterosexual transmission of HIV in New York City were due to unprotected sex with an injecting drug user. In Manipur, India, the infection rate among non-injecting wives of intravenous drug users was estimated to be 45 per cent (Panda et al. 2000, 2001). In China, the spread of the virus accelerated after the infection extended out from injecting drug users in Yunnan province to Guangdong and Xinjiang through sexual transmission by IDUs to non-injecting

HIV/AIDS and intravenous drug use

sexual partners (Folch et al. 2002; Friedman et al. 1994, 1998; Zheng et al. 1994). The trend of sexual transmission of the virus by IDUs was also observed in the former Soviet countries, particularly in the Baltic region and in South America (Dehne et al. 2000). The increase in infected female partners, combined with a rise in infected female IDUs, also generated a further bridge for the virus that was based on inter-uterine mother-to-baby transmission. In Uruguay, 40 per cent of babies born with HIV in 2002 had a drug-injecting mother, while UNICEF reported a rise in the number of mother-to-baby cases of transmission in the Russian Federation and particularly within Ukraine (UNICEF 2003).

While the problem of IDU-related HIV was serious and growing, there were methodological problems in determining the line of causality. This was particularly the case for IDUs who engaged in unprotected sexual activity with commercial sex-workers, a second high-risk group of people. In this instance the IDU could become the bridge from one infected group, commercial sex-workers, to an uninfected group, the IDUs. There was a high level of interaction between male injecting drug users and the commercial sex industry. In Calcutta, India, 71 per cent of male injecting drug users reported frequent sex with a sex-worker (Panda et al. 1998). Surveys in Bangladesh found that 33 per cent of injecting drug users interviewed had visited sex-workers in the previous month. Less than one-fifth reported using condoms (Saidel et al. 2003). A quarter of injecting drug users interviewed in Hanoi and 20 per cent in Da Nang, Vietnam, had visited sex-workers over the previous year. Less than 20 per cent had used condoms (Tung 2001).

Underscoring the difficulties in determining lines of causality in HIV infection, some female commercial sex-workers were also themselves IDUs (Platt 1998; Power and Nozhkina 2002). For example, studies of female injecting drug users in Russia found that between 15 and 50 per cent were engaged in commercial sex acts to finance drug addiction (Amirkhanian et al. 2001; Dehne and Kobyshcha 2000; Grassly et al. 2003; Lowndes et al. 2002). Studies from Canada and the UK showed that between 14 and 50 per cent were involved in sex work (Archibald et al. 2003).

A rise in promiscuous sexual behaviour during the 1990s further increased the possibility of a wider epidemic in those countries vulnerable to an HIV jump from IDUs to the general population. This not only included the former Soviet states and the Asian countries, but also North America and Western Europe where a trend of people engaging in sexual activity at a younger age, with more partners and without protection, was identified (Amirkhanian et al. 2001). Changes in patterns of sexual activity combined with a rise in injecting drug use have consequently created a highly favourable environment for the spread of HIV.

Conclusion

The global drug-injecting population is estimated to be 13 million people, of whom one-quarter are women. An estimated 2 to 3 million past and current injecting drug users worldwide have HIV/AIDS, with 110 countries reporting IDU-related HIV epidemics to the World Health Organization. It is thought that the HIV epidemic in post-Soviet countries is still at a rudimentary stage and that it will spread across the wider population in the second half of the 2000s. China is expected to have an infection rate of 10 million by 2010.

These statistics and trends pose an acute dilemma for the international drug control system. They first demonstrate that the UN control apparatus did not anticipate or move pro-actively to avert an increase in drug use and drug trafficking through the former Soviet states. This raises serious questions as to the functioning and capacity of the drug control institutions. Second, there was no immediate and effective assistance to weak and fragile states that was necessary to help them defend their borders. Third, development aid and economic assistance to the region was not significant enough to prevent the drug trade emerging as a source of employment and wealth opportunity. The external finances that were provided through bilateral and multilateral mechanisms were skewed towards security sector reform, which is to say enforcement of prohibition, while demand-side issues were neglected. Finally, the philosophy of prohibition and the policies and laws that are in place to achieve this impeded the adoption of social policies and healthcare practices that could reduce the vulnerability of IDUs and the wider community to HIV/AIDS. This is explored in the following chapter.

12 | International drug control and HIV/AIDS

International drug control, the agencies that enforce it and the philosophy of prohibition that underpins it, have exacerbated the threat posed by the AIDS virus. This is evident on two levels. First, drug control is an obstacle to effective intervention against the spread of the virus through programmes that are based on principles of harm reduction.

The philosophy of harm reduction directly contradicts the principle of prohibition that has shaped the organizational and operational precepts of international drug control. While prohibition emphasizes abstinence from drugs that have no legitimate medical value, a position enforced by drug control, harm reduction accepts that people find it hard to abstain from drugs that they have become dependent on or addicted to. It is a pragmatic concept in that it accepts that certain types of behaviour cannot be stopped. It is also non-judgemental, rising above moral, spiritual or social censure of 'risky' behaviour. Harm reduction consequently aims to minimize the negative health consequences that are associated with 'risky' behaviours in order to prevent them from becoming a threat to public health. Projects such as the distribution of clean needles to IDUs and oral opiate substitution treatment drugs such as methadone, both of which are informed by harm reduction principles, have been condemned by drug control bodies for condoning and facilitating drug use.

The emphasis on criminalization in drug control policies has also led to the stigmatization of intravenous drug users, their marginalization and, usually, their incarceration on drug-related offences. This increases the risk associated with their behaviour, both to themselves, the IDU community and wider society.

Harm reduction and injecting drug use

NEEDLE EXCHANGES For those who inject drugs, the provision of clean injecting equipment is the equivalent of providing condoms to those at risk from sexual transmission of HIV/AIDS. A number of needle and syringe exchanges have been introduced in different regions as part of public health initiatives. These provide IDUs with clean, sterile equipment and facilities to dispose of used needles and syringes. Harm reduction is achieved through the exchanges in the following way. Through the provision of clean equipment, the need for IDUs to share is eliminated and this reduces the risk that they will be exposed to the virus. And just as condom use can reduce exposure to other sexually transmitted diseases, the provision of clean injecting equipment can limit infection from other blood-borne and potentially fatal diseases to which IDUs are exposed, such as hepatitis C. The advantages accruing to the wider, non-injecting community are substantial. By reducing the possibility of transmission within the IDU user group, the risk to the sexual partners and children of IDUs is also reduced. Moreover, by taking dirty injecting equipment out of circulation, the exchanges reduce the risk of infection or injury that can be caused by the random discarding of needles (Open Society Institute 2001).

SUBSTITUTION THERAPY Drug substitution therapy such as methadone maintenance programmes also fall under the harm reduction rubric. These have a dual function; first, they can move drug users away from injecting drugs such as heroin and towards oral administration of an opiate substitute. If this can be achieved, the problem of addiction and dependency can be tackled by gradually reducing the prescribed dose of methadone. Even if medically supervised drug substitution treatment fails, simply maintaining the addiction with a substitute can eliminate the need to inject and the dangers implicit in injecting such as infection with blood-borne diseases and also the risk of overdosing. Access to substitution treatment also reduces the need for drug users to finance drug purchases through activities such as crime and prostitution.

Exchange schemes and methadone maintenance project sites can also provide a number of other important services such as: access to screening and testing facilities; information about welfare, legal and medical services; educational programmes that teach IDUs how to clean their equipment and administer their drugs through non-injecting routes; and the provision of support for the families and children of IDUs. Harm reduction programmes can therefore promote the social reintegration of the marginalized drug user.

Box 12.1 Harm reduction initiatives

- The provision of information explaining to injecting drug users how to administer narcotic drugs non-intravenously, i.e. orally or through smoking.
- The provision of opiate alternatives such as methadone.
- Needle and syringe exchange programmes, which provide users with clean equipment and provide a disposal facility for used needles.
- Information on how to clean and sterilize injecting equipment, i.e. with bleach.
- The provision of condoms for injecting drug users in order to counter sexual transmission of the virus to non-injecting partners.
- Legal and medical referral services for drug users.
- Screening for other diseases and infections, such as sexually transmitted infections, hepatitis C and tuberculosis.

The utility of harm reduction Harm reduction programmes have two important benefits. First, they are cheap to administer. In exchange for the outlay on disposable syringes, which typically cost less than 20 cents (US), health services are saved the expense of treating an HIV positive drug user and non-injectors who can become part of the chain of infection (Lurie et al. 1993). In its analysis of needle exchange programmes in Kathmandu, Nepal and Washington, the WHO estimated the cost per exchange scheme client to be in the region of $3. This contrasts favourably with the estimated lifetime cost of treating one HIV infected person, which is put at $120,000 (ibid.). Evaluating harm reduction programmes in Belarus, the World Health Organization concluded that: 'One HIV infection could be averted for as little as US$68 – a powerful example of the favourable cost effectiveness of such interventions.' In a 1991 review of needle and syringe programmes in Australia, it was estimated that the cost per life saved was in the region of US$200, contributing to HIV treatment cost savings of $150 million (Feacham 1995).

Harm reduction programmes do not require complex and expensive education and training for administrators so they also minimize human resource costs. The budgetary savings that can be made in national health spending are consequently substantial and this is an important consideration for financially strained countries in the developing world and the post-communist countries. Exchange programmes also contribute to reductions in law enforcement costs, although no significant research supporting this has been conducted (Hernandez et al. 1996). As these projects are small in scale, typically being run from mobile units, pharmacies, community facilities or small clinics, they can serve as an important social welfare presence in socio-economically deprived communities and in countries where national provision has collapsed.

Harm reduction programmes are also highly effective in containing the transmission of HIV and this is particularly the case for needle and syringe exchanges (Commonwealth Department of Health and Ageing 2002; Holtgrave et al. 1998; Stimson et al. 1998). A WHO study of eighty-one cities around the world compared HIV infection rates among injecting drug users in cities with needle and syringe provision with those that had no provision. In the fifty-two cities that did not have needle distribution and exchange facilities, HIV infection rates increased by an average of 5.9 per cent per year. In the twenty-nine cities that ran exchange schemes, HIV infection rates decreased by an average of 5.8 per cent per year (World Health Organization 1994).

In Belarus, a harm reduction programme in Svetlogorsk was found to have reduced the number of drug users sharing equipment from 92 per cent in 1997 to 35 per cent by 1999 (Vickerman and Watts 2002). Targeted programmes in Switzerland, Nepal, Thailand, the USA, the Netherlands, Britain and Australia reported similar success in reducing unsafe practices and infection rates (Jarlais 1992; Maharjan et al. 1994; Normand et al. 1995; Span 1996; Suwanee et al. 1994;

Watters 1994). Feacham's (1995) review of needle and syringe programmes conducted in Australia in 1991 found that they had saved the lives of an estimated 3,000 people.

Timely intervention and integrated provision are the key to success, with efforts to contain the spread of infection enhanced if there is early introduction of comprehensive harm-reduction-based programmes. The Open Society Institute found that the most effective exchange programmes had been launched when the HIV infection rate among the national community of injecting drug users was less than 5 per cent. Success was also determined by accessibility and availability, with the most effective initiatives providing IDUs with comprehensive and regular provision. Trust between the health worker and injecting drug user was a further significant determinant of programme effectiveness (Jarlais et al. 1998; Open Society Institute 2001).

Because of their record of success, harm-reduction-based initiatives are advocated by the world's leading medical and scientific bodies and the ten UN agencies grouped within UNAIDS. Starting with experiments with needle exchanges in Switzerland in the early 1980s, governmental and non-governmental organizations have introduced IDU-targeted projects around the world. These operate in Iran, Kazakhstan, Poland, the UK, Australia, Spain, the Netherlands, Canada, Brazil and Vietnam. The prison population has been an important focus for these activities, specifically government-led programmes.

Injecting drug use and prisons

Injecting drug use is a problem throughout the prison system, regardless of a country's level of development or the nature of its penal structure. From Canada to Mexico, Sweden to Thailand, intravenous drug use is prevalent in penal settings despite restrictions on distributing, acquiring and using controlled drugs within prisons. Surveys based on small samples of inmates have found injecting rates that vary from over 70 per cent in some Australian, European and Asian prisons to a more typical figure of 30 to 40 per cent of inmates. While the majority of prisoners who inject drugs administered narcotics intravenously before they were sentenced to prison, an estimated 10 per cent of incarcerated IDUs began injecting once they had entered the prison system (Bollini 2001).

Restrictions imposed on obtaining clean injecting equipment within prisons ensured that the practice of sharing needles and syringes was more common than in a non-prison setting. This has combined with other high-risk HIV transmission behaviours, such as sexual relations between prisoners and tattooing, to create a dangerous environment for virus transmission within which prisoners are confined. The result, as seen at Glenochil prison in Scotland in 1993, can be mini-epidemics of HIV/AIDS within the prison population. Once inmates are released from prison, or if allowed conjugal rights with visiting partners, bridges out of the infected prison population can be quickly built.

International drug control and HIV/AIDS

While the relationship between prisons, injecting drug use and HIV is well established in Western Europe, North America and the Oceanic countries, it is only a recently identified trend within the former Soviet states and communist countries of Eastern Europe. Positive HIV tests from newly admitted prisoners in the Russian Federation, for example, rose from seven in 1993 to nearly 8,000 in 2000. In Ukraine eleven prisoners were identified as HIV positive during the period 1987 to 1994. In 1997 alone, there were 2,939 (ibid.).

With the support of the WHO and UNAIDS, needle cleaning initiatives have been piloted in prisons (Jürgens and Bijl 2001). As with parallel projects among the non-prison population, the results have been encouraging. A study of European prisons conducted in 1991 found that needle cleaning initiatives had become institutionalized after successful trials and none of the prisons reverted to a policy of non-intervention (ibid.). Prison-based needle exchange projects, a step up from needle cleaning projects, were first piloted in Switzerland in 1992. An external audit of a needle distribution project at the Swiss Hindelbank women's prison, which was launched in 1994, found improvements in the health of inmates, a decrease in needle sharing and also that no new cases of HIV or hepatitis had been reported since the introduction of the exchange.

The utility of methadone maintenance projects in prisons has also been recognized. This is particularly the case for new prisoners who were following methadone programmes before incarceration. Without access to methadone once in prison, it is likely that this group of people will revert to injecting behaviour. For this reason, the WHO guidelines *HIV/AIDS in Prison* endorses methadone prescribing in instances were a prisoner was already receiving treatment, and prison-based methadone programmes have been introduced in Australia, Canada and Western European countries.

These harm reduction projects are still in their infancy and only twenty-two countries have introduced a full range of harm reduction policies, combining needle distribution, methadone maintenance and educational programmes. They include Iran, where an estimated 2.8 per cent of the general population are IDUs, as are an estimated 20 per cent of the Iranian prison population. Nearly a quarter of Iranian prisoners are HIV positive (Catania 2004). Harm reduction programmes are recognized as effective and necessary by the world's most authoritative academic, medical and public health organizations. They also face powerful resistance. As a result, they remain an exception rather than a mainstream element of national health policies.

Opposition to harm reduction

Dispute over the utility and morality of harm-reduction-based measures has generated profound tensions within the machinery of international narcotics control, among separate agencies of the United Nations and between individual countries. The opponents of harm reduction constitute a powerful lobby and their influence has enabled them to block the roll-out of harm reduction programmes. They include the International Narcotics Control Board (INCB), which is responsible for monitoring compliance with the international drug conventions; the USA, Sweden and Japan, who are three of the largest donors to the UNODC; conservative politicians and religious interests and a host of 'family'-based grassroots groups.

There are five arguments against harm reduction. It is first argued that the presence of exchange facilities within communities sends a negative message to non-drug-using members of society. As an example of this, President Bill Clinton's drug 'czar', the director of the Office of National Drug Control Policy, Barry McCaffrey, blocked federal funding of needle exchange programmes in 1998 on the basis that they were irresponsible and sent out the wrong message to children (ONDCP 1998b). A second point of opposition is based on the claim that drug-related crime and violence would flourish in areas where exchange projects are located. There is, however, no evidence to support the link between increased criminality or initiation into drug use correlating with the presence of exchange facilities. On the contrary, the evidence suggests that the exchanges reduce incidences of acquisitive crime and drug-related disorder in those areas where they are located (Human Rights Watch 2003).

A third criticism is grounded in 'medical' terminology. Opposition to harm reduction from this perspective holds that such policies do not benefit the individual drug user as they perpetuate rather than address problems of addiction and dependency. Drug substitution programmes, educational projects that emphasize non-intravenous administration and needle exchanges are all seen as 'band aid' solutions that fail to reduce individual reliance on narcotic substances. The most vocal, and in some cases influential, opponents of harm reduction reject this philosophical approach on the grounds that it is part of a wider campaign for the legalization of controlled drugs (Du Pont and Voth 1995; Stoker 2001). This view has been shaped by a conservative rejection of what are perceived to be libertarian ideals. Hostility to harm reduction is thus located within a broader anti-liberal critique that rejects drug use along with other indicators of 'deviance' such as homosexuality, abortion and atheism. Speaking on the history of the harm reduction movement, Peter Stoker of the British National Drug Prevention Alliance claimed: 'This movement, piously promoted in the name of treating drug users with respect, was in fact an exercise in radical politics' (Stoker 2001). The promotion of harm reduction is conceptualized as a great conspiracy that is international in dimension and which has been executed incrementally over three decades, starting with the 'responsible use' strategies that were promoted in the mid-1970s.

The most influential argument against harm reduction, and the position that has been effective in blocking the expansion of this type of programming, is the claim that harm-reduction-based policies contradict the international drug conventions of 1961, 1971 and 1988. These oblige signatory states to eliminate the use of drugs that have no legitimate medical or scientific value and to criminalize possession, a position that is most explicit in the 1988 convention and which was reinforced by the 1998 UNGASS declaration. Opponents of harm reduction consequently argue that these services are illegal, contrary to the spirit of the conventions and legitimize drug use. This perspective also views harm reduction philosophies as condoning the trade in illicit drugs and thereby sustaining demand, production and trafficking. This position is held by the INCB.

THE INCB AND HARM REDUCTION In a succession of annual reports, the INCB reiterated its view that harm-reduction-based policies contradicted the fundamentals of the international drug conventions. In 2002, the INCB condemned the 'crusade' in favour of harm reduction and the body's president Dr Philip O. Emafo spelt out the INCB line: 'To promote drug use illicitly through the giving out of needles or through providing rooms for drug abusers to inject themselves without supervision of medical practitioners would, to me, amount to inciting people to abuse drugs, which would be contrary to the provisions of the conventions' (UNODC 2002).

In 2003, the INCB emphasized that 'The operation of such facilities remains a source of grave concern. The Board reiterates that they violate the provisions of the international drug control conventions' (INCB 2003). This was followed in 2004 by a statement reaffirming the body's view that needle exchange programmes violated the conventions and direct criticism of those countries that had introduced exchange programmes, with Switzerland and the Netherlands specifically condemned by the INCB.

Given its influence within the UNODC, the hostility of the USA to needle and syringe programmes has reinforced the position of the INCB. According to one former employee of the body, US officials strenuously lobby meetings convened by the Commission on Narcotic Drugs on harm reduction; ultimately: 'everyone understood – no needle exchange, no harm reduction and certainly nothing like prescription of heroin' (Cindy Fazey quoted in Wolfe 2004).

The position of the INCB and those national governments, such as that of the USA, that endorse conservative interpretations of the international drug conventions, directly contradicts that of UNAIDS, of which the UNODC is a member. As early as 1992, the WHO stated that national demand reduction programmes should primarily focus on minimizing the harm associated with the use of narcotics (WHO 1993a). The position of the INCB contradicts this and the 1999 Action Plan for Demand Reduction that committed signatories to offering harm-reduction-based services. The INCB position also went against the Declaration of Commitment on HIV/AIDS that was adopted at the 26th Special Session of the UN General Assembly in 2001 and which required signatories to promote harm reduction programmes and expand the provision of clean injecting equipment by 2005.

The line followed by the INCB and those countries that have allied with the body on the question of harm reduction also runs contrary to the position assumed by regional organizations, such as the European Union. The European Union Strategy on Drugs (2000–04), for example, emphasized harm reduction strategies as a central element of demand reduction policies.

The legality of harm reduction The international drug conventions do have some flexibility in interpretation. For example, the 1961 convention requires states to 'take steps' to restrict drug use to medical and scientific purposes but it does not specify what these should be. Moreover, the preamble to the 1988 convention is explicit in stating that narcotics consumption does not have to be treated as a punishable offence. Although the main body of the document makes it clear that there is a preference for possession and consumption to be criminalized, it is recognized that the development of national law is the autonomous responsibility of sovereign states. This view was upheld by legal experts at the UNODC in their analysis of the legality of harm reduction measures in a report commissioned by the INCB in 2002. The findings were rejected by the INCB but leaked to the public.

This legal reality has led one critic of the INCB to conclude: 'The Board is misinterpreting the Conventions and oversteps its mandate when it tries to influence or control the internal policies of governments as regards the use of controlled drugs' (Jelsma 2003). While the thirteen-person INCB strives to maintain a single international position and a rigid interpretation of the conventions, national responses to HIV/AIDS need to be pragmatic and informed by the specificities of the domestic situation. Moreover, the INCB does not have the authority nor is it qualified to pronounce on harm reduction, among a number of other drug-related issues, over and above expert groups. This is particularly the case given that those appointed to the INCB come from backgrounds in drug diplomacy, policing and criminology. Further to this, many of the INCB members are advanced in age and this reinforced the view of critics that the body was comprised of 'the dinosaurs of UN drug control', self-interested in maintaining the body's influence while remaining detached from modern realities (Jelsma cited in Wolfe 2004).

A problem caused by drug control?

While the decision to inject drugs is down to the individual, the prohibition of drugs influences the choices that are made (Wodak n.d.). Drug users who inject do so for four principal reasons, all of which are influenced by the way in which the international drug control system operates. The primary driver of injecting drug use is low levels of drug purity. This in turn is linked to either a shortage of the drug in question or the drive for increased profits by dealers, leading them to cut the drug with additives. These two scenarios – shortage and profit motive – result directly from the model of drug prohibition. People also inject because they cannot afford to sustain a more expensive sniffing or smoking habit so they administer intravenously as this is more cost effective. But when controlled drugs are cheap and pure, users will smoke or sniff rather than inject (ibid.). Hence a large number of drug seizures, which is a measure of success for the drug control bodies, would have the counter-productive effect of increasing injecting behaviour, needle and syringe sharing and HIV/AIDS transmission. Injecting behaviour is also driven by the need to achieve a more intensive high. User problems in this area could be addressed through the provision of more and better funded treatment services; however, the focus on supply-side activities and the channelling of drug control finances into this angle of the drug trade has led to a deficit on treatment spending.

The emphasis on criminalization that is implicit in the international drug conventions and national laws also exacerbates the threat posed by HIV/AIDS. For example, the discarding of dirty needles, one of the key 'public' dangers linked to IDUs, has been linked to policies that criminalize the carrying of drug paraphernalia (Eicher 1996; Kin 1995; Friedman et al. 1989; Wodak n.d.). Moreover, as a result of the emphasis on the criminalization of drug-related behaviour, harm-reduction-based programmes operate in a complex and hostile environment in the majority of countries and their legality is constantly open to challenge from governments and drug enforcement agencies seeking to uphold their commitments under the conventions. Cogent examples include the situation in the USA. In the late 1970s, drug paraphernalia laws were introduced to prevent the sale of items such as bongs, hookahs and water pipes. This legislation was used to block the sale and distribution of injecting equipment in the 2000s. In the view of Human Rights Watch: 'Despite the well documented effectiveness of syringe exchange programs and other measures that encourage the use of sterile injection equipment, these interventions in the United States are scattered, lack support, and in the worst cases are forbidden by law' (Human Rights Watch 2003).

Even in those countries that have more liberal drug legislation and that have gone the furthest in developing harm reduction initiatives, expansion of the programmes has been limited as a result of INCB criticism, ongoing disputes over their legality and domestic opposition at local or regional level. Australia, for example, is recognized as a lead country for harm reduction, but, as Wodak notes, programmes there are limited in reach:

> At present in Australia there are between 30,000 and 100,000 IDUs, injecting anywhere between one and four times a day. This means that there may be anywhere between 40 and 60 million injections of street drugs in Australia per annum. Currently, between 2 million and 3 million sterile needles and syringes

are provided annually. It is unlikely that this level of intervention is sufficient to achieve the maximum reduction in spread of HIV infection in this population.

The situation in post-communist countries The clash between conservative drug laws that criminalize users and the need for effective and immediate health interventions is forcefully represented by the situation in the former Soviet countries, that is to say, those countries experiencing an IDU-driven HIV epidemic. The UNODC took a lead role in advising governments in these states on the drafting and implementation of drugs legislation and policies. The legal framework that developed and was subsequently institutionalized established punitive criminal sentences for possession and use (Malinowska-Sempruch 2003). As a result, there has been a sharp increase in the number of people convicted for drug-related offences in these countries, the majority of them IDUs, and a related surge in the prison population. In the first twelve months following the introduction of new drugs legislation in Russia, there was a five-fold increase in drug-related convictions. An estimated 20 per cent of the 800,000 prisoners in Russian jails and 40 per cent of all Russian women in prison were convicted on drug-related charges (Bollini 2001; Wolfe 2004). In turn, this created a burgeoning problem of prison-based HIV epidemics.

The adoption of strict counter-narcotics legislation also contributed to a climate of hostility and violence towards drug users in the post-Soviet states. In the context of an IDU-fuelled HIV epidemic, this was an obstacle to effective treatment and outreach work:

> We've heard reports of parents in Central Asia watching their children die of overdoses, so afraid of police harassment of the entire family that they will not bring them to a hospital. This type of fear, shame and silence breeds HIV [...]
> One cannot have a serious discussion about HIV prevention among groups that are prosecuted, harassed by the police, and humiliated in work camps in Central Asia. (Malinowska-Sempruch 2003)

In a number of Eastern European and former Soviet countries, methadone has been scheduled as a controlled drug. This has further circumscribed the development of harm reduction programmes, as the distribution of methadone is classified as drugs trafficking. Precisely because the model of drugs legislation adopted in these states was developed in collaboration with the UNODC, national governments have been able to reject harm reduction programmes on the basis that these violate their commitments under the conventions.

Conclusion

Although an increasing number of countries reject the position of the INCB and the counter-productive strategy of pursuing drug prohibition, there has been no united effort to push for harm reduction to be adopted as a guiding principle of the drug control machinery, or for the drugs conventions to be revised. This is unfortunate given that the conventions themselves are outdated and provide an ineffectual basis for a coherent international response to HIV/AIDS. Relics of the Cold War period, two of the principal conventions were written before the advent of HIV/AIDS. The 1988 convention was introduced at an early stage of the epidemic and almost a decade before the emergence of the IDU-driven pandemics in the post-Soviet countries. Moreover, the zero-tolerance, criminalization emphasis of the conventions as policed by the INCB has been stepped up concurrent with the global spread of HIV/AIDS. As the 'war on drugs' accelerated in the 1980s and into the 1990s, many transition countries, such as those in the former Soviet Union, looked to the INCB for a lead on drugs policy. The end result is that states with snowballing rates of HIV infection have anti-drug regimes that leave no room for harm reduction policies and there is insufficient flexibility in the drug laws for a coherent response to a potentially catastrophic public health threat.

13 | Cultivation and drug production: the environmental costs

The greening of the drugs issue

The 'drug debate' has traditionally focused on the effects of drugs on the individual, the community and wider society. Drug policy and assessments of the impact of drugs have consequently been 'anthropocentric' or human-centred in approach. Over the past decade, however, there has been a growing interest in, and analysis of, the impact that the cultivation and production of drugs has on the environment. There is a growing body of evidence demonstrating that supply-side activities have a damaging effect on the environment. This damage is cumulative and it has accelerated in line with the increase in drug consumption and production in the 1990s and 2000s.

The incorporation of an environmental dimension into the drug debate, and awareness of the issue, stems from a number of developments. The most significant of these has been the increased use of aerial technologies in counter-narcotics operations. Aerial surveillance systems have provided graphic evidence of land degradation and the destruction of forestry in drug cultivation and production areas. Improved monitoring of environmental standards and the use of new technologies to assess levels of, for example, water and air pollution, have further enhanced understanding of the impact of supply-side activity on the environment and local ecologies. This information has become available at a time of heightened popular environmental awareness and concern over deforestation, climate change and greenhouse gas emissions. As the study of the contemporary drugs trade has incorporated environmental issues into analysis and debate, appeals to popular environmentalism have been used to legitimize more assertive supply-side suppression strategies. Environmental protection has also emerged as a key element of the drug prohibition narrative.

The former Jamaican Prime Minister Edward Seaga was one of the first politicians to highlight the negative impact of drug cultivation on the environment. In a televised address in 1986, he emphasized the damaging consequences of extensive cannabis cultivation in the north central and south central areas of the island on Jamaica's environmental and ecological systems. The broadcast aimed to build support for a controversial US-backed government campaign to stem the rapid growth of cannabis cultivation and trafficking that had escalated during the 1970s (Nahas 1985). More recently, US authorities have sought to tap into environmental awareness as part of domestic demand-side strategies. The Office of National Drug Control Policy's 2003 National Youth Anti-Drug Media Campaign adopted as its central message the claim that ending drug use was a way of protecting the environment. The organization ran a public service announcement that featured the characters 'Nick and Norm' in which one explained to the other the environmental damage caused by methamphetamine and cocaine production. Launching the campaign, the then Director of the ONDCP, John Walters, stated:

> Those who enjoy and care about our planet's natural resources should be troubled by the environmental consequences of the drug trade [...] Concerned young people and adults should think about the global impact of the drug trade the next time they and their peers discuss what they can do to sustain a healthy environment here in the US and abroad.

While there is evidence of an increasingly problematic drug-related environmental issue, the qualitative and quantitative information supporting these assessments is unreliable. Moreover, the extent to which drug prohibition and supply-side eradication strategies contribute to the damage caused is significantly under-assessed in the existing literature and official documentation.

The environmental costs of narcotic plant cultivation

Deforestation Deforestation is acknowledged to be a major global issue. It is associated with a host of problems that are most immediately felt in the developing world and the tropics, where the majority of the world's rainforests are located. Three key concerns predominate. The first is the threat of ecological imbalance that results from the impact of forestry losses on surrounding animal and plant species. Second, there are land concerns that relate to soil erosion and the depletion of soil nutrients that follow from forest clearance. These increase the risk of flooding and they reduce the quality of land available for agricultural planting. A final issue is the impact of deforestation on the atmosphere and climate change. Particular concern has focused on the deforestation of tropical rainforest. This is because the 1,000 million ha of global rainforest are critical to the regulation of the global biosphere and the limiting of the greenhouse effect. The tropical rainforests are also home to an estimated 13 million rare and distinct plant and animal species. Around 11 to 16 million ha of rainforest are cleared every year and research suggests that the current rate of deforestation will lead to the eradication of all tropical forests by 2030 (UNFAO 2001, 2005).

Population and economic pressures linked to rising demand for land, food and natural resources are recognized as the principal causes of deforestation and these pressures are seen to have been exacerbated by globalization (Brown and Pearce 1994; Cropper and Griffiths 1994; Lipton and Longhurst 1989; Van Kooten and Bulte 1999; Williams 2003). Many developing countries have privatized publicly-held land and extractive industries such as mining in accord with the neoliberal policy recommendations of multilateral financial organizations.

This has contributed to the acceleration of deforestation as commercial logging, mining and agriculture have typically proceeded outside, or in the absence of, a regulatory framework (Barraclough and Ghimire 2000; Hellin and Higman 2003; Simon 1998). Financial pressures in developing countries are also viewed as having exacerbated deforestation by leading the state or sections of the population to engage in the export of rare and lucrative timbers, as has been the case in Afghanistan, Myanmar and Thailand (Hurst 1990; Saba 2001).

DEFORESTATION AND DRUG CULTIVATION The cultivation of narcotic plants is increasingly recognized as a driver of deforestation. The impact of drug-related deforestation in countries such as Colombia and Peru is seen as particularly severe and deleterious because of the ecological significance of these areas. The Peruvian Amazon contains more than 300 species of tree, in contrast to the 200 species found in Southeast Asian forests and the 120 species found in Central Africa. Scientists have warned that deforestation for coca cultivation in Peru could lead to the elimination of a 'genetic frontier' as rare plant and animal life dependent on the forests in the region loses its natural habitat. Aside from being the world's largest cocaine producer, Colombia is one of the most ecologically diverse and species-rich countries on the planet. It is estimated that 10 per cent of the world's plant and animal species are to be found in the country, many of which are unique to Colombia.

The planting of coca and opium poppies is preceded by the clearing of tracts of forest areas; typically low altitude humid forests in the case of coca and high altitude forests in the case of opium poppies. In the Upper Huallaga area of Peru, forest clearances for coca cultivation are estimated to have led to the deforestation of over 1 million ha since the 1970s. This represents 10 per cent of the total amount of deforestation in the Peruvian Amazon (Dourojeanni 1992). In Colombia, coca cultivators destroyed an estimated 1.4 million ha of tropical humid forest between 1990 and 2000 (Colombian Ministry of National Defence 2002). The US State Department points to rainforest loss in the region of 2.4 million ha for the whole of the coca producing Andean region over the past twenty years.

It is difficult to estimate the impact of opium poppy cultivation because little systematic research has been conducted in the Golden Triangle or Golden Crescent countries. In relation to Afghanistan, the world's largest opium poppy cultivator, 'Work done by international agencies is scant, [the issue] has not yet been addressed and requires responsible research' (Saba 2001). Statistical information is available on overall rates of deforestation in some of these opium poppy cultivating countries. In its examination of the period 1961 to 1985, the US State Department established that the annual rate of deforestation along the Thai–Myanmar border, an important cultivation zone, was in the region of 130,000 ha. Deforestation rates in Thailand were estimated to be 280,000 to 300,000 ha per year (La-Ongsri 1992).

The clearing of forest areas by narcotics cultivators has been cited as the cause of a number of natural disasters. In May 1986, Jamaica experienced floods that were attributed to the deforestation of hillside forests for cannabis cultivation. It was this experience that prompted Seaga's televised address. Deforestation, soil erosion and the build-up of sedimentary deposits in waterways stemming from coca production in the Huallaga valley were blamed for flooding and landslides in Peru in 1987 and in the Chontayacu river valley area of the country in 1982. Similar problems of deforestation damaging watersheds and water catchment areas were reported in Thailand (Sadoff 1991) and opium poppy cultivation in Myanmar has been linked to soil erosion and flooding in southwest China (Huang 1998).

Land management The environmental damage caused by deforestation is compounded by the techniques of the cultivators. In terms of those responsible for planting coca, a distinction has to be drawn between traditional planters cultivating for the licit coca economy and 'new' planters (González Posso 2000). The new planters are typically migrants from urban areas engaged in illicit production. The traditional planters manage the land appropriately and use cultivating practices that are sustainable and attuned to ecological cycles. In Peru and the Yungas area of Bolivia, licit coca was planted in dedicated areas and in wells that ran to around 80 cm in depth. As the plants matured they were transferred to fields or terraces. Legal coca farmers rotated coca with other crops such as cassava, corn or manioc in order to replenish the soil. As a result of these practices, the average life of a legal coca plantation in Bolivia and Peru was estimated to be between fifteen and twenty years.

The bulk of illicit cultivation is, however, conducted by new planters who do not employ the land management practices or cultivating techniques of traditional coca farmers. The new planters employ slash and burn techniques in cultivation areas in order to increase the rate of raw plant material production. This approach is primitive, intensive and it rapidly degrades the land. The harvesting and weeding practices of the new planters are also environmentally degrading. The use of pickaxes and shovels skims around 10 to 15 cm of topsoil and contributes to soil erosion (Scott and Ullmer 1992; Schaefer 1994). The new planters also engage in single crop production. This practice of mono-cropping contrasts unfavourably with the system of crop rotation that is used in traditional agriculture and is essential for the preservation of land. It also creates problems of food security for those living in cultivating areas.

Colombian cultivators usually abandon cultivation plots after three to four years. In the Golden Triangle region, poppy cultivators are reported to move on after harvesting only two or three crop cycles, although little detailed research has been conducted in this area (US State Department 2001).

NATURAL PARKS A further environmentally destructive aspect of illicit drug cultivation is the strategy of planting in natural parks and nature reserves. In Colombia 4,600 ha of coca and 199 ha of poppy were planted in protected natural parks in 2000, with 14,500 ha deforested in preparation for planting (Colombian Ministry of National Defence 2002). In Bolivia, 15,000 ha of forests in the Isibora Secore National Park were replaced by coca plantations. In Peru, the national parks of Tingo Maria, Abiseo, Manu and Yanachaga-Chemellen were overrun by coca producers in the 1970s. Two national forests, the Alexander Von Humboldt Park and Apurimac Park, were also invaded by coca cultivators (Dourojeanni 1992). This problem was not confined to South America. Opium poppy cultivators in Thailand planted in official reserves such as the Doi Chang Das Wildlife Sanctuary in Chiang Mai Province (Armstead 1992).

The USA also had a significant problem of illicit cultivation in protected areas. The Forestry Service of the Department of Agriculture claimed that it faced a 'tremendous challenge' in eradicating illicit cannabis cultivation in national parks in California, Hawaii, Kentucky, Tennessee, Arkansas and Missouri. Between 1997 and 2003, over 3 million cannabis plants, equivalent to 3,000 mt, were eradicated on National Forest Systems land (Gaffrey 2003). The Sequoia and Kings Canyon national park – '850,000 acres (344,000 hectares) of pristine wilderness 200 miles north of Los Angeles' – had a significant problem of illicit cultivation by Mexican cartels. In the period January to September 2005, authorities in California destroyed over a million cannabis plants that had been planted in the reserve (Glaister 2005). Illicit planting in protected sites was driven by two things. First, these areas are secluded and remote, and this allows cultivation to be hidden from enforcement officials. Second, eradication programmes such as chemical fumigation are legally prohibited in these parks, by either national laws or international conventions, and this has made them highly attractive to cultivators.

CHEMICALS AND CULTIVATION The use of fertilizers and biocides such as herbicides, pesticides and fungicides in the cultivation process is a further means by which illicit planting contributes to environmental degradation. Constantly striving to obtain higher yields and more sales revenue, cultivators have increased the use and strength of fertilizers and pesticides in the growing process. Andean cultivators were reported to rely heavily on highly toxic contraband chemical products prohibited in the USA and European countries on environmental grounds (Thoumi 2003: 168). Underscoring the volume of the chemical input, the Colombian Defence Ministry estimated that 4.5 million litres of herbicides, insecticides and fungicides were used in the cultivation of coca in the country in 2000. Paraquat, endosulfan and clordano, all highly toxic herbicides, were the most frequently used. These chemicals are applied without regard for their impact on the health of planters, the surrounding community or the fragile ecology of cultivation areas. The fertilizers and biocides run into the soil, where they deposit nitrogen and phosphorous residue that renders the soil sterile, a situation that in turn contributes to the high turnover of land. They can also run into downstream waterways, with damaging implications for public health and ecological systems.

Drug production and the environment

The conversion of drug plant material into coca and heroin is a highly toxic process that relies on a significant chemical input. The production of these two drugs requires acids, such as sulphuric, hydrochloric and nitric acid; solvents, including ethyl and sulphuric ether, acetone, toluene and kerosene; bases, like sodium and calcium carbonate, sodium and potassium hydroxide and ammonia, and oxidizers such as potassium permanganate (Osorio-Bryson 1992). As drug production increased in the 1990s, so did the overall volume of chemicals used in the production process. It is estimated that 600 million litres of chemicals are used annually in the cocaine production process in South America. During the 1990s in Peru, more than 2 metric tons of chemical waste were generated for every hectare of coca processed into cocaine (US State Department Bureau for International Narcotics and Law Enforcement Affairs 2003). Figures released by the Colombian National Police showed that the conversion of one hectare of coca into cocaine base and then cocaine required 10 litres of sulphuric acid, 38 litres of acetone and nearly 2 kilos of potassium permanganate. The amount

TABLE 13.1 Chemicals used in the processing of cocaine base and cocaine, Colombia, 2000

Compound	Measure	Amount per hectare	Total
Plaster	Kilos	658	107,522,751
Sodium bicarbonate	Kilos	3,14	513,380
Gasoline	Litres	2,190	357,741,451
Sulphuric acid	Litres	10	1,709,379
Ammoniac	Litres	15	2,564,069
Water	Litres	2,093	341,875,946
Dissolvent	Litre	114.04	18,621,286.72
Ethyl acetate	Litres	57.02	9,310,643.36
Acetone	Litres	38.01	6,207,095.57
Chloridric Acid	Litres	28.78	4,698,771.34
Potassium permanganate	Kilos	1.90	310,697.74
Activate carbon	Kilos	0.38	62,139.55

Source: Colombian National Police, *Antinarcotics – Crop Eradication Area*, July 2001

of gasoline used in coca leaf processing for the year 2000 was equivalent to 6.8 days of gasoline consumption in Colombia.

On completion of the production process this assortment of chemicals and other waste by-products are indiscriminately dumped, usually into rivers and streams, or buried. This has created a high risk of chemical waste exposure for humans, animals, aquatic life and the environment, a situation that has been accentuated by the trend of constructing processing laboratories and encampments close to rivers and other water sources.

Environmental aspects of drug production in the developed world There is growing concern in the consumer countries of the developed world over the environmental impact of rising levels of methamphetamine production. One of the largest producer countries is the USA, where methamphetamine production has spread from urban centres such as California into remote, rural locations in the 2000s. Underscoring the scale of the problem, 8,971 clandestine methamphetamine laboratories were uncovered in the country in 2000. By 2002, this had risen to 15,353 (*The Economist* 2003c). The chemicals required for the production of methamphetamine include pseudoephedrine and lithium, which can be easily obtained 'over the counter'. The production process itself is highly combustible and dangerous. These chemicals produce toxic fumes when cooked and, as a result, manufacturing sites such as kitchens and garages can become contaminated with carcinogenic chemical by-products. As with the chemical residue left from heroin and cocaine manufacture, the toxic and corrosive waste products of methamphetamine production are dumped in water supplies or buried. Given that every kilogram of manufactured methamphetamine produces in the region of 7 kilograms of waste, the scale of this environmental pollution and the cost of subsequent clean-up operations are considerable.

Drugs and the environment: a credible debate?

Drug-related environmental damage and pollution are worrying trends and are expected to increase as production levels of all drugs continue their inexorable rise. However, both the nature and the scale of the problem are not fully understood and the statistical indicators that have been produced are considered unsophisticated and unreliable. The funding of investigations into the relationship between the drugs trade, deforestation, pollution and public health has not been a priority for national or international control bodies and this is particularly problematic given the stress now placed on the links between drugs and the environment. It is consequently difficult to evaluate the scale of drug-related environmental damage, despite the increasing importance of the 'green' angle to the anti-drugs narrative.

The methodological problems A particular difficulty in conducting environmental impact assessments and collating information on the impact of drug production is the lack of reliable macro-data. For example, statistics on the rate of global deforestation are contradictory and disputed by national governments, environmental organizations and the UN. Without a clear indication of the overall rate of deforestation, it is acutely difficult to quantify the level of deforestation that is attributable solely to the drugs industry. Further to this, very little is known about the scale and impact of other illicit industries such as logging, which occurs in many of the areas associated with drug production. Unless the impact of different types of illicit activity is disaggregated, the contribution of drug production cannot be determined. Moreover, the extent to which high rates of deforestation can be attributed to illegal activities has been questioned. Álvarez, for example, critiqued figures released by US and Colombian counter-narcotics agencies that showed 79 to 97 per cent of deforestation in Colombia during the period 1990 to 1995 was related to narcotics cultivation. As this period included the promotion of legal commercial activities in frontier areas by the Colombian government, it is possible that neoliberal-inspired policies rather than drug production were responsible for deforestation, with drugs serving as a convenient scapegoat for government policy (Álvarez 2002). Complicating the Colombian picture further, the Colombian Instituto de Estudios Ambientales (Institute of Environmental Studies) claimed that forest cover in the country actually increased by 3.3 million ha between 1986 and 1996. Similar challenges exist in trying to separate out drug-related deforestation in Myanmar and Thailand from illegal logging.

The impact of migration is also inadequately incorporated into the analysis of drug-related deforestation (Thoumi 2003: 169). Population, land and economic pressures in cultivating countries have led peasants to move into and exploit remote, virgin areas of territory. Disturbed and deforested land identified by aerial surveillance is commonly assumed to be under drug cultivation, without follow-up investigation on the ground. There is also a lack of reliable data on the chemical waste generated by the drug production process. Statistics provided by the UNODC, which are used as the basis for policy and the existing academic literature on the environmental costs of the drug industry, are compiled from figures for chemical production and purchases that are submitted by individual states to the control bodies. There has been no large-scale, field-based testing of water and soil and those investigations that have been conducted 'on the ground' have been limited and contained, thereby providing only 'snap-shots' of the problem.

Enforcement and environmental damage Supply-side policies that are intended to eliminate cultivation and production, such as plant eradication programmes and the dismantling of production facilities, indirectly influence the rate of drug-related environmental damage in two respects. First, it is only because drugs are illegal that their value is high. As long as the cultivation of coca and opium poppy remains lucrative and more fiscally rewarding than engagement in the formal economy, illicit cultivation and production will continue and the scale of drug-related damage will continue to rise. The illegal nature of cultivation and production processes also means that there is no mechanism for safely disposing of toxic chemical by-products.

Second, enforcement activities compound the negative environmental costs of drug production because they lead cultivators and producers constantly to relocate and exploit new land. As the planter runs the persistent risk of arrest or crop eradication, there is no incentive to invest in the land, only to deforest, exploit and move on. 'Successful' enforcement operations, therefore, have the counter-productive effect of driving cultivation and production into increasingly remote and fragile areas, as reflected in the rise of cultivation in protected parks. Displaced cultivators in countries such as Colombia, Afghanistan, Thailand and Myanmar have also relocated to mountainous terrain, where their operations can be hidden from aerial and land surveillance. In the case of coca, this has in turn contributed to the production of higher volumes of purer cocaine. Grown at 1,000 metres above sea level, a coca plant can reach a metre high, with a typical alkaloid content of 0.70 per cent. When grown at 3,000 metres, the plant reaches 3 metres in height and the alkaloid content increases to 1 per cent (Osorio-Bryson 1992).

Conclusion

A link has been established between the cultivation and production of drugs and a host of environmental and public health problems. However, the extent to which the policy of suppressing supply-side activities and prohibiting drugs has contributed to and exacerbated the environmental costs of drug production has not been explored in the existing, limited body of research, or acknowledged by drug control authorities. Consequently it is difficult to determine if, in environmental terms, supply-side repression policies do more harm than good. If the impact of aerial fumigation strategies, an increasingly important element of supply-side eradication programming, is incorporated into the analysis, it becomes evident that drug prohibition is making an increasingly large contribution to environmental degradation.

14 | Anti-drug policies and the environment: the role of chemical fumigation

Since the time of Harry J. Anslinger's protracted incumbency of the Federal Bureau of Narcotics, US officials have been in search of a cheap, effective 'magic bullet' that would permanently eliminate illicit drugs at source. In the early 1970s it was believed that chemical fumigation was the solution to the perennial problem of cultivators replanting after eradication. The spraying of drug plants such as coca with chemicals that killed them was heralded as the elusive silver bullet that would terminate the supply of illicit drugs.

These early hopes were frustrated for reasons that are outlined in this chapter. However, fumigation remained a central weapon in the US-led 'war on drugs'. Chemical fumigation was seen to have advantages over manual eradication, specifically when delivered from planes. With aerial spraying, a wider expanse of cultivation could be destroyed than could be covered by the slow and laborious task of manual eradication. Aerial spraying allowed enforcement agencies to penetrate remote territory and the strategy of aerial dispersion reduced the risk of attack from cultivators or rebel groups operating in cultivation areas. Chemical fumigation was a central element of the US-funded Plan Colombia launched in 2000, and the US government of President George W. Bush sought to extend chemical eradication programmes into neighbouring Andean countries and the opium poppy cultivating regions of Southwest Asia. However, chemical fumigation was highly controversial on environmental and political grounds and it faced intense, globalized resistance.

US fumigation strategies in historical context: the Mexican experience

Aerial fumigation was introduced as a weapon in the original 'war on drugs' launched by President Nixon in 1969. The incorporation of this strategy into supply-side programming followed from a strengthening of the prohibition tendency within the White House during the Nixon administration that was also reflected in the punitive sentencing procedures introduced under the 1970 Controlled Substances Act (Baum 1996). Chemical fumigation was perceived as an advanced weapon in the drugs war and trials were conducted on cannabis plantations in Florida, cannabis having been classified as a Schedule 1 drug in the 1970 legislation, along with heroin and LSD.

In 1975, US promotion of chemical fumigation shifted focus to Mexico, a key source country. During the 1960s, Mexico supplied an estimated 90 per cent of cannabis consumed in the USA (2,700 mt) and 70 to 80 per cent of heroin on the American market (6 to 8 mt) (Astorga 2004; Craig 1978). US drug enforcement officials proposed chemical crop destruction to Mexican officials in 1969. Viewing it as a gross violation of Mexican sovereignty, Mexican officials, 'using diplomatic language of course, told us to go piss up a rope' according to G. Gordon Liddy who served on Nixon's Presidential Task Force Relating to Narcotics, Marijuana and Other Dangerous Drugs (Galen Carpenter 1985). In response to the Mexican rebuttal, the Nixon administration launched Operation Intercept. Imposed without negotiation with Mexican authorities, Intercept caused economic chaos and massive disruption to cross-border flows as US authorities rigorously exercised the 'maximum application of the right to search' for drugs being trafficked into the USA (Liddy cited in ibid.).

Intercept ended within a fortnight of its launch after diplomatic protests from Mexico and an agreement on the part of the Mexican authorities to intensify eradication and interdiction efforts and to co-ordinate these with the USA. An American-sponsored chemical fumigation programme was the backbone of this new pro-active and co-operative approach.

Before addressing the impact of the Mexican fumigation campaign, two longer-term effects of Intercept should be mentioned as they substantiate the balloon effect thesis. The stop and search tactics employed by US officials during Intercept's brief operation led traffickers to develop alternative distribution routes for the heroin and cannabis that had traditionally been transported into the USA by road. Small planes and boats subsequently assumed a higher level of importance in distribution activities and this opened up a host of new trafficking routes. Secondly, the initial vacuum of cannabis supply created by Intercept boosted cannabis cultivation in the USA and the level of illicit imports from Jamaica.

Drawbacks and protest In its initial phase, the Mexican fumigation campaign was directed against opium poppy plantations in the northwest of the country. It rapidly evolved into a campaign focused on cannabis plantations in the states of Sinaloa, Chihuahua and Durango. Fumigation was successful in reducing cultivation and supply of opiates and cannabis but it had two problematic side-effects that drastically reduced public confidence in chemical fumigation strategies. First, and again reflecting the balloon effect, cannabis and opium poppy cultivation relocated from fumigated areas in the north to the south of Mexico and into Colombia. The leading trafficking organizations escaped interdiction and moved their headquarters to the commercialized state of Jalisco. This 'gave them a better point of departure for the internationalisation of their operations' (Astorga 2004: 91). Chemical fumigation in the northwest of Mexico was consequently linked to an increase in the volume of cannabis and heroin supplies to the USA; the diversification of trafficking routes; the fragmentation of trafficking organizations; and a growing inter-relationship between Mexican producers and

Colombian trafficking groups, such as the Ochoa brothers, whose Medellín cartel included Pablo Escobar, Jose Rodriguez Gacha and Carlos Lehder and which controlled distribution on the US West Coast, and the Cali cartel controlled by the Rodriguez Orejuela brothers, Jose Santacruz Londono and Helmer Herrera-Buitrago, which supplied the East Coast.

The second problem with the Mexican fumigation campaign was the public health consequences of spraying plants with poisonous chemicals. The toxic herbicide Paraquat was used to spray Mexican cannabis cultivation. Mexican farmers and traffickers subsequently offloaded the fumigated crops on to American consumers. After Paraquat-contaminated marijuana was seized by customs officers in five US cities, there was a backlash against aerial spraying in the USA. While the US Environmental Protection Agency allowed a maximum Paraquat contamination level in foodstuffs of 0.05 parts per million, the confiscated cannabis samples were reported to have an average Paraquat content of 177 parts per million, with a high of 655 recorded (Rogers 1978). A campaign to end US sponsorship of Paraquat spraying was mobilized by the National Organization to Reform the Marijuana Laws (NORML). Their lobby activities gained support and media coverage amid growing public concern that people who had inadvertently consumed Paraquat-contaminated cannabis would suffer heart, lung, liver or kidney damage, poisoning or death. The effects of burning or inhaling Paraquat were not known at the time and there was no known antidote to Paraquat poisoning.

There were also public health concerns and reports of Paraquat-related illness among Mexican villagers in the areas sprayed. However, protests against fumigation were brutally suppressed by the Mexican security forces that had responsibility for executing Operation Condor, the national anti-drug programme. Astorga claims: 'Those hardest hit by Operation Condor [...] were not the drug lords but large numbers of peasants in the region, who were tortured, sent to prison, or removed from their communities of origin' (Astorga 2004: 91).

Reversal, restoration and resistance The campaign against Paraquat spraying gained an important victory in 1978, with a decision by the US Congress to terminate funding for the Mexican fumigation programme. Two years later, the American Environmental Protection Agency introduced strict controls on the use of Paraquat; Chevron, the US manufacturer of the product, was reported to have withdrawn its support for the use of Paraquat in the Mexican programme. In 1983, the US Federal Center for Disease Control confirmed the public health concerns raised by NORML. It reported that 9,000 Americans could have been poisoned by Paraquat-sprayed cannabis (Anderson 1981).

These developments did not diminish support for chemical fumigation within the US executive and drug control apparatus. After assuming office in 1980 and declaring his own 'war on drugs', Ronald Reagan succeeded in reversing the congressional block on the funding of overseas fumigation initiatives after the

US Supreme Court reinstated executive authority over federal funding of anti-drug initiatives in 1983. Although re-legitimized, chemical fumigation was not rolled out across the Andean cultivator and producer countries. This was despite the surge in cocaine production in the region in the 1980s and 1990s. Fumigation faced intense opposition from the Bolivian, Colombian and Peruvian governments amid concerns that it would lead to destabilizing protests from cultivators and provoke violence from trafficking organizations. The relationship between these countries and the USA was strained and conflictive during this period and, as a result, US support for eradication activities was limited to financial and technical assistance, capacity building and intelligence sharing. In order to insulate themselves from US pressure, the Bolivian and Peruvian governments introduced legislation that prohibited fumigation within the national territory. This was on the grounds that herbicide use was detrimental to the health and interests of rural communities and the environment.

Chemical fumigation was not prohibited in Colombia and, like their Mexican counterparts, the Colombian authorities had launched an aerial chemical fumigation programme against cannabis cultivation in 1978. Paraquat was initially trialled and this was followed by tests involving Ticlopyr in 1985 and Tebuthiuron and Glyphosate in 1986. By the second half of the 1990s, the Colombian authorities were spraying 100,000 acres per year with chemical herbicides (Embassy of Colombia 1998).

Contemporary fumigation strategies: Plan Colombia

In 1999, political developments in Colombia presented the US government with a strategic opening to pursue source focused eradication programmes in the most important supply country. During the presidency of Ernesto Samper Pizano (1994–98), relations between Colombia and the USA had degenerated amid allegations that Samper had received $6 million in election campaign contributions from the Cali cartel. The US authorities refused to certify Colombia as co-operating in the 'war on drugs' in 1996 and 1997, resulting in the country's diplomatic isolation and reduced access to multilateral lending. The tensions in bilateral ties were relieved when Samper's successor, Andrés Pastrana, assumed office in 1999 (Ruiz 2001).

Pastrana pursued close and amicable ties with the administration of President Bill Clinton and, in emphasizing his commitment to decisive action against the drugs trade in Colombia, Pastrana succeeded in obtaining US certification in 1999 and $1.3 billion in support for his administration's development programme, Plan Colombia. Pastrana's original Plan Colombia was costed at $13 billion. It was expensive because it sought to achieve a decisive break from cultivation and production and the government determined that this could be achieved only with substantive and sustainable economic support to cultivators.

US officials overhauled Plan Colombia, turning it 'from a peace plan into a battle plan' (Livingstone 2002: 152). Nearly 80 per cent of the financing provided by the USA was ring-fenced for military assistance, with the entire funding package dependent on Colombian acceptance of an eradication strategy based on aerial fumigation (Kirk 2004: 260; Livingstone 2002; Ruiz 2001). Underscoring the skewing of resources between alternative development and eradication, direct military assistance to the Colombian armed forces totalled $860.3 million, with an additional $519.2 million in assistance to the police. By contrast, funding for alternative development totalled $68.5 million, $13 million for judicial reform and just $3 million for dialogue promotion and peace negotiations (Livingstone 2002). The USA provided an additional $300 million in military assistance to the Colombian armed forces, and this made Colombia the third largest recipient of US defence aid after Israel and Egypt.

GLYPHOSATE The herbicide Glyphosate was used in Plan Colombia. It is produced by Monsanto and marketed under the brand name Roundup. Glyphosate was approved for general use by the American Environmental Protection Agency in 1974 and the product was marketed in South America from the mid-1970s. Glyphosate was widely used in agriculture and it was classified by the US Environmental Protection Agency as a herbicide of relatively low toxicity. Reflecting the small level of risk associated with its use, it was classified as a Category III toxin. Users were required to exercise caution in handling the product as over-exposure was linked to vomiting, stomach and intestinal illness, lung enlargement, pneumonia and mental confusion.

Glyphosate was highly effective when applied to coca and, in contrast to Paraquat, it had no purported damaging effects on public health. According to the *Glyphosate Fact Sheet* produced by the US State Department, Glyphosate 'poses virtually no risk to humans, animals, or the environment [...] it is in fact one of the least harmful herbicides on the world market [...] less toxic than common salt, aspirin, caffeine, nicotine and even Vitamin A'. Glyphosate was also promoted as an environmentally benign chemical as it did not percolate downwards into soil when applied to plants and this reduced the risk of land contamination. It was also soluble in water, eliminating the possibility of damage to aquatic ecosystems or pollution of water supplies.

After the launch of Plan Colombia in 1999, the Colombian authorities annually sprayed over 100,000 hectares of coca plantings with Glyphosate. Fumigation activities were concentrated in Putumayo, Caquetá and Guaviare, the most important coca cultivating departments.

The impact of chemical fumigation with Glyphosate

Cultivation levels It is difficult to state with precision the impact that chemical fumigation had on coca cultivation levels. The data for eradication, cultivation and potential cocaine manufacture were intensely disputed and significant differences existed between the figures presented by the US Office of National Drug Control Policy and the UNODC. Figures from the 2005 *World Drug Report* indicated that chemical fumigation had a significant impact on coca cultivation levels. These were more than halved from the period of Plan Colombia's launch in 1999 until 2004, as demonstrated in Table 14.1 below.

TABLE 14.1 Fumigation and cultivation in Colombia, 1997–2004

	Eradication reported (hectares)	Cultivation levels (hectares)	Potential cocaine manufacture (metric tons)
1997	44,123	79,400	350
1998	69,155	101,800	435
1999	44,157	160,100	680
2000	61,574	163,300	695
2001	95,898	144,800	617
2002	126,933	102,000	580
2003	136,828	86,000	440
2004	139,161	80,000	390

Source: UNODC (2005a)

However, despite progress made in reducing the total area under cultivation, Colombia remained the world's largest coca cultivator and cocaine producer. By 2004, five years after the introduction of intensive fumigation, Colombia had a potential cocaine manufacturing capacity of 390 metric tons. There were also indications that the utility of fumigations strategies was negated by the balloon effect. Coca cultivation and cocaine manufacturing increased in both Peru and Bolivia during the implementation of Plan Colombia. The balloon effect was also observable within Colombia. As Table 14.2 indicates, fumigation did reduce cultivation levels in traditional growing areas such as Putumayo, Guaviare and Caquetá. At the same time, cultivation increased in departments that had previously been marginal to the planting process such as Antioquia, Nariño and Bolivar.

The success of fumigation strategies cannot be judged on the basis of cultivation reduction alone. At the street level in consumer countries, aerial eradication had no impact on supply. Cocaine continued to be widely available, the purity of cocaine imports continued to increase and the average price of a gram of cocaine in the USA continued to fall, dropping from $145 in 1997 to $106 by 2003.

The sustained fall in cocaine prices, despite progress in reducing cultivation, pointed to two fundamental problems with source eradication policies

TABLE 14.2 The balloon effect in Plan Colombia

	March 1999	August 2000	November 2001	December 2002	December 2003	% change 2002–03
Putumayo	58,297	66,022	47,120	13,725	7,559	-45
Norte de Sant- ander	15,039	6,280	9,145	8,041	4,471	-44
Guaviare	28,435	17,619	25,553	27,381	16,163	-41
Cauca	6,291	4,576	3,139	2,120	1,443	-32
Caquetá	23,718	26,603	14,516	8,412	7,230	-14
Meta	11,384	11,123	11,425	9,222	12,814	39
Nariño	3,959	9,343	7,494	15,131	17,628	17
Bolivar	5,897	5,960	4,824	2,735	4,470	63
Antioquia	3,644	2,547	3,171	3,030	4,273	41
Boyaca	-	322	245	118	594	403

Source: UNODC (2004d).

like fumigation. As discussed in Chapter 8, the bulk of profits in the drug trade are realized at the retail end. Because cultivators rather than distributors are the primary focus of supply eradication policies, the net effect of cultivation reductions is relatively limited. As Leogrande and Sharpe (2000) explain:

In 1997 the price of coca leaf needed to make a pure kilo of cocaine was $300. Refined and ready for export from Colombia, it was worth $1,050. The cost of smuggling that kilo into the United States raised its price in Miami to $20,000, and black market distribution costs raised its retail price in Chicago to $188,000. This means even an incredibly successful crop eradication program that tripled the price of coca leaf to $900 would raise retail prices in the United States imperceptibly.

Fumigation may also have catalysed a 'bio war' with cultivators. At the end of 2004, Colombian officials claimed to have identified new strains of coca that grew to double the height of a standard coca plant and yielded eight times the typical alkaloid content of a leaf. The existence of 'super coca' was used to account for the sustained fall in cocaine prices and the increase in drug purity. Two theories were put forward to account for this development in coca agriculture: excessive use of fertilizer and experimentation with genetically modified coca. The super coca story underscored the possibility that fumigation could be 'defeated' by scientific and technological advances that ensured the sustainability of coca in Colombia and the cocaine trade more generally (BBC Online News, 7 December 2004).

There were serious doubts as to the sustainability of the reductions in cultivation achieved between 1999 and 2004. In order to make progress in eradication, fumigation had to be progressively intensified and the geographical area sprayed extended. This created a serious dilemma for policy-makers because there was evidence that fumigation with Glyphosate during Plan Colombia had detrimental effects on the health of the residents of sprayed areas and that it damaged crops, livestock and local ecologies.

Health and the environment In 1996, health problems and damage to crops and livestock were reported in Guaviare and Putumayo after fumigation with Glyphosate during a domestic Colombian coca crop reduction campaign (Cox 1995; Lloyd 1997; Youngers 1997). Despite documented problems with Glyphosate, it was applied intensively during Plan Colombia. As in 1996, there were immediate reports of illness among residents of the areas fumigated. Local health authorities and non-governmental organizations documented symptoms that included hair loss, nausea, respiratory problems, abdominal pains and diarrhoea. Particularly severe cases were reported in young children. Nearly 200,000 animals, including dogs, livestock and fish were reported dead in Putumayo and it was claimed that non-coca agricultural crops had been sprayed and killed as a result of fumigation (TNI et al. 2001; Kirk 2004; Livingstone 2002; Knight 2000; Brauchli 2001; Rohter 2000). The Colombian ombudsman received over 8,000 health-related complaints from people resident in the fumigated departments (TNI 2005b). Health problems linked to Glyphosate were also reported in provinces of Ecuador that bordered Putamayo and Nariño (Lucas 2000; TNI 2005c). Medical and local authorities reported respiratory illnesses, animal deaths and the devastation of crops such as yucca and maize.

Critics of Glyphosate fumigation pointed to three aspects of the spraying campaign to account for the problems reported. First, aerial dispersion of the herbicide was conducted at an altitude of 15 metres or less in the case of coca and 30 metres or less for opium poppies. The risk to pilots of being shot down by insurgents at this height was low, with the danger increasing in line with a fall in altitude. Critics argued that spraying at this height contravened the guidelines on the use of Glyphosate. These recommended spraying from a height of between 10 and 3 metres. The altered exposure conditions may have had unanticipated health and environmental consequences. Dispersal from this height would also have caused the Glyphosate to drift, making the targeting of coca crops difficult and leading to cross-border pollution.

Second, it was claimed that the Glyphosate mix used in the Colombian fumigation exercise violated the manufacturer's instructions as it was used at a dosage of 23.7 litres per hectare and not the recommended 2.5 litres per hectare (TNI 2001a). In addition, the formulation of the spray used was a mixture of chemical additives and not 'pure' Glyphosate. This was not made evident to the public when the spraying campaign was initiated and non-governmental organizations had to engage in an intense lobbying campaign in order to obtain the information that Cosmo Flux-411F and Cosmo-InD were being dispersed with Glyphosate (ibid.). Those directly affected by the aerial fumigation campaign in Colombia and Ecuador were peasants and indigenous people. These groups were traditionally marginal to the political process and, in the Colombian case, vulnerable to repression and coercion by the state, left-wing insurgents and right-wing paramilitaries. These people were also poor and isolated from state provision of basic welfare and health services, including access to clean water. This may have made them more vulnerable to Glyphosate-related illnesses.

At the end of 2000, indigenous leaders from Putumayo, Guaviare, Meta and Caquetá, the Organization of Indigenous Peoples of the Colombian Amazon (OPIAC) and the Colombian affiliate of the Pesticides Action Network lodged an official complaint with the Colombian ombudsman. They claimed that Glyphosate spraying was killing food crops, contaminating water supplies and creating severe health problems. This was in turn creating food shortages, driving people away from their homes and impeding progress in developing agricultural alternatives to coca. A subsequent investigation by the Colombian ombudsman vindicated their claims. In his final report, the ombudsman stated that fumigation had:

> Destroyed not only illegal crops [...] but also other crops necessary for subsistence [...] These persons and the communities are facing both the ruin of their family economy as well as a serious hunger problem. Given the precarious conditions of this group of people, the action by the State can be seen as a violation of their right to subsistence, which translates into a grave harm to the physical integrity and dignity of the families and their members.

The ombudsman also criticized the lack of co-ordination between agencies responsible for Plan Colombia and concluded by claiming the fumigation campaign had been counter-productive: 'The intention was to foster a policy that would strengthen the community and move it away from marginality and illegality. However, the arbitrary behaviour described herein has produced the opposite effect to the one desired' (Ombudsman Resolution, No. 004, 12 February 2001).

The fumigation campaign and the problems experienced by residents of the areas sprayed provided an important insight into the political impact of eradication strategies. These were shown to be profoundly undemocratic and closed from scrutiny or criticism even though they touched on issues of state sovereignty, accountability and transparency.

The politics of fumigation

The knowledge vacuum Although chemical fumigation was the central element of the crop eradication strategy of Plan Colombia, neither the US nor the Colombian government conducted assessment missions or data collection exercises before commencing intensive aerial fumigation. Limited to negligible research existed on large-scale Glyphosate fumigation exercises and the UN drug control apparatus had never carried out a large-scale investigation into the health, economic or environmental effects of chemical spraying in cultivation areas. As a result, no indicators were available that would have allowed the impact of Glyphosate spraying to be tracked over time. There was also no project to collate information measuring the effect of Glyphosate spraying on the environment or human health as the fumigation programme progressed. As a consequence, no mechanism existed to evaluate claims of damage to human health or to evaluate the impact of chemical fumigation on alternative development programmes (Robert F. Kennedy Memorial Center for Human Rights 2002).

The Colombian government did establish the Inter-institutional Technical Committee in 2000. The role of the committee was to oversee and advise on aerial eradication, but its remit was limited. The Colombian government also contracted an independent environmental monitor who accompanied the Anti-narcotics Directorate of the Colombian National Police on fumigation missions. Both initiatives failed as substitutes for a systematic toxicity study. The US Congress did respond to concerns over the health and environmental effects of the fumigation programme by attaching a series of environmental conditions to foreign aid appropriation bills after 2002. This made aid disbursements to Colombia dependent on the presentation of a report by the State Department and the Environmental Protection Agency detailing the effects of the spraying campaign. This did not satisfy anti-fumigation protesters or enhance understanding of the wider social and environmental impact of chemical eradication. The Environmental Protection Agency based its assessment on information provided by the State Department and the body did not have the authority to conduct its own independent research: 'What's more, the EPA assessments were conducted without the benefit of information specific to the local environment in Colombia [...] As a result, fundamental questions about the effects of the spray programme go unanswered' (Lemus et al. 2004).

Sovereignty and democracy In Colombia there was no national debate in relation to the sweeping changes that were made to the original Plan Colombia before the revised US-sponsored, militarized version went into effect. The implementation of chemical fumigation subsequently proceeded without negotiation or discussion with the residents of the affected departments, the citizens of Colombia or the governments and residents of neighbouring states such as Ecuador. This may have been due to concerns that the promotion of a debate on eradication would have led to protests, as it had done in Bolivia and Peru. In Colombia, the 1996 Glyphosate trial galvanized the largest rural mobilizations in the country's history, with an estimated 240,000 people demonstrating against the government's eradication policies (Youngers 1997; Blickman and Felsma 1998).

The failure to conduct a broad-based consultation process violated the constitutional right of indigenous peoples to participate in government decisions that affected their territories or endangered their survival. President Pastrana also overrode the criticism and recommendations of those institutions that were meant to check and balance the executive, such as the ombudsman, congressional representatives and the comptroller general. Those agencies responsible for overseeing environmental protection and public health programmes were bypassed or ignored, as were democratically elected representatives at the state and community level. The manner in which aerial eradication was executed also violated Law 30 of 1986. This required the approval of environmental and public health agencies before the implementation of fumigation policies.

Because Plan Colombia was conceived and executed in a wholly undemocratic manner, no mechanisms of accountability or 'ownership' of aerial fumigation policies existed (Lemus et al. 2004). As a result, those affected by Glyphosate spraying had to pursue compensation through a bureaucratic labyrinth. Redress was particularly difficult to achieve in Plan Colombia because responsibility for fumigation had been outsourced by the US State Department to the US firm DynCorp Aerospace Technologies for $170 million. In an attempt to establish culpability for Glyphosate damage, the International Labour Rights Fund brought a lawsuit against DynCorp on behalf of the Ecuadorian groups in 2001. DynCorp was charged with infanticide, human rights abuses and environmental damage against 10,000 people. In a letter to the chief executive of DynCorp, Paul Lombard, the president of the ILRF painted a graphic picture of the social and emotional trauma caused by the fumigation campaign:

> Imagine that scene for a moment – you are an Ecuadorian farmer, and suddenly, without notice or warning, a large helicopter approaches, and the frightening noise of the chopper blades invades the quiet. The helicopter comes closer, and sprays a toxic poison on you, your children, your livestock and your food crops. You see your children get sick, your crops die. (<www.apfn.org/enron/dyncorp.htm>)

Chemical fumigation was a product of elite, inter-governmental negotiations between the Colombian and US administrations. This underscored the authoritarian nature of anti-drug strategy development and the central role of the USA in devising regional anti-drug approaches. Given the power and influence that the USA had over the Colombian government at this time, it is open to question how far the Colombian president would have been able to resist US eradication plans and strategies, in turn pointing to a diminution of Colombian state sovereignty.

Ethics and war Plan Colombia raised important ethical questions relating to the use of fumigation strategies in countries experiencing civil conflict. First, chemical eradication exacerbated a pre-existing problem of population displacement and food insecurity. An estimated 1.5 million Colombians were displaced due to rural violence in the late 1990s. Chemical fumigation in the 2000s increased the rate of population displacement while the fumigation campaign itself detracted from the need to address the social problems caused by the on-going civil conflict.

Second, US sponsorship of chemical fumigation was acutely problematic given that the focus of eradication activities was those areas controlled by the left-wing insurgent group, the FARC. Critics argued that the US administration had deliberately entangled its anti-drug programming with its anti-communist and then anti-terrorist campaigns. In this interpretation, the financial support and training made available to the Colombian armed forces under the framework of anti-drug operations masked direct US engagement in the Colombian conflict and military support for the Colombian government (LeoGrande and Sharpe 2000). For US officials, this blurring of the two 'wars' against drugs and terrorism was necessary because the two were inseparable. Fumigation was seen as functional in the anti-terrorist context as it eliminated the financial base and consequently the military capacity of the FARC. Hence, while opponents of fumigation claimed that the programme undermined the search for peace and dialogue, the US maintained that only through weakening the FARC would the Colombian state be in a position to force the insurgent organization into negotiations.

This link between terrorism and drugs was used to detract from the claims of health problems and illness in sprayed areas. It was also used to denigrate the campaign against fumigation with critics of the strategy condemned by the US and Colombian governments as supporters of terrorism and the drugs trade. In his response to the International Labour Rights Fund claim against DynCorp, Paul Lombard, the chief executive of Dyncorp, wrote that the anti-fumigation campaign was: 'Notably, consistent with the drug cartel's objectives, the complaint also seeks to permanently enjoin further spraying of coca and opium poppy [...] Considering the major international issues with which we are all dealing as a consequence of September 11, none of us need to be sidetracked with frivolous litigation the aim of which is to fulfil a political agenda.' The terminology of the fumigation debate obscured important technical, ethical and political questions arising from the strategy.

By way of a conclusion

In November 2004, people living in Nangarhar province in the east of Afghanistan reported sickness, diarrhoea, eye infections and skin complaints after unidentified aircraft sprayed opium poppies in the districts of Khogiani and Shinwar with 'snow'. Echoing events in Colombia and Ecuador, agricultural crops and livestock were reported to have been killed and soil contaminated. Following its own investigation into the claims, the Afghan transitional government confirmed that an unidentifiable substance had been sprayed and that this had occurred without the authorization of the government.

The US administration had promoted a policy of chemical eradication of opium poppies in the country as part of its Plan Afghanistan announced in 2004. This dedicated $152 million of funding to eradication projects and $120 million to alternative development. The head of the transitional government, Hamed Karzai, rejected the strategy on public health and environmental grounds, and the British government, the US partner in the reconstruction of Afghanistan, did not support it. Although the US controlled the airspace over Afghanistan and was engaged in intense surveillance in the Tora Bora mountains located within the affected area, it denied that it had authorized or conducted fumigation trials, and US officials had no knowledge as to who could have conducted the spraying. It was widely suspected that that a US agency was responsible for the spraying, which was thought to be a secret trial (Graham 2004; Meo 2004; *New York Times* 2004; Burke 2004; *Pakistan Tribune* 2004; *Wall Street Journal* 2005; TNI 2005a).

The USA continued to support and develop fumigation strategies despite the limitations of this approach in Colombia. Trials were conducted by US authorities into the use of Tebuthiuron, also known as 'spike'. Spike had the potential to overcome the problems associated with the use of Glyphosate in Colombia. It could be dispersed in pellet form so it was not susceptible to drift and it could be accurately targeted. The pellets could not be washed away as they landed directly in the soil and this in turn reduced the need for multiple spray flights. There was vocal criticism of the spike trials but the largest obstacle to the roll-out of a spike-based eradication programme was the opposition of Dow AgroSciences, the manufacturer of Tebuthiuron. Dow rejected the use of spike in Colombia on the grounds that the product was unsuitable for dispersion in humid and rainy climates. The company was also concerned that the chemical could damage aquatic organisms.

The move by Dow followed the earlier decision by Chevron to block the use of Paraquat in Mexico. The pattern of chemical manufacturers withdrawing their consent for their products to be used in fumigation programmes was also repeated at an early stage of Plan Colombia when the British chemical manufacturer ICI was reported to have blocked the use of Cosmo Flux in the Glyphosate spray mix (Barnett and Hughes 2000). The absence of comprehensive testing and data gathering by US, Colombian and UNODC authorities rendered chemical manufacturers vulnerable to litigation by affected communities, a situation that prompted the manufacturers to limit their exposure by preventing their products from being used.

Rather than analysing and exploring fundamental policy dilemmas, such as the balloon effect and the economic 'logic' of participation in the drugs trade, the USA maintained that suppression strategies had to be escalated not revised.

The momentum of this logic was that the search for a 'magic bullet' would continue. Against the backdrop of limited success with Glyphosate, the USA began pursuing an even more controversial and revolutionary approach to crop eradication. This is examined in the following chapter.

15 | The new magic bullet: bio-control solutions

In the early 2000s, research was conducted into naturally-occurring drug-plant-killing fungi or mycoherbicides that included *Fusarium oxysporum*, which kills coca, and *Pleospora papaveracea* and *Dendryphion penicillatum*, which attack opium poppy. The research was led by the USA and supported by the UK and the UNODC. It was hoped that mycoherbicides would be superior to man-made chemicals in drug crop eradication campaigns and they emerged as the 'magic bullet' of future drug control strategies. However, the development of myco-herbicide-based strategies caused alarm within the international community. Regional organizations, non-governmental organizations and individual nation-states from Brazil to Kenya expressed concern that mycoherbicide dispersal would have a profoundly negative and irreversible impact on the environment. It was also argued that the development and use of mycoherbicides would violate international conventions on the conduct of warfare, bio-weapons control and environmental protection.

The evolution of the mycoherbicide strategy

Supporters of mycoherbicide solutions believe aerial fumigation with plant-killing fungi has numerous advantages over the use of Glyphosate or spike. Taking the case of *Fusarium oxysporum*, the fungus lives naturally in the soil and particularly soil planted with coca. When applied in mass doses, the *Fusarium* attacks the coca plant and its sustained presence in the sprayed area prevents subsequent coca planting. This in turn meant that, unlike Glyphosate, *Fusarium* did not have to be reapplied. The fungus was additionally seen as superior to man-made chemical products because it was host-specific. This meant that it would not jump from plant type to plant type. Consequently, direct target-ing of coca cultivation would not be required and risks to other crops such as yucca, cotton and maize removed. A further purported benefit of *Fusarium*-based fumigation was that the fungus had no detrimental effect on human or animal health, aquatic systems or the wider ecology as all were exposed to the fungus 'naturally' in the environment.

Interest in the use of *Fusarium oxysporum* for the biological control of coca developed after two devastating outbreaks of the fungus at a soft drinks research plant in Hawaii in the 1970s. The Hawaiian experience alerted US researchers at the Department of Agriculture to the existence of the fungus, although *seca seca*, as the fungus was known in the Andean region, was recorded as having killed extensive areas of coca in Peru as early as 1932. After *Fusarium oxysporum* was identified, efforts quickly followed to determine, isolate and reproduce the chemical causative agents of the disease in coca plants. The US Department of Agriculture continued to conduct research into the biological control of coca throughout the 1980s, and after preliminary trials demonstrated the effectiveness of the fungus, the US Congress allocated $23 million to *Fusarium* research under the three-year Master Plan for Mycoherbicides to Control Narcotic Crops in 1998 (Bigwood 2000; Hogshire 1998, 2000). The funding aimed to push existing research to 'operational' level.

The timing of the *Fusarium* funding initiative was significant as this was the period of congressional debate over Plan Colombia. A number of Republican Party representatives in the Congress and Senate saw the US-funded plan as an opportunity to trial the work on *Fusarium* in coca control. In a letter to President Clinton, the Senate Majority Leader and the House Speaker, Republican members Trent Lott and Dennis Hastert, called for the deployment of mycoherbicides in the coca producing zones controlled by the FARC. In March 2000, Republican congressman Benjamin Gilman added an amendment to Plan Colombia. This required the Colombian government to agree to the use of 'tested, environmentally safe mycoherbicides'. The Republican mycoherbicide lobby subsequently accepted President Clinton's proposal for Glyphosate spraying over *Fusarium* use. This was taken as a tacit acknowledgement by the Republican Party that the mycoherbicide initiative was controversial and that it could be open to legal challenge (Jelsma 2000).

Supporters of mycoherbicide programmes in the USA subsequently sought to build support for the initiative within the multilateral framework of the UNDCP. The idea that anti-American sentiment might be an obstacle to achieving international support for bio-control measures led to an internal State Department 'action request' from Secretary of State Madeleine Albright in 2000 that called for UNDCP support, funding and control of the mycoherbicide project. The American government shared the costs of developing mycoherbicide research and provided the UNDCP with twelve years of work into *Fusarium*. The move reflected the tradition of US authorities working within international counternarcotics frameworks to gain support for unilaterally developed and controversial programme initiatives.

The role of the UNDCP Research scientists employed by the UNDCP had been engaged in mycoherbicide research under the auspices of the Expert Group on Environmentally Safe Means of the Eradication of Illicit Narcotic Plants. This body, which exchanged data and research on chemical and biological control agents, was set up in the aftermath of the Mexican marijuana Paraquat scandal. The UNDCP was not, however, supportive of the research initiatives of the group and requests for funding increases were rejected. It was not until the late 1990s, and with strong encouragement from the USA, that the UNDCP announced plans to test biological control agents. The focus of the UNDCP initiative was not coca but opium poppies, with the research assessing the impact of the fungi *Pleospora papaveracea* and *Dendryphion penicillatum*, which had been discovered in diseased opium poppies in Central Asia.

The UNDCP research was based in Uzbekistan at the Institute of Genetics and Experimental Biology. It commenced in 1998 with the bulk of the costs borne by the British government. British interest was driven by the fact that Afghanistan was the most important heroin source country. British and US research was consequently complementary; while the USA focused on coca-killing fungi, reflecting the specific 'threat' posed by cocaine from South America, the UK developed the opium side of the mycoherbicide initiative, with both countries deferring identification of the research with their own national and security interests by working under the framework of the UNDCP.

Progress in the development and testing of the opium-poppy-killing fungus was rapid. By mid-2003, the fungus had been tested on 200 different plant species and agricultural crops in Uzbekistan, Kyrgyzstan and Tajikistan. Howard Stead, the head of the scientific section of the UNDCP, reported that the mycoherbicides had not infected plants other than opium poppies and that 'studies to date have provided no evidence that the fungus may cause environmental damage' (TNI 2004; Kozlova 2003).

In 2000, after US authorities had provided the UNDCP with its research into *Fusarium oxysporum*, the Colombian authorities entered into negotiations with the UNDCP to experiment with the fungus in Colombia. The extent to which the Colombian officials arrived at this decision independently of the USA was subject to speculation. The draft of the joint agreement between the UNDCP and the Colombian government claimed the Colombian research initiative would allow for the development of an environmentally safe and effective biological control agent for coca that would be available for use in other coca cultivating countries (Herron 2000; Jelsma 2000; Sunshine Project 2002).

Experimentation and opposition As was the experience with the introduction of Glyphosate spraying under Plan Colombia, the proposed Colombian experiment with mycoherbicides was not subject to national debate within Colombia itself, again reflecting the anti-democratic nature of source eradication initiatives and programming. However, potential objections bypassed at the national level did present themselves in regional organizations. The Organization of American States objected vigorously to the proposed deployment of *Fusarium* in Colombia. Strong opposition also emanated from the Andean Community, the regional body comprising Bolivia, Colombia, Ecuador, Venezuela and Peru, and in September 2000 a committee of the organization, the Andean Committee of Environmental Authorities, issued a declaration that rejected the use of the fungus as a tool for the eradication of illicit crops. The Brazilian government lodged its objections directly with the General Secretary of the UN, Kofi Annan, while the Peruvian authorities introduced legislation in March 2000 to prohibit the use of bio-control agents for the eradication of coca in its territory, a move that was followed by Ecuador in July 2000. Hostility was also expressed in Europe, with the European Parliament voting against the deployment of *Fusarium* by 474 votes to 1. The surge of hostile criticism and legal resolutions extended from European and South American countries to states in Africa and it culminated in the decision by Colombian authorities to jettison the trials (Bigwood 2000; Marsh 2004; Sunshine Project 2002).

The *Fusarium* debate

The international backlash against the use of mycoherbicides in Colombia pointed to a minimal level of confidence in the use of biocides despite the reassurances of the UNDCP and US government that *Fusarium* was a cost-effective, reliable and environmentally sound method of eradicating coca. Underpinning this was an intense dispute over the scientific evidence that *Fusarium* was safe for dispersal. A second important point of contention related to the legal and political ramification of mycoherbicide use as an offensive weapon in the drugs 'war'.

The scientific questions

MUTATION The argument that the *Fusarium* fungus is host-specific and does not damage non-coca crops was contested. Research conducted in Peru during the early 1990s showed high concentrations of *Fusarium* led to the devastation of tomatoes and maize crops. It was not until 1999 when the Department of Environmental Protection (DEP) in Florida criticized plans for trials with strains of *Fusarium* against cannabis that the host specificity argument was subject to critical scrutiny. Dr David Struhs of the DEP argued that *Fusarium* was capable of evolving and that this made other crops vulnerable to attack from the fungus (Kleiner 1999; *St Petersburg Times* 1999). Although the DEP's criticisms were rejected by the Florida 'drugs czar' Jim McDonough, the Republican Governor Jeb Bush suspended the project.

Research conducted by Bigwood and Plowman supported the DEP position. The two scientists re-examined the fungus that attacked the Hawaiian coca plants and they concluded that the outbreak was not attributable to diseased coca seedlings imported from Peru, as had been assumed by the US Department of Agriculture; instead, their work pointed to a fungus native to Hawaii as having mutated, triggering the Hawaiian outbreak. The 'remote possibility' that the fungus could mutate and was not host-specific was acknowledged by the UNDCP in confidential documents obtained from the body's Vienna office by the BBC Television documentary programme 'Britain's Secret War on Drugs' (*Panorama*, BBC, 2 October 2000). However, the mutation claim was dismissed by the US government, the head of the Office of National Drug Control Policy, Barry McCaffrey, and federal government-funded researchers, including Dr David Sands, an expert in mycoherbicides and a pioneer of their use in counter-narcotics operations. Sands rejected the mutation argument as a 'mathematical impossibility' and he claimed that if *Fusarium* were able to mutate and target other plants, this would have occurred in nature.

ENVIRONMENTAL IMPACT A second controversy related to the impact of fungus dispersion on the soil. Research showed that high volumes of *Fusarium* fungus spores rendered soil sterile. This first came to the attention of scientists following a fatal outbreak of *Fusarium* in the Soviet Union in 1949. After investigating the disease, the Soviet scientist N. A. Krasil'nikov reported that a high concentration of the fungus had left land infertile. The Florida DEP reiterated the soil sterility claim and argued that *Fusarium* could remain active in the soil for up to forty years, thereby preventing the land from being put to other agricultural use (Kleiner 1999). This had implications for local ecologies as well as the livelihoods of rural farmers.

METHODOLOGY A third point of contention related to the methodological approach taken by American scientists in their *Fusarium* research. Critics argued this was flawed as it focused on a specific protein in the fungus, 24kDa, the compound identified as triggering the wilting of the coca plant. Department of Agriculture scientists did not conduct detailed research outside the work on 24kDa and they specifically neglected to test for and analyse toxins associated with the *Fusarium* genus (Bigwood and Stevenson 2000).

All fungi release toxins; some are benign and even beneficial, but this is not the case with *Fusarium*. The toxins released by the fungus include Fumonisin B1, which is carcinogenic in mammals and humans; Nivalenol, which can cause fever, nausea, leukaemia and vomiting in cases of overexposure; the highly toxic Mycotoxin T2; Deoxynivalenol, also known as Vomitoxin which, as the name implies, is linked to vomiting and diarrhoea in humans; and Fusariotoxin. Animal experiments with Fusariotoxin led to toxicity and death. Research conducted by the Colombian Centre for International Physics showed exposure to *Fusarium* toxins to be fatal for people with low levels of immunity and malnutrition, that is to say, those problems specifically associated with marginal socio-economic groups engaged in drug plant cultivation or living close to cultivation areas (Vullimay 2000).

TRANSFERABILITY Critics also argued that mycoherbicides posed a real danger to the environment when strains of the fungus were transferred between countries, as it was not known how the fungus would react in a non-native environment. This followed the isolation in the late 1980s of a strain of *Fusarium* called EN4. It was this compound that the Colombian authorities were encouraged to use in the much disputed mycoherbicide research programme. However, the

EN4 strain was not derived from the Colombian coca plant, *Erythroxylum coca*, but from a Hawaiian species of the *Erythroxylum* genus, *Erythroxylum novogranatense*. The research scientist who isolated EN4, Dr David Sands, maintained that this did not reduce the effectiveness or safety of EN4 because *Fusarium* was genus- and not species-specific. It would therefore attack only the genus *Erythroxylum*. There were 100 different plant species of this genus, of which only a handful could be used in the production of cocaine. Critics argued that the exposure of varieties of *Erythroxylum* plants to *Fusarium* would have devastating consequences for the ecological systems that depended on these non-cocaine producing plants (Sunshine Project 2000).

The direction of mycoherbicide research

A further divisive issue was the claim that research scientists in the USA were developing a more virulent strain of the *Fusarium* fungus. This followed the isolation and sequencing of the gene encoding of 24kDa protein. This triggered concerns that future research would focus on a modified fungus with an enhanced pathogenicity, or ability to kill coca. Ultimately, however, the biggest concern was the secrecy surrounding mycoherbicide research and the fear that, once released, the unpredictable fungus would be beyond human control. According to Dr David Struhs of the Florida Department of Environmental Protection: 'it is difficult if not impossible to control the spread of the *Fusarium* species' (Fichtl 2000).

The politics of mycoherbicides

Those countries, regional organizations and non-governmental organizations opposed to the use of *Fusarium* and the *Dendryphion penicillatum* and *Pleospora papaveracea* in eradication programmes based their objections on two arguments. First that the use of plant-killing fungi violated international conventions and domestic laws protecting biodiversity and limiting and controlling the development, export and use of biological weapons. Related to this, a second concern was the social, political and environmental ramifications of the use of fungi, particularly within the context of civil conflict. It was feared that the use of mycoherbicides in the 'drug war' would set a precedent for the use of other plant-killing fungi in intra- and inter-state conflicts, thereby rolling back the progress that had been made in controlling bioweapons.

A violation of international conventions?

ENMOD The most relevant conventions in terms of the mycoherbicide debate were the Convention on the Prohibition of Military or Any Other Hostile Use of Environmental Modification Techniques (ENMOD) of 1977 and the Biological and Toxin Weapons Convention (BTWC) of 1972. These two conventions were part of a patchwork of international agreements that regulated the conduct of war and protected the environment and civilians in conflicts. ENMOD prohibits the modification of the environment for hostile purposes, through, for example, the lighting of forest fires, deforestation, artificially stimulated changes to weather patterns, the triggering of earthquakes or crop destruction with biocides as offensive or defensive strategies in war (Chamorro and Hammond 2003).

The ENMOD emerged from international concerns over the military strategies employed by the USA in the anti-communist conflicts in Vietnam and Laos in the 1960s and 1970s. US scientists had sought to trigger monsoon conditions in order to block the supply of weaponry and reinforcements to enemy fighters in South Vietnam under 'Operation Popeye', and chemical herbicides, most notoriously Agent Orange, were used as a form of advanced technological warfare against the guerrilla operations of the communists. Building on research conducted by the USA Department of Defense into the biological destruction of the Asian rice crop in the Second World War, forests and agricultural areas in Vietnam were sprayed in order to expose combatants hiding in jungle areas and to prevent them from replenishing food stocks (Whitby 2001). Approximately 10 per cent of Vietnamese territory was sprayed with Agent Orange between 1962 and 1971, causing environmental devastation that was pronounced in the south of the country. The use of Agent Orange had a catastrophic effect on human health and it was linked to cancers, birth defects, spontaneous abortions and mental health problems (Pesticide Action Network 2004). In 1972 the US government renounced the use of climate modification techniques for hostile purposes, a move that laid the foundations for the ENMOD negotiations.

BTWC In contrast to the ENMOD, which prohibits the use of environmental modification techniques but not research into them, the BTWC prohibits the development, stockpiling and export of bioweapons, including those that can be used to spread disease and to kill food crops. The draft protocol of the BTWC lists the *Fusarium oxysporum* and the toxins Fusariotoxin and Vomitoxin as biological agents of war. There are no exemptions within the BTWC for those biological agents that are contained in the convention so, if listed, they cannot be used by a national government within its own territory or deployed in self-defence (Chamorro and Hammond 2003).

The question of biological warfare The USA and also the UK maintained that the use of *Fusarium* would not violate the international conventions or constitute an act of biological warfare on four counts. First, mycoherbicide programmes would be conducted only with the consent of the government of a cultivating country. Second, it was argued that coca, opium poppies and cannabis are weeds and not agricultural crops. Consequently these plants do not fall under the scope of the ENMOD or BTWC, thereby legitimizing the export of *Fusarium* strains such as EN4. The third argument in defence of mycoherbicide use was the claim that the international drug conventions superseded the international bioweapons conventions. Article 14 of the United Nations Convention against Illicit Traffic in Narcotic Drugs and Psychotropic Substances of 1988, for example, commits signatories to the elimination of narcotics cultivation. For supporters of myco-herbicides, specifically the US lobby, this responsibility prevailed over obligations enshrined in other conventions. This led into a fourth, US-specific, defence of mycoherbicides. This was the claim that the national security of the USA was under attack from drugs trafficked from South America. Consequently, if the use of *Fusarium* was construed as an act of warfare, this was a legitimate response on the part of the USA. Biowarfare was self-defence, a response shaped by the specific and unique nature of the enemy. Dr David Sands, for example, argued in the *Panorama* programme that countries and people engaged in drug plant cultivation 'are unleashing a chemical, a drug, on our children, an addictive drug [...] I think they should suffer the consequences of that decision'.

There were a number of problems with this mycoherbicide defence. As the experience of Colombia demonstrated, it may be possible to gain the consent of the government of a cultivating country to fumigate crops, but not necessarily the people. Given the covert and anti-democratic nature of source eradication programme development, there were real concerns that the notion of consent implicit in the US and UK argument was weak and limited. Related to this, the US arsenal of legislative measures used to punish states deemed not to be co-operating in anti-drug efforts raised concerns as to the extent to which a government would be able to defend national sovereignty and deflect pressure to apply mycoherbicides. Finally, the government of a country where there was both drug plant cultivation and civil conflict might agree to mycoherbicide programmes and then use this type of fumigation as a tactical weapon against insurgents. Reform of both the ENMOD and the BTWC would be necessary to delimit the possibility of mycoherbicides being developed and deployed outside the international system of bioweapons control. Both conventions were criticized as anachronistic as they did not address the new challenges posed by contem-porary post-Cold War conflicts (Bradford n.d.; Chamorro and Hammond 2003; Environmental Law Institute 1998).

The challenge of US unilateralism

Despite vocal international opposition, support for mycoherbicide-based strategies persisted in the USA. In December 2002, the Republican member for Florida, John Mica, called on the US Congress to introduce mycoherbicides in Colombia. In his view: 'things that have been studied for too long need to be put into action'. While the Colombian government did not accept the export of *Fusarium* from the USA in 2000, it did explore the development of a native fungus, the so-called *hongo criollo*, with the UNDCP; the US authorities maintained an active dialogue on mycoherbicide use with their Colombian counterparts.

As with the allegations of covert US fumigation of opium poppy plants in Afghanistan in 2004, there was speculation that the USA had secretly trialled mycoherbicides in South America. In 1984 and 1989 there was an outbreak of *Fusarium* in the Upper Huallaga valley of Peru and reports by local farmers of planes dispersing gases. During Plan Colombia, the environmental lobby group Accion Ecologica conducted tests in the Sucumbios region of Ecuador that bordered the Colombian coca cultivating department of Putamayo. These indicated a heightened presence of the *Fusarium* fungus. The implication of the finding was that either *Fusarium* had been sprayed in Colombia or that a connection existed between Glyphosate spraying and the presence of the fungus. Those sceptical about America's conduct of its 'drug war' lean towards the former interpretation, but there are over fifty peer-reviewed scientific articles supporting the proposition that a scientific connection between Glyphosate and *Fusarium* exists. While the precise nature of the linkage was unclear, the possibility of a connection reinforced the argument that insufficient research was conducted into the impact of spraying concentrated herbicide solutions.

Conclusion

Aerial spraying of mycoherbicides to eliminate cultivation at source will not be an effective weapon in the drugs 'war'. Biocide strategies are part of the supply-side-focused approach that has been repeatedly shown to be ineffective in reducing cultivation and production. If international hostility is overcome and mycoherbicide-based programmes become the future shape of source-focused programming, the balloon effect suggests that cultivation will simply be displaced, as has been the case with all other supply-side-focused initiatives. Ultimately, mycoherbicide spraying, like glyphosate-based eradication campaigns, does not address the reason why people are engaged in the cultivation and production of drugs. Moreover, even if the distant utopia of a cocaine-, heroin- and cannabis-free world were realized by the mass dispersal of living fungi, this would not reduce the persistent and historic demand for stimulants. The use of mycoherbicides would radically redefine the rules of the game in the drugs war and a counter-response would be expected, although its nature and shape are unknown.

The international drug control apparatus and the USA have set unrealistic policy goals and this has driven and legitimized the quest to develop more effective weapons in the drugs 'war'. This process has occurred without the development of national and international frameworks that allow for a meaningful debate on the future of eradication strategies. Even more problematic, mycoherbicide research has been conducted covertly and outside the mechanisms of oversight and accountability. In the USA, mycoherbicide research was promoted through a $3 million federal grant to Dr David Sands for his work at Montana State University-Bozeman. It was not until a decade later that his research fell into the public domain after a tip-off to the National Organization for the Reform of Marijuana Laws in March 1999. Details of the research were released only after the NORML launched a legal challenge against Montana State University.

The rise of the mycoherbicide option, despite the strong and persistent opposition of the majority of countries, is a testament to the absence of democratic and broad-based input into drug control strategies, the dominance of the USA in setting the drug agenda and the continued neglect of basic humanitarian issues in drug control policies. As the 'drug war' progresses into the twenty-first century, it is evident that policy direction will be determined by an increasingly narrow group of economic, political and religious interests based in the USA. There is little to distinguish this situation from that which prevailed at the launch of the international campaign to prohibit drugs a century ago.

16 | A note on hemp

The case of hemp illustrates the fundamentally counter-productive and arbitrary nature of the international drug control system. Hemp is one of the most versatile and useful plants known to man. A recent count put the total number of uses for its long, medium and short core fibres, seed, seed oil and seed meal at 25,000 (Anderson 1998). It is also an environmentally friendly agricultural crop. It requires no herbicides or pesticides and it is a soil builder. In this respect, it is one of just a handful of crops that enhance soil structure and leave the soil in better condition than when first planted.

Hemp is also a member of the *cannabis sativa* family and as a result, it has been subject to regulation by the international drug control system. This is despite the fact that industrial hemp has a negligible content of psychoactive D9-tetrahydrocannabinol (THC) or cannabinoids. While cannabis has a THC ranging from 3 to 16 per cent, the THC content of industrial hemp is typically less than 1 per cent: 'You would need to smoke a joint the size of a telegraph pole to get high' (Tangi 1998).

The case of hemp has divided the USA and the international community within the control system. As the 'war on drugs' escalated in the 1980s, so did interest in the use of hemp. The plant is now being rehabilitated and is at the centre of international efforts to develop environmentally friendly, sustainable alternatives to a range of manufactured products and damaging natural resource extraction practices. While Asian, Oceanic, African and European countries have embraced regulated industrial hemp production and support a reform of the existing regime regulating cannabis, authorities in the USA remain deeply hostile to the legalization of the crop. For the Office of National Drug Control Policy, legalizing industrial hemp cultivation would 'send the wrong message' to the public at large, particularly young people 'at a time when adolescent drug use is rising rapidly'. From this perspective, the legalization of hemp would mean 'the de facto legalization of marijuana cultivation' (ONDCP 1997). Reform of the legislation relating to hemp has consequently emerged as a divisive issue at both national and international level and one that poses real dilemmas for the system of narcotics control. As this chapter demonstrates, hemp, like Cuba, is a peculiarly American fixation.

A brief history of hemp

Hemp was one of the first non-food industrial plants to be cultivated and the history of its domestication dates back 5,000 years (Mignoni 1997). From around

8,000 BC until the beginning of the twentieth century, it was the most important and widely cultivated agricultural crop on the planet. Rope, sails, rigging, clothes, textiles, paper and fishing nets were made from the strong, durable, water- and salt-resistant hemp fibre. Hempseed was a primary food source for humans and birds and the oil of the hempseed was traditionally used as an alternative to butter in Russia and Central European countries. The oil is one of the most nutritious known and a complete protein source. It contains essential amino acids and two essential fatty acids, omega-3 and omega-6 (Deferne and Pate 1996; Fleischmann 1998; Roulac 1997). The oil was also used for paints, lubricant, varnishes and as fuel for lamps.

Hemp is a dioecious plant, meaning that it has both male and female parts. It uses the sun more efficiently than any other plant, enabling it to grow rapidly in one season, and it flourishes in virtually any soil or climatic condition. Native to Asia, it is believed to have first been domesticated in China where hemp fibres were used for the production of textiles and paper (Lu and Clarke 1995). By around the sixth century BC, the cultivation of the plant extended to Turkey and into Europe. There was a surge in demand for hemp in Europe in the fourteenth century. Starting in Italy, hemp cultivation expanded rapidly, a development linked to rising demand for rope and rigging by merchant traders (Mignoni 1991; Roulac 1997). The use of hemp fibres in textile and paper manufacture was widespread in Europe by the sixteenth century and, as the value of the crop was recognized, its cultivation was extended across the colonies of the Spanish, French and British empires.

The Spanish monarchy imposed mandatory hemp crop cultivation quotas in South America in the mid-sixteenth century and British and Chinese authorities set jail terms on farmers reluctant to cultivate hemp in the seventeenth and eighteenth centuries. The export of hempseed from China was a capital offence. The Puritans took hemp to North America in the seventeenth century and, after cultivation of the plant was made mandatory, it dominated agricultural production in the Mid-West agricultural belts of Massachusetts, Connecticut, Virginia and particularly Kentucky. Hemp was legal tender in the USA until the early 1800s and this meant that taxes could be paid to the American government with hemp for nearly 200 years (Herer 1998).

Russia was historically the world's leading exporter of hemp and access to hemp supplies has been cited as a motivating factor or strategic consideration in a number of historical conflicts. These include the war between the UK and the USA in 1812 and Napoleon's decision to invade Russia in the same year (Herer 1998; Roulac 1997). After a long history as one of the most important agricultural crops, hemp cultivation experienced a rapid decline at the turn of the twentieth century. Two factors account for this: technological progress and the launch of international narcotics control.

The economic causes of hemp's decline

The hemp industry started to suffer a reversal in North America and Europe at the end of the nineteenth century. Technological developments, the emergence of new resource sectors and advances in engineering and mechanics made hemp use redundant as new challengers emerged. Hemp was acutely disadvantaged during this period owing to the heavy labour input associated with its processing. Agricultural labourers had to break the stalks of the plant with a small machine known as the hand break in order to separate the fibre from the core, an arduous task that made hemp uncompetitive.

The first challenge to hemp came from within the textile sector. The replacement of the hand cotton gin (invented in 1793) with industrial gins drastically reduced costs in the cotton industry, making cotton textiles and clothing cheaper to produce. The development of artificial fibres such as Rayon in the 1880s, followed by synthetic fibres in the early 1900s, accelerated the pace of hemp's decline. The utility of hemp was set back further following the invention of steam and petroleum engines and the advent of the steam ship. Demand for hemp-based rope products collapsed, as did the need for hemp fibres for fishing nets, cordage and rigging, as cheaply produced synthetic competitors moved into the market.

The hemp industry was undermined by developments after the First World War, particularly in the USA, traditionally one of the largest hemp cultivating countries. As part of its reparation payments to the USA, Germany surrendered the patents on a number of manufactured products that were considered revolutionary for their time. They included non-biodegradable plastic and petrochemical fibres developed by the German firms I.G. Farben and I.G. Corporation. After 1936, these were licensed to the US firm DuPont, the leading supplier of munitions to the American government. Plastic and petrochemical fibres and other new fibres, such as Nylon, which was invented in 1935, quickly came to dominate the textile, clothing, rope, twine and cordage markets.

DuPont was also responsible for placing synthetic petrochemical oil on the domestic consumer market. This further undercut demand for hemp as the synthetic petroleum was marketed as a cheap and effective substitute for hempseed oil (Herer 1998). The rise of fossil fuels and the petroleum industry had dire ramifications for hemp and, as the market share of kerosene and petroleum for lighting expanded in the 1930s, demand for industrial hemp and hempseed oil declined. Hempseed oil was also replaced in food production following the commercialization of margarine, which was first developed in France in the mid-nineteenth century as an alternative to butter. The market for margarine expanded in the first half of the twentieth century after purified beef fat, the principal but expensive ingredient in early margarine, was replaced by hydrogenating oils. First patented in 1903, these vegetable-based oils made margarine manufacture cheaper, with low costs driving the expansion of the sector.

Hemp was also sidelined by the growth and industrialization of wood pulp-based paper manufacture after the American inventor Charles Fenerty made the first paper from wood fibres in 1838. By the end of the nineteenth century, advances in pulp paper technologies meant that it was timber-based paper and not hemp paper that was serving the massively expanding market for toilet paper, newsprint, wallpaper and corrugated paper products.

The quest for sustained hemp use Attempts were made to reverse hemp's decline. The Chemurgy Group of engineers and scientists that included Henry Ford, Thomas Edison and George Washington Carver were deeply hostile to the rise and use of non-renewable resources because of their impact on the environment and agriculture, and also because they increased US reliance on foreign suppliers. The Chemurgy group developed the manufacture of hemp-based fibre, bio-plastic, paints and lubricants by combining agriculture and organic chemistry and pioneered research into hemp-based biomass alternatives to fossil fuels through a process called pyrolysis. This involved the burning of the hemp plant pulp and its processing into petroleum, methanol, methane and charcoal (Anex 2003; Herer 1998; Roulac 1997; Shurtleff and Aoyagi 1997).

The Chemurgy group also resolved the intractable problem of high labour costs in the harvesting and processing of hemp when George Schlichten patented the decorticator in 1916. The machine mechanically separated the hemp fibres, leaving the pulp behind. This slashed processing costs and labour input. With the invention of the decorticator, paper-making costs could be halved and it was estimated that for each acre of land turned over to hemp, 5 acres of forest would be conserved. The enormous potential benefits for the hemp-pulp industry after the invention of the decorticator were emphasized in the journal *Popular Mechanics*, which in a 1938 issue referred to hemp as a 'new billion dollar crop' (Herer 1998; Roulac 1997). The article went to press two months after legislation controlling hemp cultivation in the USA was introduced.

The political causes of hemp's decline

By the 1930s, hemp processing had advanced significantly and appeared to be enjoying a reversal of fortunes. This was stifled and rolled back as a result of political factors. In 1937 the Marihuana Tax Act was introduced in the USA. This required manufacturers, importers and distributors of cannabis to register with the federal authorities. Transactions had to be detailed on compulsory order forms, with a tax of $1 per ounce imposed for the transfer of the plant to registered people and $100 per ounce to those not registered. There was no distinction in the legislation between cannabis (resin and herb) and industrial hemp (Bonnie and Whitebread 1999).

The Federal Bureau of Narcotics, which assumed responsibility for enforcement of the Act, was zealous in its enforcement of the controls in hemp producing states (Bonnie and Whitebread 1999; Herer 1998; Roulac 1997). The legislation and resulting bureaucracy and taxation crippled the hemp industry, even though it did not prevent individual states from licensing hemp production. The legislation also undermined investor confidence in the new hemp-related technologies that were being developed.

The failure to distinguish between the different types of cannabis in the legislation was subsequently carried into the international drug conventions and the domestic laws of signatory states. As with coca, cultivation and production were permitted in some countries but only when strictly controlled. Even after THC was identified in 1964, providing empirical evidence of the distinction between hemp and cannabis, national drug laws and the international conventions did not revise the scope of the controls. On the contrary, the national laws in many European and English-speaking countries increased the criminal penalties for cannabis cultivation, production, distribution and use after the 'war on drugs' was declared by President Nixon in 1968 and domestic laws were modified in line with the 1961 Single Convention on Narcotic Drugs.

TABLE 16.1 Hemp: world harvested area, 1948–97 (average thousands of hectares per period)

Period	Hectares
1948–52	1,085
1961–65	633
1974–76	562
1985–88	385
1989–91	198
1992–94	145
1995–97 (estimated)	130

Source: FAO cited in Mignoni (1997)

The hemp conspiracy The early inclusion of hemp in the international drug conventions and national drug legislation can be attributed to ignorance. THC had not been identified at this time and so the failure to distinguish between a psychoactive and non-psychoactive plant can be understood as an unfortunate mistake that came at a grave cost to the hemp industry. There is, however, an alternative explanation. In the view of some critics, the controls imposed on hemp were motivated by the economic interests of a politically powerful and inter-connected group of interests in the USA that had invested heavily in new technology and resource sectors. From this perspective, hemp posed a threat to the commercial viability of these interests and it was consequently the victim of a conspiracy that sought to eliminate the hemp industry through the 1937 Marihuana Tax Act (Roulac 1997; Herer 1998).

The inception and progress of the 1937 legislation was quite extraordinary. Finance and narcotics officials drew up the Marihuana Tax Act in a highly secretive manner and this prompted the American Medical Association to criticize the Treasury Department for drafting the bill 'without any intimation, even to the profession, that it was being prepared' (Bonnie and Whitebread 1999). Limited evidence was taken and congressional scrutiny of the bill was negligible. The damaging social effects of cannabis use constituted the principal justification for the legislation yet the findings of three major inquiries into cannabis use – the Indian Hemp Drugs Commission (1893–94), the Panama Canal Zone Report (1925) and the 1938 La Guardia Commission – were ignored.

The timing of the legislation is acutely significant from the conspiracy perspective. The petrochemical, wood pulp paper and synthetic fibre manufacturing sectors had gained market dominance over hemp-based products by the first decade of the twentieth century. Major and on-going investments had been made by leading economic groups as they sought to consolidate their position, reduce production costs and expand the mass market for manufactured products and energy produced from non-renewable resources. In the timber sector, for example, the media owner William Randolph Hearst and his Hearst Paper Manufacturing Division, Kimberly Clark, had collaborated with DuPont to develop chemical pulping with sulphate. The process, which stripped the woody glue from timber fibres, was patented by DuPont in 1937. It vastly reduced costs in the pulp paper industry, allowing the sector to shift away from the expensive process of mechanized pulping. The introduction of Schlichten's decorticator and advances made in the mechanization of hemp harvesting in the 1930s threatened to undercut wood pulp paper production costs. Progress in hemp technologies would consequently have posed a major financial and commercial challenge, not only to the chemical and paper industries, but also to the petrochemical and synthetic fibre sectors.

The lobby groups that cohered around the architect of the Marihuana Tax Act, Herman Oliphant, are significant as they corresponded directly with these interests. DuPont executives gave secret evidence to Oliphant during the development of the legislation and advised him on commercial and marketing issues. The chief financing for the DuPont projects came from the Mellon Bank of Pittsburgh and this included funding for DuPont's purchase of a controlling share of General Motors, a key competitor to Henry Ford of the pro-hemp Chemurgy Group in 1920. Mellon Bank also financed the expansion of the wood pulp and timber industry. Andrew Mellon himself had served as Secretary of the Treasury during the presidency of Herbert Hoover and, while in office, Mellon appointed Harry Anslinger to the post of head of the Federal Bureau of Narcotics. Anslinger was married to Andrew Mellon's niece. Evidence that DuPont had an 'inside track' on Treasury policy in the run-up to the introduction of the Marihuana Tax Act is found in the 1937 company report. In this, DuPont encouraged investors to keep faith in the firm's new synthetic, petrochemical products, particularly as 'radical changes' in government policy were to be expected. In the words of the report, the revenue-raising powers of government were to be 'converted into an instrument for forcing acceptance of sudden new ideas of industrial and social reorganization' (Herer 1998).

Anslinger had a solid working relationship with William Randolph Hearst and, as discussed in Chapter 3, FBN officials fed sensational stories of cannabis-related acts of violence to Hearst's papers, which in turn campaigned vigorously in favour of the cannabis restrictions promoted by Anslinger and mobilized public support for the legislation. From the hemp conspiracy perspective, control of cannabis stemmed from domestic commercial lobbies in the USA and not the 'moral entrepreneurs' of prohibition.

HEMP FOR VICTORY! One of the great and often recounted ironies of the legislative move against hemp in the USA during this period was that the USA was forced radically to revise its position on the crop less than five years later, at the height of the Second World War. Following the Japanese Imperial Army's invasion of the Philippines, strategically important supplies of Manila hemp to the US navy were cut off. In response, the US Department of Agriculture promoted a mass hemp cultivation campaign. Central to this was the 1942 film *Hemp for Victory*. After glorifying the historical contribution of hemp to US economic development and instructing farmers on growing techniques and how to obtain permits for cultivation, the film concluded with a patriotic rallying cry to all Americans to produce hemp:

> This is Manila hemp from the Navy's rapidly dwindling reserves. When it is gone, American hemp will go on duty again; hemp for mooring ships; hemp for tow lines; hemp for tackle and gear; hemp for countless naval uses both on ship and shore. Just as in the days when Old Ironsides sailed the seas victorious with her hempen shrouds and hempen sails. Hemp for victory. (Transcript, USDA *Hemp for Victory*)

An estimated 60,000 tons of cannabis had been destroyed annually in the USA following the introduction of the 1937 legislation (Davenport Hines 2001: 277). Over 300,000 acres of hemp were planted during the Hemp for Victory campaign. With the conclusion of the war in 1945 all permits were rescinded, criminal penalties reimposed and enforcement stepped up. The last hemp harvest in the USA was carried out in the 1950s.

The contemporary hemp revolution

After decades of decline and criminalization, industrial hemp is enjoying an unexpected rebirth. Starting with France in 1982, European countries have amended existing legislation in order to decouple hemp and cannabis. Spain reintroduced hemp cultivation in 1986 and by 2005 eleven other Western European countries were participating in the European Union hemp harvest. Hemp production in the former communist countries of Romania, Poland, Hungary, Russia and the Balkan states also resumed after a sustained decline after the Second World War, while Canada and Australia introduced regulated hemp production in the second half of the 1990s. In 2005, thirty-three countries were producing hemp, with the commercial expansion of the $5.5 million per annum industry (Hoffman 1998) taking place within the framework of strict licensing controls that varied from country to country.

Accounting for the hemp renaissance The enormous interest in hemp is attributed to a number of factors, the most important of which is popular concern over ecological issues and demand for environmentally sound products made from renewable and sustainable resources. Hemp has supplied a growing market for natural fibres and textiles that are produced without the use of chemicals and pesticides. Hemp jeans, hemp knitwear, hemp bedding and hemp bags are durable, long-lasting and increasingly popular as production technologies have been refined and the softness of the product enhanced.

The second major growth area for hemp has been in paper production and this has been driven by resource and security concerns related to wood pulp paper. Global consumption of wood-based paper has surged over the past twenty years, growing at an unsustainable rate of 3 per cent per year. Timber resources are not considered adequate given the scale of market demand, and recycling has made only a minor contribution to the overall preservation of timber stocks. Moreover, recycled wood pulp paper is of low quality and its lack of resistance to mechanization processes means that it cannot be used in the production of cardboard or other forms of packaging. Aside from the destruction of timber, pulp paper production has a further environmental cost stemming from the use of dioxins and other toxic chemicals in pulp and paper processing.

In the context of a chronic deficit in wood pulp, rising demand for paper and concerns over the environmental costs of wood pulp paper production, interest in the use of paper manufactured from hemp has surged. This has been reinforced by security concerns based on the fear that diminishing forestry reserves will ultimately be monopolized by timber cultivating countries, to the detriment of states with limited forestry resources. Wood pulp paper is also expensive to purchase and has to be paid for in hard currency on the international market. This will make paper increasingly inaccessible to developing countries, with ramifications for book and newspaper use, manufacturing capacity and resource dependence of these states on the developed world. In this context, the expansion of hemp production and processing in the developed world would open up the possibility of national textile and paper production in these countries in addition to cost savings on imported manufactured goods and paper from industrialized nations.

A note on hemp

It was concerns over the dependence of European countries on external and predominantly US textile and fibre imports that initially led the EU to develop hemp production as part of a policy of diversifying farming in the late 1960s. A 10 per cent subsidy was provided to hemp farmers to encourage production and this was reduced to 7.5 per cent in 1998 as the sector developed. In order to qualify for the subsidy and be licensed for hemp production, farmers are required to purchase seeds listed on an EU register that have a THC content of less than 0.3 per cent. Current investment in research aims to develop a hemp strain with zero THC. As a result of these policies, there has been a large increase in the area of hemp harvested in the EU, which has risen from 5,840 hectares in the period 1980–82 to 15,233 for 1995–97 (Mignoni 1997).

The high price of oil, dependence on overseas suppliers that are typically fragile or unstable states, and dwindling reserve levels have enhanced interest in the development of environmentally friendly, domestically manufactured energy alternatives to fossil fuels, and this includes hemp. Hemp-based biomass fuels are free from metals and sulphur and burning them does not increase carbon dioxide levels in the atmosphere so they do not contribute to pollution or the greenhouse effect. For supporters of hemp, a future of cars powered on pressed hempseed oil is an increasingly viable possibility. The potential contribution of hemp-based products to industry and cosmetics are also increasingly recognized, with the market for hemp-based concrete, insulation material, bio-plastic, composite board, animal bedding, shampoo and soap expanding worldwide.

A further growth area for hemp-based products is the food, beverages and nutritional supplement sector. The health value of hempseed oil, while long acknowledged by scientists and botanists, is now increasingly recognized by the public. Concerns over nutritional deficiency, obesity and rising cancer rates linked to the consumption of heavily processed and fatty foods, particularly in industrialized countries, has translated into an expansion of the market for a vast range of hempseed and seed oil-based products rich in polyunsaturated fatty acids. Hemp sodas, hemp ice cream, hemp bread, hemp chips, hemp beer, hemp pasta and hemp bars count among the list of new hemp-based products.

A final factor that has promoted interest in hemp relates specifically to the commercial interests of the agricultural sector. The declining profitability of grain and vegetable crops combined with efforts by national governments to reduce tobacco smoking and consequently tobacco crops has increased the importance of hemp as a commodity in itself; as a rotational crop; and as a substitute for tobacco. Hemp production is being widely promoted by hemp and farming lobbies as a means of reversing rural decline. As an example of this trend the New Zealand Hemp Industries Association produced the *Five Minute Guide to Industrial Hemp* as part of its campaign for regulated hemp trials similar to those introduced in Australia in 1997. According to the *Guide*, hemp could fetch $1,000 to $10,000 per hectare, three times the value of other crops.

Although it is acknowledged that hemp will remain a niche sector dominated by small and medium enterprises, the growth potential continues to drive interest in the crop.

The US position America is the only industrialized country in the world that continues to block hemp farming. The continued prohibition of a domestic hemp industry has led to mobilized protests from US farmers and legal challenges to the Drug Enforcement Administration and Office of National Drug Control Policy position that hemp legalization would signal the de facto legalization of cannabis. Officials from the DEA and ONDCP have directly linked the campaigns for hemp and cannabis legalization, with the former presented as a subterfuge or 'Trojan horse' for the latter.

In an attempt to deflect these allegations, the key hemp lobby groups, such as the North American Industrial Hemp Council, have distanced themselves from the cannabis legalization movement and drafted celebrity endorsers including politician Ralph Nader, actor Woody Harrelson and the former head of the CIA James Woolsey to support the hemp campaign. The potential value of hemp to depressed rural areas and recognition of the distinction between cannabis and hemp have led state authorities in North Dakota, Virginia, Hawaii, Idaho, Illinois, Minnesota, Montana, New Mexico, Wisconsin and Vermont to authorize or examine the possibility of authorizing hemp production. However, as the DEA has responsibility for licensing, limited progress has been made in developing a regulated US hemp sector. In 2000, the DEA issued the first and only licence for hemp trials since the 1950s for small-scale experiments in Hawaii. Underscoring the complexity of the US position, hemp-based products can be imported into America, either as finished articles or for further manufacture, a situation that US farmers argue discriminates against and disadvantages them in the international market.

Aside from its objections to industrial hemp on law enforcement and public health grounds, federal authorities in the USA have rejected the argument that the crop is economically viable and potentially lucrative. The ONDCP has argued that cheaper alternatives to hemp exist and that the potential market is overestimated by agricultural lobby groups. Further to this, the USA is not seen to have a comparative advantage in hemp production, particularly given the competition from countries like China that have low labour and production costs.

Conclusion

The hemp issue poses a major dilemma for international and national drug control regimes. It underscores the extent to which drug control was built on pseudo-science, insufficient empirical inquiry and vested economic interests. That the distinctions between hemp and cannabis were recognized over thirty years ago and yet the conventions and many national laws still do not reflect this, underscores the rigidity and arcane nature of the control system. Countries have fractured on the issue of legalization and, as a result, growth of the international market will be constrained. Without a revision of hemp controls at the international level, legitimate hemp producers will continue to face marketing obstacles and the possibility of criminal sanction.

As an example of the current confusing state of hemp controls, the Body Shop inadvertently risked prosecution on drug-related offences in Sweden and Hong Kong for marketing hemp-based lotions in 1998. Hemp is still classified with cannabis as an illegal drug in both countries. In Canada, farmers have launched writs against the DEA after the seizure of hemp-based products such as birdseed, on the grounds that this violates the North American Free Trade Agreement that prohibits restrictions on trade between Canada, the USA and Mexico. Commercial pressures have contained efforts by federal authorities in the USA to curb the market for hemp-based foods and, in a landmark ruling in 2004, a San Francisco Federal Appeal Court found that the DEA did not have the authority to seize hemp-based products. By retaining the prohibition of hemp in the context of globalization, economic change and scientific progress, the USA and the UN have undermined the credibility of the control system.

By way of a conclusion

It is essential that the international community confronts the crisis of the current drug control model. To fail to do so would be a negation of duty and it would have potentially catastrophic implications for human health, human security and also global political stability. Unless a way is found of eliminating the profit motive in the drug trade, the problems and policy dilemmas that are currently being experienced will persist and deepen. Increasing levels of repression and accelerating the application of current control strategies have been shown not to work and it is a testament to the lack of democracy and transparency in drug policy formulation that this situation has been able to continue.

There are powerful political and financial vested interests in the current system but these have to be addressed and removed if the dangers posed by harmful drugs are to be confronted. This book has shown that the USA is the key player in international drug policy. Until US drugs policy and US foreign policy are decoupled, no progress can be made in revising drug laws so that they are in touch with contemporary realities. The USA has gained institutional control of the drug policy agenda and this has chronically limited the space for debate, revision and revitalization of the policy agenda. In this context, the largest obstacle to change and progress is the ideology of prohibition. This has to be recognized as an arcane and discredited principle and jettisoned in favour of more pluralistic ideas and approaches.

Drug policy options are usually understood as a choice between the current prohibition-based system and complete legalization. Between these two options there is a middle ground of regulation. There is a broad and on-going debate as to whether legalization or regulation would reduce the problems caused by current strategies and allow for progress in the campaign to reduce the harm caused by some drugs. The current regulatory system that limits access to alcohol and tobacco, stimulants responsible for more violence, addiction and death than drugs, is usually cited as the way forward. However, current debates and evaluations of policy options have tended to be framed with reference to national politics. This is problematic because the international community has to negotiate the way ahead collectively. Because of the trans-national nature of the drugs industry, it will be impossible for diffuse and fragmented drug policy frameworks to emerge. It is therefore difficult to state what the future of drug policy should be, as the optimal model needs to reflect national experiences and national judgements.

Nation-states are currently limited in their capacity to shape their drug policies, despite the enormous divergence in national drug experiences. There is no space to debate or trial new options, while current policy responses have been shown to be counter-productive and limited in imagination. Globalization, free trade and neoliberalism have made the old drug control model redundant and anachronistic. Adapting to modernity will require a change of revolutionary proportions. This will be fiercely resisted, but without an overhaul of founding principles, institutions and vested interests, the international community will continue to waste millions of dollars and ruin millions of lives in the pursuit of an unrealizable end.

Bibliography

Abdelnour, Z. (2001) 'The Revival of Lebanon's Drug Trade', *Middle East Intelligence Bulletin*, Vol. 6, no. 3.

Abel, E. (1980) *Marijuana, the First Twelve Thousand Years*. New York: Phenum Press.

Abraham, M. (1999) 'Places of Drug Purchase in the Netherlands', Tenth Annual Conference on Drug Use and Drug Policy, Vienna. <www.cedro-uva. org/lib/abraham.places.pdf>.

Abramson, H. (ed.) (1967) *The Use of LSD in Psychotherapy and Alcoholism*. New York: Bobbs-Merrill.

Adams, E. and N. Kozel (eds) (1985) 'Cocaine Use in America, Introduction and Overview', Rockville, MD: National Institute on Drug Abuse.

Addison, T., P. Le Billon and S. Murshed (2001) 'Conflict in Africa: The Cost of Peaceful Behaviour', United Nations University, Discussion Paper No. 2001/51 <http://www.wider.unu.edu/ publications/dps/dp2001-51.pdf>.

Adler, F. (1898) 'The Parting of the Ways in the Foreign Policy of the United States', *International Journal of Ethics*, October.

Allen, C. (1981) 'To be Quechua: The Symbolism of Coca Chewing in Highland Peru', *American Ethnologist*, Vol. 8, pp. 157–71.

Álvarez, M. (2002) 'Forests in the Time of Violence: Conservation Implications of the Colombian War'. <www.columbia. edu/%7Emda2001/>.

Amatangelo, G. (2001) 'A First Step Toward Reform of the Drug Certification Process', *Cross Currents: Washington and the Americas*, Vol. 10, no. 2.

Amirkhanian, Y., J. Kelly and D. Issayev (2001) 'AIDS Knowledge, Attitudes and Behaviour in Russia: Results of a Population-based, Random-digit Telephone Survey in St. Petersburg', *International Journal of STD and AIDS*, vol. 12, no. 1, pp. 50–7.

Amnesty International (2001) 'Bolivia: Chapare–Human Rights Cannot be Eradicated Along with the Coca Leaf', International Press Release, 25 October.

Andersen, S. and V. Berridge (2000) 'Opium in Twentieth Century Britain: Pharmacists, Regulations and the People', *Addiction*, Vol. 95, pp. 23–36.

Anderson, A. (1998) 'Let's be Adult About This', *New Scientist*, 21 February.

Anderson, P. (1981) *High in America: The True Story Behind NORML and the Politics of Marijuana*. New York: Viking Press.

Andreae, P. (1915) *The Prohibition Movement in Its Broader Bearings upon Our Social, Commercial, and Religious Liberties*. Chicago, IL: Felix Mendelsohn.

Andreas, P. (1998) 'The Political Economy of Narco-corruption in Mexico', *Current History*, no. 97, pp. 160–5.

Anex, R. (2003) 'Something New Under the Sun: The Industrial Ecology of Biobased Products, *Journal of Industrial Ecology*, Vol. 7, no. 3–4.

Anslinger, H. (1937) 'Marijuana: Assassin of Youth', *American Magazine*, Vol. 24, no. 1. <www.redhousebooks.com/ galleries/assassin.htm>.

Anslinger, H. and W. Tompkins (1953) *The Traffic in Narcotics*. New York: Funk and Wagnalls.

Archibald, C., D. Reid, Y. Choudri and S. Cule (2003) 'HIV Among Injecting Drug Users and Spread to the General Population: Putting the Cart Before the Horse', *International Journal of Drug Policy*, Vol. 14, no. 11, pp. 75–8.

Armstead, L. (1992) 'Illicit Narcotics Cultivation and Processing: The Ignored

Environmental Drama', *Bulletin on Narcotics*, no. 2, pp. 9–20.

Arthur, C. (1998) 'UK: Cannabis Campaign: Report Boost for Cannabis', *Independent*, 18 February.

Asbury, H. (1950) *The Great Illusion: An Informal History of Prohibition*. New York: Doubleday.

— (2002) *The Barbary Coast: An Informal History of the San Francisco Underworld*. New York: Thunder's Mouth Press.

Ashley, R. (1975) *Cocaine, Its History, Uses and Effects*. New York: Warner Books.

Ashton, R. (2002) *This is Heroin*. London: Sanctuary.

Astorga, L. (2004) 'Mexico: Drugs and Politics', in M. Vellinga (ed.), *The Political Economy of the Drug Industry: Latin America and the International System*. Tampa: University of Florida Press.

Austin, G. (1979) *Perspectives on the History of Psychoactive Substance Use*. Rockville, MD: National Institute on Drug Abuse.

Austin Kerr, K. (ed.) (1973) *The Politics of Moral Behavior: Prohibition and Drug Abuse*. Reading: Addison Wesley.

Baan Commission Report (1972) Werkgroep Verdovende Middelen, *Rapport van de Werkgroep Verdovende Middelen*. The Hague: Staatsuitgeverij.

Bagley, B. (ed.) (1994) *Drug Trafficking in the Americas*. Boulder, CO: Lynne Rienner.

Bagley, B., and J. Tokatlian (1992) 'Dope and Dogma: Explaining the Failure of US–Latin American Drug Policies', in J. Hartlyn, L. Schoultz and A. Varas (eds), *The US and Latin America in the 1990s – Beyond the Cold War*. Carolina: University of North Carolina Press.

Bailey, T. (ed.) (1968) *The American Spirit: United States History as Seen by Contemporaries, Vol. II*. Boston, MA: D.C. Heath.

Ballentine, K. and J. Sherman (eds) (2003) *The Political Economy of Armed Conflict: Beyond Greed and Grievance*. Boulder, CO: Lynne Rienner.

Barnett, A. and S. Hughes (2000) 'Plan Colombia; British Chemical Company ICI Pulls Out of Cocaine War', *Observer*, 1 July.

Barraclough, S. and K. Ghimire (2000) *Agricultural Expansion and Tropical Deforestation*. London: Earthscan Publications.

Bartz, D. (2000) 'U.S. Presses Colombia to Use Herbicide on Coca', *Reuters*, 25 July.

Bastos, I., M. de Fatima de Pina and C. Szwarcwald (2002) 'The Social Geography of HIV/Aids among Injection Drug Users in Brazil', *International Journal of Drug Policy*, Vol. 13, no. 2, pp. 137–44.

Bauer, L. and S. Owens (2004) 'Justice Expenditure and Employment in the United States, 2001'. Washington, DC: US Department of Justice, Bureau of Justice Statistics.

Baum, D. (1996) *Smoke and Mirrors: The War on Drugs and the Politics of Failure*. Boston, MA: Little, Brown.

Beck, J. (1998) '100 Years of "Just Say No" Versus "Just Say Know": Re-evaluating Drug Education Goals for the Coming Century', *Evaluation Review*, Vol. 22, no. 1.

Becker, G., M. Grossman and K. Murphy (1991) 'Rational Addiction and the Effect on Consumption', *American Economic Review*, Vol. 81, pp. 237–41.

Becker, H. (1963) *Outsiders; Studies in the Sociology of Deviance*. Glencoe: Free Press.

— (1992) 'Impact Evaluation of Drug Abuse Resistance Education (DARE)', *Journal of Drug Education*, Vol. 22, no. 4.

Beeching, J. (1975) *The Chinese Opium Wars*. London: Harcourt Brace Jovanovich.

Behr, E. (1996) *Prohibition: Thirteen Years that Changed America*. New York: Arcade Publishing.

Bell, S. (1998) 'Body Shop's Hemp Products Blow Up: A Storm in France', *The Times*, 28 August.

Berger, S. (1998) 'UK: Cannabis "Safer than Alcohol"', *Daily Telegraph*, 19 February.

Bergquist, C., R. Penaranda and G. Sanchez (eds) (2001) *Violence in Colombia 1990–2000: Waging War and Negotiating Peace*. Wilmington, DE: Scholarly Resources.

Berridge, V. (2001) 'Altered States: Opium and Tobacco Compared', *Social Research*, Fall.

Berridge V. and G. Edwards (1981) *Opium and the People: Opiate Use in Nineteenth Century England*. London: Allen Lane.

Bewley-Taylor, D. (2001) *The United States and International Drug Control, 1909–1997*. London: Continuum.

— (2003) 'Challenging the UN Drug Control Conventions: Problems and Possibilities', *International Journal of Drug Policy*, Vol. 14, pp. 171–9.

Bigwood, J. (2000) *'The Drug War's Fungal "Solution' in Latin America'*, Andean Seminar Lecture Series sponsored by GWU and WOLA. <www.jeremybigwood. net/Lectures/GWU-WOLA-JB/ GWUNov2000.htm>.

— (2001) 'Toxic Drift: Monsanto and the Drug War in Colombia', *CorpWatch.* <www.corpwatch.org/print_article. php?&id=669>.

— (2002) 'The Drug War's Fungal "Solution" in the Amazon', Society for the Anthropology of Lowland South America. Annapolis, Maryland, 8 June. <www.jeremybigwood.net/Lectures/ SALSA/Annapolis2002.htm>.

— (2003) 'The Toxic War on Drugs GM Crop Weed Killer Linked to Powerful Fungus', *Counterpunch.* <www. counterpunch.org/bigwood08232003. html>.

Bigwood, J. and S. Stevenson (2000) 'Drug Control or Bio Warfare?', *Mother Jones* website. <www.motherjones.com/news/ feature/2000/05/coca.html>.

Bing, L. (1992) *Do or Die: For the First Time, Members of America's Most Notorious Gangs – the Crips and the Bloods – Speak for Themselves*. New York: Perennial.

Bischke, P. (2003) 'Pleasure Drugs and Classical Virtues: Temperance and Abstinence in U.S. Religious Thought',

International Journal of Drug Policy, Vol. 14, pp. 273–8.

Blickman, T. and M. Jelsma (1998) 'Coca Fumigation Hinders Colombian Peace Negotiations', TNI Briefing Paper, November.

Blum, R. (1969) *Society and Drugs*. San Francisco, CA: Jossey-Bass.

Blumenson, E. and E. Nilsen (1998) 'The Drug War's Hidden Economic Agenda', *The Nation*, 9 March.

Boister, N. (2001) *Penal Aspects of the U.N. Drug Conventions*. The Hague, Boston and London: Kluwer Law International.

Bollini, P. (ed.) (2001) *HIV in Prisons: A Reader with Particular Relevance to the Newly Independent States*. Geneva: World Health Organization. <www.euro. who.int/document/E77016.pdf>.

Bonnie, R. and C. Whitebread (1999) *Marijuana Conviction: A History of Marijuana Prohibition in the United States*. New York: Lindesmith Center.

Booth, M. (1999) *Opium: A History*. New York: Thomas Dunne.

— (2004) *Cannabis: A History*. New York: Thomas Dunne.

Bouvier, M. (2001) *Whose America? The War of 1898 and the Battles to Define the Nation*. Virginia: Praeger.

Bradford (n.d.) *Bradford Project on Strengthening the Biological and Toxin Weapons Convention*. <www.brad.ac.uk/ acad/sB.T.W.C./other/bw-bradproj. htm>.

Bragg, R. (1999) 'Marijuana-Eating Fungus Seen as Potent Weapon, but at What Cost?', *New York Times*, 27 July.

Brauchli, C. (2001) 'Plan Colombia: US May be Wading into a Posionous Quagmire', *Boulder Daily Camera*, 24 February.

Brecher, E. and editors of *Consumer Reports Magazine* (1972) 'Consumers Union Report on Licit and Illicit Drugs'. <www.druglibrary.org/schaffer/Library/ studies/cu/cumenu.htm>.

Brereton, W. (1882) *The Truth about Opium*. London: Allen.

Brook, T. and B. Tadashi Wakabayashi

(eds) (2000) *Opium Regimes: China, Britain, and Japan, 1839–1952*, Berkeley: University of California Press.

Brown, J., G. Ita and G. Kreft (1998) 'Zero Effects of Drug Prevention Programs: Issues and Solutions', *Evaluation Review*, Vol. 22, no. 1.

Brown, K. and D. Pearce (1994) 'The Causes of Tropical Deforestation: The Economic and Statistical Analysis of Factors Giving Rise to the Loss of the Tropical Forests', Centre for Social and Economic Research on the Global Environment. London: UCL Press.

Bruun, K., L. Pan and I. Rexed (1975) *The Gentlemen's Club: International Control of Drugs and Alcohol*. Chicago, IL: University of Chicago Press.

Buergin, R. (2000) '"Hill Tribes" and Forests: Minority Policies and Resource Conflicts in Thailand', SEFUT Working Paper Series, no. 7. University of Freiburg.

Bulletin on Narcotics (1949) 'Opium Production Throughout the World', Vol. 1, no. 4.

— (1953) 'History of Heroin', Vol. 2, no. 3. Geneva: UNODC.

— (1956) 'The Paris Protokoll of 1948', Issue 1.

Bureau for International Narcotics and Law Enforcement Affairs (2003) 'Fact Sheet: Narcotics Certification Process FY 2003', Washington, DC.

Bureau of Western Hemisphere Affairs, US Department of State (2001) *The Aerial Eradication of Illicit Crops: Answers to Frequently Asked Questions on the Environment*. <www.drugwarfacts. org/environm.htm>.

Burke, J. (2004) 'British Troops Wage War on Afghan Drugs', *Observer*, 5 December.

Burnett, V. (2003) 'Afghan Opium Cultivates New Converts', *Boston Globe*, 17 August.

Burrows, D. and G. Alexander (2001) 'Walking on Two Legs: A Developmental and Emergency Response to HIV/AIDS among Young Drug Users in the CEE/ CIS/Baltics and Central Asia Region: A Review Paper', Geneva: UNICEF. <www. unicef.org/evaldatabase/index_14412. html>.

Buscaglia, E. and W. Ratliff (2001) 'War and Lack of Governance in Columbia: Narcos, Guerrillas, and U.S. Policy', *Essays in Public Policy*, no. 107. New York: Hoover Institute Press.

Butler, W. (2003) *HIV/AIDS and Drug Misuse in Russia: Harm Reduction Programmes and the Russian Legal System*. London: International Family Health.

Cashman, J. (1966) *The LSD Story*. Greenwich: Fawcett Publications.

Castle, D. and R. Murray (2004) *Marijuana and Madness: Psychiatry and Neurobiology*. Cambridge: Cambridge University Press.

Catania, H. (2004) 'Progressive Harm Reduction in Iran's Prisons', *Harm Reduction News*, Fall.

Catýn, T. (2003) 'Adviser Quits Over "Corruption" at U.N. Agency', *Financial Times*, 2 November.

Caulkins, J., C. Rydell, W. Schwabe and J. Chiesa (1997) *Mandatory Minimum Drug Sentences: Throwing Away the Key or the Taxpayers' Money?*. Santa Monica, CA: RAND Corporation.

Center for AIDS Prevention Studies, 'Does Needle Exchange Work?' University of California. <www.epibiostat.ucsf. edu/capsweb/needletext.html>.

Centre for International Policy's Colombia Programme (2002) 'Impacts in Ecuador of Fumigations in Putumayo as Part of Plan Colombia', Report on Verification Mission. <www.ciponline.org/colombia/02121301.htm>.

Centre for International Policy's Colombia Project (n.d.) 'DynCorp in Colombia'. <www.ciponline.org/colombia/dyncorp. htm>.

Chamorro, S. Pimiento and E. Hammond (2003) 'Addressing Environmental Modification in Post-Cold War Conflict', Sunshine Project/Edmonds Institute. <www.edmonds-institute.org/pimiento. htm>.

Chase Eldridge, D. (1998) *Ending the War on Drugs: A Solution for America*. New York: Bridge Works Publishing.

Chatterjee, S. (1988) *A Guide to the International Drugs Conventions*. London: Commonwealth Secretariat.

Chaudhury, S. (2003) *From Prosperity to Decline: Eighteenth Century Bengal*. Delhi: Manohar Publishers.

Chillier, G. and L. Freeman (2005) 'Potential Threat: The New OAS Concept of Hemispheric Security', Washington Office on Latin America Special Report.

Chouvy, P. (2003) 'Myanmar's War: Likely Losers in the Opium War', *Asia Times*, 24 November.

Claridge, D. and D. Diehl (2002) *A Spy for All Seasons: My Life in the CIA*. New York: Scribner's.

Clark, N. (1976) *Deliver Us from Evil: An Interpretation of American Prohibition*. London: W. W. Norton.

Clawson, P. and L. Rensselaer (1999) *The Andean Cocaine Industry*. London: Palgrave Macmillan.

Clutterbuck, R. (1995) *Drugs, Crime and Corruption: Thinking the Unthinkable*. New York: New York University Press.

Coffman, T. (2003) *Nation Within: The Story of America's Annexation of the Nation of Hawaii*. Hawaii: EpiCenter.

Cohen, P. (1990) 'Drugs as a Social Construct', Dissertation, University of Amsterdam.

— (1999) 'Shifting the Main Purposes of Drug Control: From Suppression to Regulation of Use', *International Journal of Drug Policy*, Vol. 10, pp. 223–34.

— (2003a) 'Bewitched, Bedevilled, Possessed and Addicted: Dissecting Historic Constructions of Suffering and Exorcism', London UKHR Conference, March. Amsterdam: Cedro.

— (2003b) 'The Drug Prohibition Church and the Adventure of Reformation', *International Journal of Drug Policy*, Vol. 14, pp. 213–15.

Cole, J. (1999) 'Religious Dissidence and Urban Leadership: Bahais in Qajar Shiraz and Tehran', *Journal of the British Institute of Persian Studies*, Vol. 37, pp. 123–42.

Collier, P. and A. Hoeffler (1999) 'Justice-Seeking and Loot-Seeking in Civil War', World Bank, Development Research Group, mimeo.

— (2001) 'Greed and Grievance in Civil War'. Washington, DC: World Bank, October.

Colombian Ministry of National Defence (2002) 'Environmental Damages of Narcotrafficking: Executive Summary', Bogota, April. <www.mindefensa.gov.co/derechos_humanos/medio_ambiente/200204environmental_damages_narcotrafficking.htm>.

Commonwealth Department of Health and Ageing (2002) 'Return on Investment in Needle and Syringe Programs in Australia'. Canberra: Department of Health and Ageing. <www.health.gov.au/pubhlth/publicat/hac.htm>.

Constable, N. (2002) *This is Cocaine*. London: MPG Books.

Cooely, J. (1999) *Unholy Wars: Afghanistan, America and International Terrorism*. London: Pluto Press.

Courtwright, D. (1982) *Dark Paradise: Opiate Addiction in America Before 1940*. Cambridge, MA: Harvard University Press.

— (2002) *Forces of Habit*. Cambridge, MA: Harvard University Press.

Cox, C. (1995) 'Glyphosate, Part 2: Human Exposure and Ecological Effects', *Journal of Pesticide Reform*, Vol. 15.

Craig, R. (1978) 'La Campana Permanente: Mexico's Antidrug Campaign', *Journal of International Studies and World Affairs*, Vol. 20, no. 2, pp. 107–31.

Cropper, M. and C. Griffiths (1994) 'The Interaction of Population Growth and Environmental Quality', *Population Economics*, Vol. 84, no. 2, pp. 250–4.

Cushman, J. (1998) 'Subterfuge for Legalization', *New York Times*, 22 March.

Dale Scott, P. (1996) *Deep Politics and the Death of J.F.K.* Berkeley: University of California Press.

Bibliography

— (1998) *Cocaine Politics: Drugs, Armies and the CIA in Central America*. Berkeley: University of California Press.

— (2003) *Drugs, Oil, and War: The United States in Afghanistan, Colombia, and Indochina*. Lanham, MD: Rowan and Littlefield.

— (n.d.) *The Official Story: What the CIA Has Admitted About the CIA Ties to Drug Traffickers*, Drug Policy Project. Institute for Policy Studies.

Davenport Hines, R. (2001) *The Pursuit of Oblivion: A History of Narcotics, 1500–2000*. London: Weidenfeld and Nicolson.

Decorte, T. (2000) *The Taming of Cocaine. Cocaine Use in European and American Cities*. Brussels: VUB University Press.

Deferne, J. and D. Pate (1996) 'Hemp Seed Oil: A Source Oil; A Source of Valuable Essential Fatty Acid', *Journal of the International Hemp Association*, Vol. 3, no. 1.

Degenhardt, L., W. Hall and M. Lynskey (2003) 'Testing Hypotheses About the Relationship Between Cannabis Use and Psychosis', *Journal of Drug Alcohol Dependency*, Vol. 71, no. 1, pp. 37–48.

Dehne, K. (2001) 'Letter to the Editor: The Emerging AIDS Crisis in Russia: Review of Enabling Factors and Prevention Needs', *International Journal of STD and AIDS*, Vol. 12.

Dehne, K., and Y. Kobyshcha (2000) *The HIV Epidemic in Central and Eastern Europe Update 2000*. Geneva: UNAIDS.

Dehne, K., L. Khodakevich, F. Hamers and B. Schwartlander (1999) 'The HIV/AIDS Epidemic in Eastern Europe: Recent Patterns and Trends and Their Implications for Policy-making', *AIDS*, Vol. 13, no. 7, pp. 741–9.

Dehne, K., V. Pokrovsky, Y. Kobyshcha and B. Schwartlander (2000) 'Update on the Epidemics of HIV and Other Sexually Transmitted Infections in the Newly Independent States of the Former Soviet Union', *AIDS*, Vol. 14, Supplement 3.

De Quincey, T. (1982) *Confessions of an English Opium Eater*. London: Penguin Books.

DiNado, J. (1993) 'Law Enforcement, the Price of Cocaine and Cocaine Use', *Mathematical Modelling*, Vol. 17, pp. 53–64.

Dolin, B. (2001a) 'National Drug Policy: The Netherlands', Report Prepared for the Senate Special Committee on Illegal Drugs. Law and Government Division, Library of Parliament.

— (2001b) 'National Drug Policy: United States of America', Report Prepared for the Senate Special Committee on Illegal Drugs. Law and Government Division, Library of Parliament.

Dorabjee, J. and L. Samson (2000) 'A Multi-centre Rapid Assessment of Injecting Drug Use in India', *International Journal of Drug Policy*, Vol. 11, no. 1, pp. 99–112.

Dorado, M. (2002) 'Drug Smuggling into Europe: The Case of Colombian Drug Couriers', unpublished research, University of Oxford.

Douglass Fyr, J. (1993) 'The Dark Side of DARE', *Village Voice*, 29 July.

Dourojeanni, M. (1992) 'Environmental Impact of Coca Cultivation and Cocaine Production in the Amazon Region of Peru', *Bulletin on Narcotics*, Issue 2, pp. 37–53.

Dowdney, L. (2004) *Neither War nor Peace: International Comparisons of Children and Youth in Organised Armed Violence*. Brazil: Viva Rio.

Draft Supplement to the Environmental Impact Statements for Cannabis Eradication in the Contiguous United States and Hawaii. Washington, DC: US Government Printing Office.

Du Pont, R. and E. Voth (1995) 'Drug Legalization, Harm Reduction, and Drug Policy', *Annals of Internal Medicine*, Vol. 123, issue 6. <www.annals.org/cgi/content/full/123/6/461>.

Earth Erowid (2003) 'The (Pseudo-)Science of the War on Drugs and the Recent Ricaurte Error'. <www.erowid.org/chemicals/mdma/mdma_research5.shtml>.

Easterbrook, M. (2001) 'Plan Colombia: Government Study Raises Doubts on

Washington's Drug-Fighting Strategy', *Associated Press*, 3 September.

Economist, The (1999) 'High in the Heartland', 4 February.

— (2001a) 'Nervous Spring', 25 January.

— (2001b) 'Spraying Misery', 19 April.

— (2001c) 'Surfeit of Pills in Thailand', 26 April.

— (2001d) 'Choose Your Poison: Who Uses Drugs, and Why', 26 July.

— (2001e) 'Big Business: The Risks are High – But So are the Rewards', 26 July.

— (2001f) 'Marching Back: Thailand's Armed Forces Show Signs of Reasserting Themselves', 6 September.

— (2002a) 'Drugs in the Andes: Spectres Stir in Peru', 14 February.

— (2002b) 'Tajikistan: Wars and Shadows of Wars', 25 July.

— (2002c) 'It's All in the Price', 26 July.

— (2003a) 'The Andean Drug Industry: The Balloon Goes Up', 6 March.

— (2003b) 'The Afghan Plague', 24 July.

— (2003c) 'Drugs and the Heartland: You Take the High Road', 27 November.

— (2004) 'Adriatic Crossing', 11 March.

Edwards, S. (2003) 'Ecuador. Illicit Drug Control Policies and Prisons: The Human Cost'. Washington, DC: Office on Latin America.

Eicher, A. (1996) 'Injecting Drug Use and HIV Risks in Churachandpur Town, Manipur State, North-east India', Abstract no. Pub.C.1175, XI International Conference on AIDS, Vancouver, Canada.

Embassy of Colombia (1998) *White Paper on Narcotics Control*. Washington, DC.

EMCDDA (European Monitoring Centre for Drugs and Drug Addiction) (2001) 'Decriminalisation in Europe? Recent Developments in Legal Approaches to Drug Use'. <eldd.emcdda.org/>.

Environmental Health Perspectives (1999) Vol. 107, no. 2.

Environmental Law Institute (1998) 'Addressing Environmental Consequences of War', Washington, DC.

Epstein, E. (1977) *Agency of Fear: Opiates and Political Power in America*. New York: G. P. Putnam and Sons.

Escohotado, A. (1999) *A Brief History of Drugs*. Vermont: Park Street Press.

Fazey, C. (2003) 'The Commission on Narcotic Drugs and the United Nations International Drug Control Programme: Politics, Policies and Prospect for Change', *International Journal of Drug Policy*, Vol. 14, pp. 155–69.

Feacham, R. (1995) *Valuing the Past, Investing in the Future: Evaluation of the National HIV/AIDS Strategy 1993–94 to 1995–96*. Canberra: Commonwealth of Australia.

Fearon, J. and D. Laitin (2003) 'Ethnicity, Insurgency, and Civil War', *American Political Science Review*, Vol. 97, pp. 75–90.

Fichtl, E. (2000) 'Washington's New Weapon in the War on Drugs', *Colombia Journal Online*, July. <www.colombiajournal.org/colombia21.htm>.

Fishel, J. (1995) 'Coca, Cocaine, Sicarios and Senderistas', in G. Turbiville (ed.), *Global Dimensions of High Intensity Crime and Low Intensity Conflict*. Chicago, IL: University of Chicago Press, Office of International Criminal Justice.

Fleischmann, A. (1998) 'Nutritional Benefits of Hemp Seeds', *Hemp Magazine*, May.

Flynn, D. and A. Giráldez (2002) 'Cycles of Silver: Global Economic Unity through the Mid-Eighteenth Century', *Journal of World History*, Vol. 13, no. 2, pp. 391–427.

Folch, C., J. Casabona and A. Esteve (2002) 'The Role of Injecting Drugs Users in the Heterosexual Transmission', XIV International AIDS Conference, Barcelona, Abstract Book, Vol. 1.

Fountain, J., H. Bartlett, P. Griffiths, M. Gossop, A. Boys and J. Strang (1999) 'Why Say No? Reasons Given by Young People for Not Using Drugs', *Addiction Research*, Vol. 7, no. 4, pp. 339–53.

Friedman, S., D. C. Des Jarlais, A. Neaigus,

A. Abdul-Quader, J. Sotheran, M. Sufian, S. Tross and D. Goldsmith (1989) 'AIDS and the New Drug Injector', *Nature*, Vol. 339.

Friedman, S., B. Jose, A. Neaigus, M. Goldstein, R. Curtis, G. Ildefonso, P. Mota and D. C. Des Jarlais (1994) 'Consistent Condom Use in Relationships Between Seropositive Injecting Drug Users and Sex Partners Who Do Not Inject Drugs', *AIDS*, Vol. 8, pp. 357–61.

Friedman, S., R. Furst, B. Jose, R. Curtis, A. Neaigus, D. C. Des Jarlais, M. Goldstein and G. Ildefonso (1998) 'Drug Scene Roles and HIV Risk', *Addiction*, Vol. 93, pp. 1403–1416.

Freud, S. (1994) *Über Coca*. Vienna: M. Perles.

Frost, L., D. Burrows and B. Murdo (2000) 'Rapid Situation Assessment (RSA) Results from the Russian Federation: Summary Report of 63 RSAs Conducted by Participants in Médecins Sans Frontières Harm Reduction Training Program in the Russian Federation, 1998–2000', 11th International Conference on the Reduction of Drug-related Harm, Jersey, UK.

Fruhling, H., J. Tulchin and H. Golding (2003) *Crime and Violence in Latin America: Citizen Security, Democracy, and the State*. Baltimore, MD: Woodrow Wilson Center Press and the Johns Hopkins University Press.

Gaffrey, A. (2003) Testimony Statement of Art Gaffrey, Forest Supervisor Sequoia National Forest, California Forest Service United States Department of Agriculture before the Subcommittee on Criminal Justice, Drug Policy and Human Resources Subcommittee on Energy Policy, Natural Resources and Regulatory Affairs Committee on Government Reform, United States House of Representatives on Drug Production on Public Lands. Three Rivers, California, 10 October.

Galen Carpenter, T. (1985) 'The U.S. Campaign Against International Narcotics Trafficking: A Cure Worse than the Disease', *Cato Policy Analysis*, no. 63.

— (2003) *Bad Neighbour Policy: Washington's Futile War on Drugs in Latin America*. London: Palgrave Macmillan.

Gamella, J. and M. Rodrigo Jiménez (2004) 'A Brief History of Cannabis Policies in Spain (1968–2003)', *Journal of Drug Issues*, Summer.

Gatto, C. (1999) 'European Drug Policy: Analysis and Case Studies', National Organization to Reform the Marijuana Laws (NORML) Foundation. <www.norml.org/index.cfm?Group_ID=4415>.

Gaughan, A. and P. Barton Hutt (2004) 'Harvey Wiley, Theodore Roosevelt, and the Federal Regulation of Food and Drugs'. Harvard Law School, Winter. <leda.law.harvard.edu/leda/data/654/Gaughan.html>.

Gedda, G. (2000) 'Colombia Tries New Drug Eradication', *Associated Press*, 7 July.

Gertz, B. (2002) 'Military Opposes Spraying Poppies', *Washington Times*, 25 March.

Gilbert, M. (2003) 'Drunk on Empire: Alcohol, Opium, the Indian National Congress and the Raj: 1891–1900', Paper presented at the conference Drugs and Empires: Narcotics, History and Modern Colonialism, Strathclyde University, April.

Gilbert Murdock, C. (1998) *Domesticating Drink: Women, Men, and Alcohol in America, 1870–1940*. Baltimore, MD: Johns Hopkins University Press.

Gillan, A. (2003) 'Bursting Point: The Drugs Mules Filling up UK Prisons', *Guardian*, 30 September.

Glaister, D. (2005) 'A Wilderness Overgrown with Dope and Danger', *Guardian*, 28 September.

Gollinger, E. (2004) *The Chavez Code*. Monroe, ME: Common Courage Press.

González Posso, D. (2000) 'Coca, Deforestation and Food Security in the Colombian Amazon Region', *Unasylva*, Issue 202.

Goode, E. and N. Ben Yehuda (1994) *Moral Panics: Social Construction of Deviance*. London: Blackwell.

Gootenberg, P. (ed.) (1999) *Cocaine: Global Histories*. London: Routledge.

Graham, B. (2004) 'U.S. Plans Assault on Afghan Heroin', *Washington Post*, 15 November.

Grassly, N., C. Lowndes, T. Rhodes, A. Judd, A. Renton and G. Garnett (2003) 'Modelling Emerging HIV Epidemics: The Role of Injecting Drug Use and Sexual Transmission in the Russian Federation, China and India', *International Journal of Drug Policy*, Vol. 14, pp. 25–43.

Gray, J. (2001) *Why Our Drug Laws Have Failed and What We Can Do About It*. Philadelphia, PA: Temple University Press.

Gray, M. (2000) *Drug Crazy: How We Got Into This Mess and How We Can Out of It*. New York: Random House.

Griffith, I. (1997) *Drugs and Security in the Caribbean: Sovereignty Under Siege*, University Park, PA: Penn State University Press.

Griffiths, P. and R. McKetin (2003) 'Developing a Global Perspective on Drug Consumption Patterns and Trends – the Challenge for Drug Epidemiology'. Vienna: UNODC.

Grinspoon, L. and J. Bakalar (1979) *Psychedelic Drugs Reconsidered*. New York: Basic Books.

Grund, J. (2001) 'A Candle Lit from Both Ends: The Epidemic of HIV Infection in Central and Eastern Europe', in K. McElrath (ed.), *HIV and AIDS: International Comparisons*. Westport, CT: Greenwood Press.

Gunder Frank, A. (1995) *Asian-Based World Economy 1400–1800: A Horizontally Integrative Macrohistory*. <www.hartford-hwp.com/archives/50/089.html>.

Gundry, J. (1890) *India's Opium Revenue: What It is and How It Should be Dealt With*. Society for the Suppression of the Opium Trade: Alexander P. S. King.

Gusfield, J. (1986) *Symbolic Crusade: Status Politics and the American Temperance Movement*. Champaign: University of Illinois Press.

Hamers, F., V. Batter, A. Downs, J. Alix, F. Cazein and J. Brunet (1997) 'The HIV Epidemic Associated with Injecting Drug Use in Europe: Geographic and Time Trends', *AIDS*, Vol. 11, no. 11, pp. 1365–774.

Harding, L. (2003) 'U.S. Helicopters in Secret Mission to Spray Afghanistan's Opium Fields', *Guardian*, 9 June.

Harding, W. and N. Zinberg (1977) 'The Effectiveness of the Subculture in Developing Rituals and Social Sanctions for Controlled Drug Use', in B. DuToit (ed.), *Drugs, Rituals and Altered States of Consciousness*. Rotterdam: A. A. Balkema.

Hargreaves, C. (1992) *Snowfields: The War on Cocaine in the Andes*. London: Zed Books.

Harrell, A. (1992) *Drugs, Crime, and Social Isolation: Barriers to Urban Opportunity*. Leinham, MD: University Press of America.

Hart, S. (1997) 'Beyond Greening: Strategies for a Sustainable World', *Harvard Business Review*, Vol. 75, no. 1.

Hartnol, R., U. Avico, F. Ingold, K. Lange, L. Lenke, A. O'Hare and A. de Roij-Motshagen (1989) 'A Multi-city Study of Drug Misuse in Europe', *Bulletin on Narcotics*, No. 41, Issues 1 and 2.

Haworth, A. (1982) 'A Preliminary Report on Self-reported Drug Use Among Students in Zambia', *Bulletin on Narcotics*, no. 3 and 4, Issue 34.

Hellin, J. and S. Higman (2003) *Feeding the Market: South American Farmers, Trade and Globalization*. London: Latin American Bureau.

Herer, J. (1998) *The Emperor Wears No Clothes: Hemp and the Marijuana Conspiracy*, SOS Freestock. Available to read on line <www.jackherer.com/>.

Hernandez, E., P. Lurie, N. Williams, K. Stafford and J. Rudy (1996) 'Needle Exchange Programs May Reduce Local Government Spending for Law Enforcement', XI International Conference on AIDS, Vancouver, Canada.

Herron, S. (2000) 'Ethnobotanical Crisis as

the US Government Attempts to Utilize Biowarfare to Unwisely Combat the War on Drugs', *Economic Botany Leaflet*.

Hill, H. (1973) 'Anti-Oriental Agitation and the Rise of Working-Class Racism', *Society*, Vol. 10, January–February.

Hillstrom, K. and L. Hillstrom (2003) *Latin America and the Caribbean: A Continental Overview of Environmental Issues*. ABC-CLIO.

Hitti, P. (1967) 'The Assassins', in G. Andrews and S. Vinkennog (eds), *The Book of Grass: An Anthology of Indian Hemp*. New York: Grove Press.

Hodgson, B. (2001) *In the Arms of Morpheus: The Tragic History of Laudanum, Morphine, and Patent Medicines*. New York: Firefly Books.

Hoffman, R. (1998) 'Hemp is Not Dope', *Farm Journal*, July/August.

Hogshire, J. (1998) 'The Drug War's Fungal Solution', *Covert Action Quarterly*, no. 64, June. (The full text of congressional debates on the subject can be read at <www. congress.gov/cgi-bin/bdquery/z?d105: HR04300:@@@L&summ2=m&>.)

— (2000) 'US Biological Roulette on Drugs', *Covert Action Quarterly*, no. 64.

Holland, J. (ed.) (2001) *Ecstasy: The Complete Guide. A Comprehensive Look at the Risks and Benefits of MDMA*. Maine: Park Street Press.

Holt, E. (1964) *The Opium Wars in China*. London: Putnam.

Holtgrave, D., S. Pinkerton, T. Jones, P. Lurie and D. Vlahov (1998) 'Cost and Cost-effectiveness of Increasing Access to Sterile Syringes and Needles as an HIV Prevention Intervention in the United States', *Journal of Acquired Immune Deficiency Syndromes and Human Retroviruses*, Vol. 18, Supplement 1.

Huang, C. (1998) 'Opium Trade: Social and Environmental Impacts', *Trade and Environmental Database (TED) Case Studies*, Vol. 8, no. 1.

Human Rights Watch (2000a) 'Key Recommendations from Punishment and Prejudice: Racial Disparities in the War on Drugs', Washington, DC: Human Rights Watch.

— (200b) 'Punishment and Prejudice: Racial Disparities in the War on Drugs', HRW Report, Vol. 12, no. 2. <www.hrw. org/reports/2000/usa>.

— (2002) 'Colombia: Terror from All Sides.' <hrw.org/backgrounder/ americas/colombia-table.pdf>.

— (2003) 'Fanning the Flames: How Human Rights Abuses are Fueling the Aids Epidemic in Kazakhstan', HRW Report, Vol. 15, no. 4.

Hunt, J. (1999) *The India–China Opium Trade in the Nineteenth Century*. Jefferson, NC McFarland.

Huntington Williams, E. (1914) 'Negro Cocaine "Fiends" New Southern Menace', *New York Times*, 8 February.

Hurst, P. (1990) *Rain Forest Politics: Ecological Destruction in South-east Asia*. London: Zed Books.

ICG (International Crisis Group) (2001) 'Central Asia: Drugs and Conflict', *Asia Report*, no. 25.

— (2003) 'Colombia: President Uribe's Democratic Security Policy', *Latin America Report*, no. 6. Bogotá/Brussels.

Ignatieff, M. (2003) 'A Mess of Intervention. Peacekeeping. Pre-emption. Liberation. Revenge. When Should We Send in the Troops?' *New York Times Magazine*, 7 September.

INCB (International Narcotics Control Board) (1995a) 'Report of the International Narcotics Control Board for 1994'. New York: United Nations.

— (1995b) 'Effectiveness of the International Drug Control Treaties', Supplement to the Report of the International Narcotics Control Board for 1994. New York: United Nations.

— (2003) 'Report of the I.N.C.B. for 2003: Measures to Reduce Harm'. Geneva: UNODC.

— (2004) 'Annual Report of the International Narcotics Control Board: Focuses on Relationship between Drug Abuse, Crime and Violence at Community Level'. Geneva: UNODC.

Inciardi, J. (1986) *The War on Drugs: Heroin, Cocaine, Crime, and Public Policy*. Palo Alto, CA: Mayfield.

Indian Hemp Drugs Commission (1969) 'Marijuana: Report of the Indian Hemp Drugs Commission 1893–1894', Silver Spring, MD: Thos. Jefferson Publishing.

Inglis, B. (1975) *The Forbidden Game: A Social History of Drugs*. New York: Scribner's.

International Herald Tribune (2004) 'Rumsfeld in Kabul for Drug Talks', 11 August.

Jain, H. (1999) *The India–China Opium Trade in the Nineteenth Century*. Jefferson, NC: McFarland.

Janofsky, M. (1998) 'Farmers Will Sue to Legalize Hemp Crops', *New York Times*, 15 May.

Jarlais, D. Des (1992) 'The First and Second Decades of AIDS Among Injecting Drug Users', *British Journal of Addiction*, Vol. 87, pp. 47–53.

Jarlais, D. Des, H. Hagan and S. Friedman (1998) 'Preventing Epidemics of HIV-1 Among Injecting Drug Users', in G. Stimpson et al. (eds), *Drug Injecting and HIV Infection: Global Dimensions and Local Responses*. London: UCL Press.

Jelsma, M. (2000) 'Fungus versus Coca: U.N.D.C.P. and the Biological War on Drugs in Colombia', *Transnational Institute Briefing Paper*, February. <www.tni.org/archives/jelsma/fungus-e.htm>.

— (2003) 'The Erratic Crusade of the I.N.C.B.', TNI Drug Policy, Briefing 4.

Jelsma, M. and T. Kramer (2005) 'Downward Spiral: Banning Opium in Afghanistan and Burma', Transnational Institute Drugs and Conflict Debate, Paper 12.

Jennings Bryan, W. (1900) 'The Paralyzing Influence of Imperialism Source', Official Proceedings of the Democratic National Convention, Kansas City, MO, 4, 5 and 6 July, pp. 205–27. <www.mtholyoke.edu/acad/intrel/bryan.htm>.

Johnson, B. (1975) 'Righteousness Before Revenue: The Forgotten Moral Crusade Against the Indo-Chinese Opium Trade', *Journal of Drug Issues*, pp. 304–26.

Johnston, L., P. O'Malley and F. Bachman (2001) *Monitoring the Future: National Survey Results on Drug Use, 1975–2000*. Volume I: *Secondary School Students* (NIH Publication No. 01-4924). Rockville, MD: National Institute on Drug Abuse.

Jordan, D. (1999) *Drug Politics: Dirty Money and Democracy*. Norman: University of Oklahoma Press.

Joseph Rowntree Foundation (2005) Drug and Alcohol Research Committee. Background and Aims. <www.jrf.org.uk/funding/research/prioritiesandcalls/priorities/darc.asp>.

Josephson, M. (1962) *The Robber Barons: The Great American Capitalists 1861–1901*. New York: Harcourt Brace International.

Joyce, E. and C. Malamud (1997) *Latin America and the Multinational Drug Trade*, Institute of Latin American Studies Series. London: Palgrave Macmillan.

Jürgens, R. and M. Bijl (2001) 'High Risk Behaviour in Penal Institutions', in P. Bollini (ed.), *HIV in Prisons: A Reader with Particular Relevance to the Newly Independent States*. Geneva: World Health Organization.

Jutkowitz, J. and Eu. Hongsook (1993) 'Drug Prevalence in Latin America and Caribbean Countries: A Cross National Analysis', *Drugs: Education, Prevention and Policy*, Vol. 1, no. 3.

Kandel, D. (2002) *Stages and Pathways of Drug Involvement: Examining the Gateway Hypothesis*. Cambridge: Cambridge University Press.

Kawell, J. (2002) 'Drug Economies of the Americas', *NACLA*, Vol. 36, Issue 2.

Kay, B. (1999) 'Violent Opportunities: The Rise and Fall of "King Coca" and Shining Path', *Journal of Interamerican Studies and World Affairs*, Fall.

Keh, D. (1998) 'Drug Money in a Changing World: Economic Reform and Criminal Finance', UNDCP no. 4.

Keire, M. (1998) 'Dope Fiends and Degenerates: The Gendering of Addiction in the Early Twentieth Century', *Journal of Social History*, Summer.

— (2001) 'The Vice Trust: A Reinterpretation of the White Slavery Scare in the United States, 1907–1917', *Journal of Social History*, Fall.

Kin, F. (1995) 'Injecting Drug Use Among Heroin Users in Malaysia: Summary of Research Findings', Report of the WHO Drug Injecting Project Planning Meeting, Bangkok, Thailand, September.

King, R. (1972) *The Drug Hang Up, America's Fifty-Year Folly*. Illinois: Charles C. Thomas.

Kirk, R. (2004) *More Terrible than Death: Drugs, Violence, and America's War in Colombia*. New York: Public Affairs Limited.

Klare, M. (2001) *Resource Wars: The Changing Landscape of Global Conflict*. New York: Henry Holt.

Klein, A. (1994) 'Trapped in the Traffic: Growing Problems of Drug Consumption in Lagos', *Journal of Modern African Studies*, Vol. 32, no. 4, pp. 657–77.

Kleiner, K. (1999) 'Operation Eradicate', *New Scientist*, 11 September.

Knickmeyer, E. (2002) 'Vice Creeps Back to Kandahar', *Guardian*, 22 February.

Knight, D. (2000) 'Plan Colombia: Fumigation Threatens Amazon, Warn Indigenous Leaders', *Inter Press Service*, 21 November.

Kobler, J. (1993) *Ardent Spirits: The Rise and Fall of Prohibition*, Cambridge, MA: Da Capo Press.

Kohl, B. and L. Farthing (2001) 'The Price of Success: The Destruction of Coca and the Bolivian Economy', *NACLA*, Vol. 34, no. 7, pp. 35–41.

Kort, M. de (1995) *Tussen patient en delinquent. Geschiedenis van het Nederlandse drugbeleid* (Between Patient and Criminal, History of Dutch Drug Policy), Dissertation, Erasmus University, Rotterdam.

Kozlova, M. (2003) 'Fungus New Weapon Against Opium', *Washington Times*, 7 August.

La Motte, E. (2003) *The Opium Monopoly*. Montana: Kessinger Publishing.

La-Ongsri, S. (1992) 'Drug Abuse Control and the Environment in Northern Thailand', *Bulletin on Narcotics*, Issue 2, pp. 31–5.

Leader, S. and D. Wiencek (2000) 'Drug Money: The Fuel for Global Terrorism', *Jane's Intelligence Review*, February, pp. 49–54.

Le Billon, P. (2001) 'The Political Ecology of War: Natural Resources and Armed Conflicts', *Political Geography*, Vol. 20, no. 5, pp. 561–84.

— (2003) 'The Political Ecology of War and Resource Exploitation', *Studies in Political Economy*, 70.

Ledebur, K. (2005) 'Bolivia: Clear Consequences', in C. Youngers and E. Rosin (eds), *Drugs and Democracy in Latin America: The Impact of U.S. Policy*. Boulder, CO: Lynne Rienner.

Lee, M. and B. Shlain (1985) *Acid Dreams: The Complete Social History of LSD, the CIA, the Sixties and Beyond*. New York: Grove Atlantic.

Leech, G. (2001) 'Death Falls from the Sky', *Colombia Journal Online*, 23 April.

Lemus, M., K. Stanton and J. Walsh (2004) 'Colombia, a Vicious Circle of Drugs and War', in C. Youngers and E. Rosin (eds), *Drugs and Democracy in Latin America: The Impact of U.S. Policy*. Boulder, CO: Lynne Rienner.

LeoGrande, W. and K. Sharpe (2000) 'Two Wars or One?: Drugs, Guerrillas, and Colombia's New Violencia', *World Policy Journal*, Fall.

Leverenz, N. A. (2004) 'Testing the Wrong Policy on Students', *Brainwash*, 19 September.

Levine, H. (1993) 'Temperance Cultures: Alcohol as a Problem in Nordic and English-Speaking Cultures', in M. Lader, G. Edwards and D. Colin Drummon (eds), *The Nature of Alcohol and Drug-Related Problems*. New York: Oxford University Press, pp. 16–36.

— (2002) 'The Secret of Worldwide Drug Prohibition: The Varieties and Uses of Drug Prohibition', *The Independent Review*, Vol. VII, no. 2, Fall, pp. 165–80.

Levine, H. and C. Reinarman (eds) (1997) *Crack in America: Demon Drugs and Social Justice*. Berkeley: University of California Press.

Lindesmith, A. (1964) *The Addict and the Law*. Bloomington: Indiana University Press.

— (1968) *Addiction and Opiates*. New York: Aldine de Gruyter.

Lindt, A. (1953) 'Achievements of the United Nations Opium Conference', *Bulletin on Narcotics*, Issue 3.

Lipton, M. and R. Longhurst (1989) *New Seeds and Poor People*. London: Unwin Hyman.

Livingstone, G. (2002) *Inside Colombia: Drugs, Democracy and War*. London: Latin American Bureau.

Lloyd, R. (1997) 'Publisher Warns about Impacts of Drug War', *World Rainforest Report*, no. 37. Lismore, NSW: Australia.

Lowndes, C., T. Rhodes, A. Judd, L. Mikhailova, A. Sarang, A. Rylkov, M. Tichonov, L. Platt and A. Renton (2002) 'Female Injection Drug Users Who Practise Sex Work in Togliatti City, Russian Federation: HIV Prevalence and Risk Behaviour', XIV International Conference on AIDS, Barcelona, July.

Lodwick, K. (1996) *Crusades Against Opium: Protestant Missionaries in China, 1874–1917*. Lexington: University Press of Kentucky.

Lowndes, C., A. Renton, M. Alary, T. Rhodes, C. Garnett and G. Stimson (2003) 'Conditions for Widespread Heterosexual Spread of HIV in the Russian Federation: Implications for Research, Monitoring and Prevention', *International Journal of Drug Policy*, Vol. 14, pp. 45–62.

Lu, X. and R. Clarke (1995) 'The Cultivation and Use of Hemp (*Cannabis sativa* L.) in Ancient China', *Journal of the International Hemp Association*, Vol. 2, no. 1, pp. 26–30.

Lubin, N. (2001) 'Central Asia's War on Drugs Takes a High Human Toll', *Eurasia Insight*, 14 May.

Lucas, K. (2000) 'Plan Colombia's Herbicide Spraying Causing Health and Environmental Problems', *InterPress Service*, 17 October.

Lurie, P., A. Reingold, B. Bowser, D. Chen, J. Foley, J. Guydish, J. Kahn, S. Lane and J. Sorensen (1993) *The Public Health Impact of Needle Exchange Programs in the United States and Abroad*, Vol. 1. San Francisco: University of California.

Lynch, T. (ed.) (2000) *After Prohibition: An Adult Approach to Drug Policies in the 21st Century*. Washington, DC: Cato Institute.

McAllister, W. (2000) *Drug Diplomacy in the Twentieth Century: An International History*, London: Routledge.

McClintock, C. (1998) *Revolutionary Movements in Latin America: El Salvador's F.M.L.N. and Peru's Shining Path*. Washington, DC: United States Institute of Peace Press.

McCoy, A. (1972) *The Politics of Heroin in Southeast Asia*. New York: Harper and Row.

— (1991) *The Politics of Heroin: Central In-telligence Agency Complicity in the Global Drug Trade*. Columbia: Lawrence Hill.

— (2003) *The Politics of Heroin: CIA Complicity in the Global Drug Trade, Afghanistan, Southeast Asia, Central America*. Columbia: Lawrence Hill.

McCraw, T. (2005) *Prophets of Regulation*. Cambridge, MA: Belknap Press.

MacFarquhar, N. (2001) 'Cattlemen in Lebanon Miss Lucre of Hashish', *New York Times*, 5 April.

McKay, A. (2003) 'Indifference, Cultural Difference, and a Porous Frontier: Drugs, Diplomacy, and the Politics of the High Himalayas', Paper presented at the conference Drugs and Empires: Narcotics, History and Modern Colonialism, Strathclyde University.

Maddison, A. and D. Johnston (2001) *The World Economy: A Millennial Perspective*.

Organization for Economic Cooperation and Development.

Maharjan, S. and M. Singh (1996) 'Street-based AIDS Outreach Program for Injecting Drug Users (I.D.U.s)', International Conference on AIDS, Vancouver, Canada.

Maharjan, S., A. Peak, S. Rana and N. Crofts (1994) 'Declining Risk for HIV Among IDUs in Kathmandu: Impact of a Harm Reduction Programme', Abstract no. 561C, X International Conference on AIDS, Japan.

Makarenko, T. (2002) 'Crime, Terror and the Central Asian Drug Trade', *Harvard Asia Quarterly*, Vol. 6, no. 3.

Malinowska-Sempruch, K. (2002) 'Central Asia's Nascent AIDS Crisis', *Harm Reduction News*, Vol. 2, Winter.

— (2003) 'Mitigating the HIV Epidemic in the Former Soviet Union: Essential Steps for a Comprehensive Response'. New York: Open Society Institute.

Mansfield, D, (1999) 'Alternative Development: The Modern Thrust of Supply-side Policy', Occasional Papers, *Bulletin of Narcotics*, Vol. VI, nos 1 and 2.

Mansfield, D. and J. Whetton (1996) 'Illicit Drugs in Developing Countries: A Literature Review'. Swansea: Centre for Development Studies, University of Wales.

Manski, C., J. Pepper and C. Petrie (eds) (2001) *Informing America's Policy on Illegal Drugs: What We Don't Know Keeps Hurting Us*. Washington, DC: National Academy Press.

Marchant, L. (2002) 'The Wars of the Poppies', *History Today*, January.

Marsh, B. (2004) 'Going to Extremes, the US-funded Aerial Eradication Programmes in Colombia'. <www.lawg. org/docs/Going2ExtremesFinal.pdf>.

May, H. (1950) 'The Evolution of the International Control of Narcotic Drugs', *Bulletin on Narcotics*, Issue 3.

— (1955) 'The Single Convention on Narcotic Drugs; Comments and Possibilities', *Bulletin on Narcotics*, Issue 1.

Meo, N. (2004) 'Karzai Grills British Officials Over "Illegal" Poppy Crop Spraying', *Independent*, 1 December.

Metzger, T. (2003) 'Descent into Hell', *Grey Lodge Occult Review*, Issue 7, year 2. <www.greylodge.org/occultreview/glor_007/dopefiend.htm>.

Michaud, J. (1997) 'From Southwest China into Upper Indochina: An Overview of Hmong (Miao) Migrations', *Asia Pacific Viewpoint*, Vol. 38, no. 2.

Mignoni, G. (1997) 'Cannabis as a Licit Crop: Recent Developments in Europe', *Bulletin on Narcotics*, Issue 1, vol. 3.

Miller, S. (1969) *The Unwelcome Immigrant: The American Image of the Chinese, 1785–1882*. Berkeley: University of California Press.

Monthly Review (2003) 'Kipling, the "White Man's Burden" and U.S. Imperialism', Vol. 55, no. 6.

Moore, J. and R. Garcia (1979) *Homeboys: Gangs, Drugs, and Prison in the Barrios of Los Angeles*. Philadelphia, PA: Temple University Press.

Moore, M. (1977) *Buy and Bust*. Lexington, MA: Lexington Books.

Morgan, H. (1981) *Drugs in America: A Social History 1800–1980*. New York: Syracuse University Press.

Morral, A., D. McCaffrey and S. Paddock (2002) 'Reassessing the Marijuana Gateway Effect', *Addiction*, Vol. 97, pp. 1493–504.

Morris, S. and N. Hopkins (2003) 'Caught in the Crossfire of Gang Violence', *Guardian*, 3 January.

Musto, D. (n.d.) *The History of Legislative Control Over Opium, Cocaine and Their Derivatives*. <www.druglibrary. org/schaffer/History/ophs.htm>.

— (1972) 'The History of the Marihuana Tax Act of 1937', *Archive of General Psychiatry*, Vol. 26, February.

— (1973) *The American Disease: Origins of Narcotic Control*. New Haven, CT and London: Yale University Press.

— (1991) 'Opium, Cocaine and Marijuana

in American History', *Scientific American*, July, pp. 20–7.

Musto, D. and Z. Sloboda (2003) 'The Influence of Epidemiology on Drug Control Policy', *Bulletin on Narcotics*, Vol. LV, nos 1 and 2.

NACLA (North American Congress on Latin America) (2001) *Widening Destruction: Drug War in the Americas*, Vol. XXXV, no. 1.

Nadelmann, E. (1990) 'Global Prohibition Regimes: The Evolution of Norms in International Society', *International Organization*, Vol. 44, no. 4.

Nahas, G. (1985) 'Critique of a Study on Ganja in Jamaica', *Bulletin on Narcotics*, Issue 4, pp. 15–29.

Nakken, C. (1996) *The Addictive Personality: Understanding the Addictive Process and Compulsive Behavior*. Center City, MN: Hazelden.

Nevamdomsky, J. (1981) 'Patterns of Self-reported Drug Use Among Secondary Students in Benedel State, Nigeria', *Bulletin on Narcotics*, Issue 33, no. 1.

New Scientist (1998) 'Marijuana Special Report: High Anxieties', 19 February.

New York Times (2004) 'Afghan Poppy Farmers Say Mystery Spraying Killed Crops', 5 December.

Normand, J., D. Vlahov and L. Moses (eds) (1995) *Preventing HIV Transmission: The Role of Sterile Needles and Bleach*, Washington, DC: National Academy Press.

O'Coffin, P. (1998) 'A Duty to Censor: U.N. Officials Want to Crack Down on Drug War Protesters', *Reason*, August/September.

ONDCP (Office of National Drug Control Policy) (1997) 'O.N.D.C.P. Statement on Industrial Hemp'. <www.whitehousedrugpolicy.gov/policy/hemp.html>.

— (1998a) *National Drug Control Strategy, 1998*. Washington, DC: ONDCP.

— (1998b) Press release: 'Drug Czar Statement on Administration Decision to Continue Ban on Use of Federal Funds for Needle Exchange Programs'. Washington, DC: ONDCP, 20 April.

— (2001) *What America's Users Spend on Illegal Drugs, 1988–2000*. Washington, DC: ONDCP, December.

— (2004) 'Price and Purity of Illicit Drugs: 1981 Through Second Quarter of 2003'. Washington, DC: ONDCP.

Open Society Institute (2001) *Harm Reduction in Principle*. Budapest: OSI.

— (2003) *Unintended Consequences: Drug Policies Fuel the HIV Epidemic in Russia and the Ukraine*. <www.soros.org/initiatives/ihrd/articles_publications/publications/unintendedconsequences_20030414>.

Ormerod, W. (1876) *Our Opium Trade with China*, Society for the Suppression of the Opium Trade: Dyer Brothers.

Osorio-Bryson, L. (1992) 'Environment and Drug Trafficking', *Bulletin on Narcotics*, Issue 2, pp. 27–9.

Painter, J. (1994) *Bolivia and Coca: A Study in Dependency*, Studies on the Impact of the Illegal Drug Trade. Boulder, CO: Lynne Rienner.

Pakistan Tribune (2004) 'Outrage Over Mysterious Spraying of Afghanistan Poppy', 15 December.

Panda, S., A. Chatterjee, S. Bhattacharjee, M. Saha and S. Bhattacharya (1998) 'HIV, Hepatitis B and Sexual Practices in the Street-recruited Injecting Drug Users of Calcutta: Risk Perception Versus Observed Risks', *International Journal of STD and AIDS*, Vol. 9, no. 4, pp. 214–18.

Panda, S., A. Chatterjee, S. Bhattacharya, B. Manna, P. N. Singh, S. Sarkar, T. N. Naik, S. Chakrabarti and R. Detels (2000) 'Transmission of HIV from Injecting Drug Users to Their Wives in India', *International Journal of STD and AIDS*, Vol. 11, no. 7, July, pp. 468–73.

Panda, S., L. Bijaya, N. Sadhana Devi, E. Foley, A. Chatterjee, D. Banerjee, T. N. Naik, M. Saha and S. Bhattacharya (2001) 'Interface Between Drug Use and Sex Work in Manipur', *National*

Medical Journal of India, Vol. 14, no. 4, pp. 209–11.

Pearson, H. (2004) 'Science and the War on Drugs: A Hard Habit to Break', *Nature*, 21 July.

Peele, S. (1985) *The Meaning of Addiction: Compulsive Experience and Its Interpretation*. Lexington, MA: Lexington Books.

— (1989) *Diseasing America, Addiction Treatment Out of Control*, Lexington, MA: Lexington Books.

Peele, S. and A. Brodsky (1975) *Love and Addiction*. New York: Taplinger.

Pegram, T. (1999) *Battling Demon Rum: The Struggle for a Dry America, 1800–1933*. Chicago, IL: Ivan R. Dee.

Pendergast, M. (1993) *For God, Country and Coca-Cola: The Unauthorized History of the Great American Soft Drink and the Company that Makes It*. London: Weidenfeld and Nicolson.

Pesticide Action Network UK (1996) 'Forgotten Victims of Agent Orange', *Pesticides News*, no. 32, p. 17, June. <www.pan-uk.org/pestnews/Pn32/pn32p17d.htm>.

— (2004) <www.pan-uk.org/pestnews/Actives/glyphosate2.htm>.

Pion Berlin, D. (2001) *Civil–Military Relations in Latin America: New Analytical Perspectives*. Carolina: University of Carolina Press.

Platt, L. (1998) *Profile of Sex Workers in Moscow*. Moscow: AIDS Infoshare.

Poole, D. and G. Renique (1992) *Peru: Time of Fear*. London: Latin America Bureau.

Porter, G. (1992) *The Rise of Big Business, 1860–1920*. Illinois: Harlan Davidson (American History Series).

Power, R. and N. Nozhkina (2002) 'The Value of Process Evaluation in Sustaining HIV Harm Reduction in the Russian Federation', *AIDS*, Vol. 16, no. 2, pp. 303–4.

Radford, T. (1998) 'U.N. Report Leaked: Cannabis "Safer than Alcohol or Cigarettes"', *Guardian*, 19 February.

Raghavan, C. (2000) 'Alarm Bells Over US Fungus Experiments Abroad', *Third World Network*, 10 May. <www.twnside.org.sg/title/alarm.htm>.

Rangel Suarez, A. (2000) 'Parasites and Predators: Guerrillas and the Insurrection Economy of Colombia', *Journal of International Affairs*, Vol. 53, Spring.

Rashid, A. (2001) *Taliban: The Story of Afghan Warlords*. London: Pan.

Recio, G. (2002) 'Drugs and Alcohol: US Prohibition and the Origins of the Drug Trade in Mexico, 1910–1930', *Journal of Latin American Studies*, Vol. 34, pp. 21–42.

Reiland, R. (1999) 'Stretch of the Litigious List', Commentary, *Washington Times*, 21 November.

Reinarman, C. and H. Levine (1997) *Crack in America: Demon Drugs and Social Justice*. Berkeley: University of California Press.

Renard, R. (2001) *Opium Reduction in Thailand 1970 to 2000, a Thirty Year Journey*. Vienna: UNDCP.

Renborg, B. (1964) 'The Grand Old Men of the League of Nations. What They Achieved. Who They Were', *Bulletin on Narcotics*, no. 4.

Renner, M. and Prugh, T. (2002) *Anatomy of Resource Wars*, Washington, DC: Worldwatch Institute.

Reports of Commissioners (1895) India (Opium), Royal Commission on Opium, Final Report, British Parliamentary Papers, 1895, Vol. 42.

Rethinking.org (2003) 'A Bitter Pill to Swallow: The Sentencing of Foreign National Drug Couriers', London. <www.rethinking.org.uk/informed/pdf/briefing5.pdf.pdf>.

Reuter, P. and V. Greenfield (2001) 'Measuring Global Drug Markets; How Good are the Numbers and Why Should We Care About Them', *World Economics*, Vol. 2, no. 4, pp. 155–73.

Revill, J. (2003) 'Scientists Admit: We were Wrong About "E"', *Observer*, 7 September.

Rhodes, T., A. Ball, G. V. Stimson, Y. Kobyshcha, C. Fitch and V. Pokrovsky

(1999) 'HIV Infection Associated with Drug Injecting in the Newly Independent States, Eastern Europe', *Addiction*, Vol. 94, no. 9, pp. 323–36.

Rhodes, T., C. Lowndes, A. Judd, L. Mikhailova, A. Sarang, A. Rylkov, M. Tichonov, K. Lewis, N. Ulyanova, T. Alpatova, V. Karavashkin, M. Khutorskoy, J. Parry and A. Renton (2002a) 'Explosive Spread and High Prevalence of HIV Infection Among Injecting Drug Users in Togliatti City, Russia', *AIDS*, Vol. 16. pp. 25–31.

Rhodes, T., L. Platt, K. Filatova, A. Sarang, M. Davis and A. Renton (2002b) *Behaviour Factors in HIV Transmission in Eastern Europe and Central Asia*. Geneva: UNAIDS.

Richards, J. (2003) 'The Opium Industry in British India', *Indian Economic and Social History Review*, Vol. 39, no. 2–3, pp. 149–80.

Robert F. Kennedy Memorial Center for Human Rights (2002) Center for International Policy, Latin America Working Group, Amazon Alliance, *Compliance with Fumigation Conditions in the Andean Counterdrug Initiative*, April. <www.ciponline. org/colombia/02041004.htm>.

Robinson, R. (1995) *The Great Book of Hemp: The Complete Guide to the Commercial, Medicinal and Psychotropic Uses of the World's Most Extraordinary Plant*. Rochester, VT: Inner Traditions International.

Rogers, M. (1978) 'Whatever Happened to Mary Jane?', *Rolling Stone*, 6 April.

Rohter, L. (2000) 'Colombians Say US Drug Spraying is Creating a Health Crisis', *San Francisco Chronicle*, 1 May.

Rose, D. (2003) 'Our Jails are Full to Bursting – and It's Almost All Down to Drugs', *Observer*, 9 February.

Ross, M. (2003) 'Oil, Drugs, and Diamonds: The Varying Roles of Natural Resources in Civil War', in K. Ballentine and J. Sherman (eds), *The Political Economy of Armed Conflict: Beyond Greed and Governance*. Boulder, CO: Lynne Rienner.

Roulac, J. (1997) *Hemp Horizons: The Comeback of the World's Most Promising Plant*. White River Junction, VT: Chelsea Green Publishing.

Ruggerio, V. and N. South (1995) *Eurodrugs: Drug Use, Markets and Trafficking in Europe*. London: Routledge.

Ruiz, B. (2001) *The Colombian Civil War*. Jefferson, NC: McFarland.

Runciman, R. (1999) 'Drugs and the Law', Report of the Independent Inquiry into the Misuse of Drugs Act 1971. London: Police Foundation.

Rush, J. (1990) *Opium to Java: Revenue Farming and Chinese Enterprise in Colonial Indonesia, 1860–1910*. New York: Cornell University Press.

Russell, D. (1998) *Shamanism and the Drug Propaganda: The Birth of Patriarchy and the Drug War*. Kalyx.com.

Ruyver, B. de, G. Vermeulen, T. Vander Beken, F. Vander Laenen and K. Geenens (2002) *Multidisciplinary Drug Policies and the UN Drug Treaties*. Maklu, Antwerpen/Apeldoorn: Institute for International Research on Criminal Policy, Ghent University (IRCP).

Saba, D. (2001) 'Afghanistan: Environmental Degradation in a Fragile Ecological Setting', *International Journal of Sustainable Develpment World Ecology*, Vol. 8, pp. 279–89.

Sadoff, W. (1991) 'The Value of Thailand's Forests Claudia', *TDRI Quarterly Review*, Vol. 6, no. 4, pp. 19–24.

Safford, F. and M. Palacios (2002) *Colombia: Fragmented Land, Divided Society*. New York: Oxford University Press.

Saidel, T., D. des Jarlais, W. Peerapatanapokin, J. Dorabjee, S. Singh and T. Brown (2003) 'Potential Impact of HIV Among IDUs on Heterosexual Transmission in Asian Settings: Scenarios from the Asian Epidemic Model', *International Journal of Drug Policy*, Vol. 14, no. 1, pp. 63–74.

St Clair, J. (2002) 'Drug War According to Dr. Mengele: Agent Green Over the Andes', *CounterPunch*, 24 December.

— (2003) 'U.S. Considers New Bioweapon Attack', *Green Left Weekly*, 22 January.

St Clair, J. and A. Cockburn (2002) 'Ecuadorian Farmers Fight Dyn-Corp's Chemwar on the Amazon', *CounterPunch*, 27 February.

St Petersburg Times (1999) 'Environmental Cures are Worse than the Disease', 27 July.

Sanello, F. and W. Travis Hanes III (2002) *The Opium Wars: The Addiction of One Empire and the Corruption of Another.* Naperville, TS: Sourcebooks.

Schaefer, B. (1994) 'Colombia, Coca Production, the Environment and Trade', *Trade and Environmental Database (TED) Case Studies*, Vol. 3, no. 2.

Schaler, J. (2000) *Addiction is a Choice.* Chicago, IL: Open Court Publishing.

Scheerer, S. (1978) 'The New Dutch and German Drug Laws: Social and Political Conditions for Criminalization and Decriminalization', *Law and Society Review*, Vol. 12, no. 4, Summer, pp. 585–606.

Schirmer, D. (1972) *Republic or Empire: American Resistance to the Philippine War.* Cambridge, MA: Schenkman.

Schivelbusch, W. (1993) *Tastes of Paradise: A Social History of Spices, Stimulants, and Intoxicants.* New York: Random House.

Schultes, R. and A. Hoffman (1992) *Plants of the Gods: Their Sacred, Healing And Hallucinogenic Powers.* Rochester, NY: Healing Arts Press.

Scott, C. and D. Ullmer (1992) 'Coca Trade and Production', *Trade and Environmental Database (TED) Case Studies*, Vol. 1, no. 1.

Scott, J. (1969) *The White Poppy: A History of Opium.* New York: Funk and Wagnalls.

Scott Palmer, D. (1992) *The Shining Path of Peru.* New York: St Martin's Press.

Shurtleff, W. and A. Aoyagi (1997) *Henry Ford and His Researchers' Work with Soybeans, Soyfoods, and Chemurgy: Bibliography and Sourcebook, 1921 to 1996.* Lafayette, CA:Soyfoods Center.

Silva Iulianelli, J., L. Guanabara, P. Pontes Fraga and T. Blickman (2004) 'A Pointless War: Drugs and Violence in Brazil', *Transnational Institute Briefing Series, Drugs and Democracy Programme*, no. 8.

Simon, J. (1998) *Endangered Mexico.* London: Latin American Bureau.

Sims, N. (2001) 'The Evolution of Biological Disarmament', *SIPRI Chemical Biological Warfare Studies*, no. 19. Oxford: Oxford University Press.

Singer, P. (2004) *Corporate Warriors: The Rise of the Privatized Military Industry*, Cornell Studies in Security Affairs. Ithaca, NY: Cornell University Press.

Sinha, J. (2001) 'The History and Development of the Leading International Drug Control Conventions', Report prepared for the Senate Special Committee on Illegal Drugs, Law and Government Division, Library of Parliament.

Smith, M. (ed.) (1992) *Why People Grow Drugs.* London: Panos Institute.

Solomon, D. (ed.) (1966) *LSD: The Consciousness-Expanding Drug.* New York: G. P. Putnam.

Span, P. (1996) 'Needle Exchanges Inject Controversy in AIDS Prevention', *Washington Post*, 16 July.

Speaker, S. (2001) 'The Struggle of Mankind Against Its Deadliest Foe: Themes of Counter-subversion in Anti-narcotic Campaigns, 1920–1940', *Journal of Social History*, Spring.

Spillane, J. (2000) *Cocaine: From Medical Marvel to Modern Menace in the United States, 1884–1920.* Baltimore, MD: Johns Hopkins University Press.

Stamler, R., R. Fahlman and H. Vigeant (1985) 'Illicit Traffic and Abuse of Cannabis in Canada', *Bulletin on Narcotics*, Issue 4, pp. 37–49.

Stares, P. (1996) *Global Habit: The Drug Problem in a Borderless World*, Washington, DC: Brookings Institute.

Steinig, L. (1968) 'The International System of Narcotics Control: Its Evolution and Main Characteristics', *Bulletin on Narcotics*, Issue 1.

Steinitz, M. (2002) 'The Terrorism and Drug Connection in Latin America's Andean Region', Centre for Strategic and International Studies, Policy Papers on the Americas, Vol. 8, study 5.

Stencel, C. (1999) 'Fungi Touted as Drug War "Silver Bullets" Face Challenges', *American Society for Microbiology*, 8 August.

Stevenson, S. (1991) 'Peru Farmers Blame U.S. for Coca-killing Fungus', *Miami Herald*, 2 June.

Stimson, G., L. Alldritt and K. A. Dolan (1998) 'Injecting Equipment Exchange Schemes: Final Report', University of London, Goldsmiths College, Monitoring Research Group, London.

Stoker, P. (2001) 'The History of Harm Reduction', World Conference on Drugs, Visby, Sweden, May.

Stolzenberg, L. and S. d'Alessio (2003) 'A Multilevel Analysis of the Effect of Cocaine Price on Cocaine Use Among Arrestees', *Journal of Criminal Justice*, Vol. 31, pp. 185–95.

Streatfield, D. (2000) *Cocaine: A Definitive History*. London: Virgin.

Sunshine Project (2000) 'Questions and Answers About Eradicating Drug Crops Using Fusarium, Pleospora, or other Biological Agents'. <www.sunshine-project.org/agentgreen/qanda.html>.

— (2002) 'An Introduction to Biological Weapons, Their Prohibition, and the Relationship to Biosafety', *Backgrounder Series*, no. 10, April.

Suwanee, R., D. des Jarlais, K. Choopanya, S. Vanichseni, P. Friedmann and J. Sotheran (1994) 'Continued Risk Reduction Among I.D.U.s in New York City and Bangkok, 1989–1993', X International Conference on AIDS, Tokyo, Japan.

Tamayo, J. (2001) 'Thriving Heroin Culture Alarms Colombian, U.S. Authorities', *Miami Herald*, 18 August.

Tangi, L. (1998) 'Seeds of Doubt Grow Over Body Shop Gift', *Hong Kong Standard*, 2 November.

Taylor Martin, S. (2001) 'U.S. Versus Them, U.S. Policy not Limited to U.S. Borders', *St Petersburg Times*, 29 July.

Thompson, T. (2002) 'Terrorist Attacks Drove Jamaican Mules to U.K.', *Observer*, 6 January.

Thoumi, F. (2003) *Illegal Drugs, Economy, and Society in the Andes*. Balimore, MD: Johns Hopkins University Press.

TNI (Transnational Institute) (2001a) 'Fumigation and Conflict in Colombia: In the Heat of the Debate', *Drugs and Conflict*, Debate Paper 2, September.

— (2001b) 'Afghanistan, Drugs and Terrorism: Merging Wars', TNI Briefing Series, no. 3.

— (2002) 'A Failed Balance: Alternative Development and Eradication', Drugs and Conflict Debate Paper 4. <www.tni.org/reports/drugs/debate4.pdf>.

— (2003) 'Alternative Development and Conflict in Colombia: Cross Purposes', TNI Briefing Series, no. 7.

— (2004) 'The Re-emergence of the Biological War on Drugs', *Drug Policy Briefing* 7, May.

— (2005a) 'Plan Afghanistan', *Drug Policy Briefing* 10, February.

— (2005b) 'The Politics of Glyphosate. The CICAD Study on the Impacts of Glyphosate and the Crop Figures', *Drug Policy Briefing* 14, June.

— (2005c) 'Aerial Spraying Knows No Borders: Ecuador Brings International Case Over Aerial Spraying', *Drug Policy Briefing* 15, September.

TNI/Acción Andina/Rapalmira Communiqué (2001) 'Forced Aerial Eradication of Illicit Crops, a Reply to the State Department', 2 September.

Tonry, M. and J. Wilson (eds) (2000) *Drugs and Crime*. Chicago, IL: University of Chicago Press.

Topp, L., C. Day and L. Degenhardt (2003) 'Changes in Pattern of Drug Injection Concurrent with a Sustained Reduction in the Availability of Heroin in Australia', *Drug and Alcohol Dependence*, Issue 70, pp. 275–86.

Trocki, C. (1999) *Opium, Empire and the*

Global Political Economy: A Study of the Asian Opium Trade. London: Routledge.

— (2002) 'Opium and the Beginnings of Chinese Capitalism in Southeast Asia', *Journal of Southeast Asian Studies*, Vol. 33, pp. 297–314.

Tullis, L. (1995) *Unintended Consequences: Illegal Drugs and Drug Policies in Nine Countries*. Boulder, CO: Lynne Rienner.

Tung, N., N. Tuan, T. Hoang, N. Hien, B. Thang, T. Kane, T. Saidel, P. Chi and H. Sara (2001) *HIV/AIDS Behavioral Surveillance Survey, Vietnam 2000*. Hanoi: National AIDS Standing Bureau, Family Health International.

Ul Haq, E. (2000) *Drugs in South Asia: From the Opium Trade to the Present Day*. London: Palgrave Macmillan.

UNAIDS (2004a) 'Epidemiological Fact Sheet by Country'. Geneva: UN. <www.who.int/emc-hiv/fact_sheets/All_countries.html>.

— (2004b) '2004 Report on the Global AIDS Epidemic: 4th Global Report'. Geneva: UN. <www.unaids.org/bangkok2004/report.html>.

— (2004c) 'The Changing HIV/AIDS Epidemic in Europe and Central Asia'. Geneva: UN. <eca.iaen.org/files/533_file_changing_hivaids.pdf>.

UNAIDS/WHO (2002) *AIDS Epidemic Update 2002*. Geneva: World Health Organization.

UNDCP (1997) *World Drug Report 1997*. Vienna: UN.

— (2000) *Report on Best Practice in Gender Mainstreaming in Alternative Development*, Independent consultants report. New York: UN.

— (2001) 'Alternative Development in the Andean Area: The UNDCP Experience', New York: UN. <www.unodc.org/pdf/publications/alt-development_andean.pdf>.

— (2002) *Afghan Opium Survey 2002*. Vienna: UN.

— (2003) *World Drug Report 2003*. Vienna: United Nations.

UNFAO (Food and Agricultural Organization of the United Nations) (2001, 2005) *State of the World's Forests*. Rome: UNFAO.

UNICEF (2003) 'Children and Young People Affected by HIV and AIDS'. Geneva: UN. <www.unicef.org/evaldatabase/files/UKR_01–005.pdf>.

United Nations (2000) 'Action Plan for the Implementation of the Declaration on the Guiding Principles of Drug Demand Reduction', Annex to resolution, General Assembly, 2 February, A/RES/54/132.

— (2001) 'Declaration of Commitment on HIV/AIDS', General Assembly 26th Special Session on HIV/AIDS, June, Article 52, A/RES/S-26/2.

UNODC (1998a) *1997 World Drug Report*. Vienna: UNODC.

— (1998b) *Economic and Social Consequences of Traffic and Abuse*. Vienna: UN.

— (2001) *2000 World Drug Report*. Vienna: UNODC.

— (2002) 'Interview with Dr. Philip O. Emafo, President of the International Narcotics Control Board (INCB)', Update. Vienna: UNODC, December.

— (2003a) *Global Illicit Drug Trends 2002*. Vienna: UNODC.

— (2003b) *Ecstasy and Amphetamines Global Survey 2003*. Vienna: UNODC.

— (2004a) *Global Illicit Drug Trends 2003*. Vienna: UNODC.

— (2004b) *Illicit Crop Monitoring Programme*. <www.unodc.org/unodc/en/crop_monitoring.html>.

— (2004c) *2003 World Drug Report*. Vienna: UNODC.

— (2004d) *Government of Colombia Coca Cultivation Survey, June 2004*. Vienna: UNODC.

— (2005a) *World Drug Report 2005*. Vienna: UNODC.

— (2005b) *Global Drug Trends*. Vienna: UNODC.

UNODCCP (1999) 'The Drug Nexus in Africa', Studies on Drugs and Crime Monograph Series. New York: UN.

— (2000) *World Drug Report*. Oxford: Oxford University Press.

US Department of Argiculture (1942) *Hemp for Victory*. <www.globalhemp. com/Archives/Government_Research/ USDA/hemp_for_victory.shtml>.

US General Accounting Office (1998) 'Report to the Honourable Charles B. Rangel, House of Representatives, Law Enforcement Information of Drug Related Police Corruption', Washington, DC.

US State Department (2000) *Fact Sheet on Mycoherbicide Cooperation*. <ciponline. org/colombia/071801.htm>.

— (2001) 'The Andes Under Siege; Environmental Consequences of the Drug Trade'. <usinfo.state. gov/products/pubs/archive/andes/ homepage.htm>#forest>.

US State Department Bureau for International Narcotics and Law Enforcement Affairs (2003) Fact Sheet: 'Environmental Consequences of the Illicit Coca Trade'. Washington, DC: Bureau for International Narcotics.

Valentine, D. (2004) *The Strength of the Wolf: The Secret History of America's War on Drugs*. London: Verso.

Van Kooten, G. and E. Bulte (1999) *The Economics of Nature: Managing Biological Assets*. Malden, MA: Blackwell.

Vann Cott, D. (2003) 'From Exclusion to Inclusion: Bolivia's 2002 Elections', *Journal of Latin American Studies*, Vol. 34, no. 4.

Vann Woodward, C. (1974) *The Strange Career of Jim Crow*, Oxford: Oxford University Press.

Varese, F. (2001) *The Russian Mafia: Private Protection in a New Market Economy*. Oxford: Oxford University Press.

Veen, N., J. Selten, I. van der Tweel, W. Feller, H. Hoek and R. Kahn (2004) 'Cannabis Use and Age at Onset of Schizophrenia', *American Journal of Psychiatry*, March, pp. 501–6.

Vickerman, P. and C. Watts (2002) 'The Impact of an HIV Prevention Intervention for Injecting Drug Users in Svetlogorsk, Belarus: Model Predictions', *International Journal of Drug Policy*, Vol. 13, pp. 149–64.

Vickerman, P. and C. Watts (2003) 'Injecting Drug Use and the Sexual Transmission of HIV: Simple Model Insights', *International Journal of Drug Policy*, Vol. 14, pp. 89–93.

Vullimay, E. (2000) 'U.S. Sprays Poison in Drugs War', *Observer*, 2 July.

Waley, A. (1985) *The Opium War Through Chinese Eyes*. London: Allen and Unwin.

Walgate, R. (2003) 'Retracted Ecstasy Paper "An Outrageous Scandal"', *The Scientist*, 16 September.

Walker, W. (1996) *Drugs in the Western Hemisphere: An Odyssey of Cultures in Conflict*. Wilmington, DE: Scholarly Resources Inc.

Wall, M. (2003) 'Estimating the Economic Impact of HIV/AIDs on the Countries of the Former Soviet Union', Economic and Statistics Analysis Unit, Working Paper 1. London: Overseas Development Institute.

Wall Street Journal (2005) 'A War on Drugs, or a War on Farmers?', 11 January.

Walton, S. (2001) *Out of It*. London: Penguin.

Warren, M. (2004) 'What Does Corruption Mean in a Democracy?', *American Journal of Political Science*, no. 48, pp. 328–43.

Watters, J. (1994) 'Trends in Risk Behaviour and HIV Seroprevalence in Heterosexual Injection Drug Users in San Francisco, 1986–1992', *Journal of Acquired Immune Deficiency Syndrome*, Vol. 7, no. 12, pp. 1276–81.

Watters, J., M. Estilo and G. Clark (1994) 'Syringe and Needle Exchange as HIV/AIDS Prevention for Injecting Drug Users', *Journal of the American Medical Association*, Vol. 271, pp. 115–20.

Webb, G. (1999) *Dark Alliance: CIA, the Contras and the Crack Cocaine Explosion*. New York: Seven Stories Press.

Weil, A. (1972) *The Natural Mind: A New Way of Looking at Drugs and the Higher*

Bibliography

Consciousness. Boston, MA: Houghton Mifflin.

Whitby, S. (2001) *Biological Warfare Against Crops*. London: Palgrave Macmillan.

White, M. (2001) 'Legalise Heroin, Says Former Police Chief', *Guardian*, 7 November.

Whitebread, C. (1995) 'The Sociology of Prohibition or the History of the Non-Medical Use of Drugs in the United States', Speech to the California Judges' Association, 1995 annual conference.

WHO (World Health Organization) (1993a) 'WHO Expert Committee on Drug Dependence: Twenty-eighth Report', WHO Technical Report, no. 836. Geneva: UN, pp. 35–6.

— (1993b) Global Programme on AIDS, 'The Costs of HIV/AIDS Prevention Strategies in Developing Countries'. Geneva: UN.

— (1994) WHO International Collaborative Group, 'Multi-city Study on Drug Injecting and Risk of HIV Infection'. Geneva: UN.

— (1995) 'Publication of the Largest Global Study on Cocaine Use Ever Undertaken', Press Release WHO/20, 14 March.

— (1998) 'WHO Did not Bow to Political Pressure in Publishing a Report on Cannabis', Press Release WHO/26, 19 February.

Wild, A. (2005) *Coffee: A Dark History*. London: W. W. Norton.

Williams, M. (2003) *Deforesting the Earth: From Prehistory to Global Crisis*. Chicago, IL: University of Chicago Press.

Williams, S. (1848) *The Middle Kingdom. A Survey of the Geography, Government, Literature, Social Life, Arts, and History of the Chinese Empire and Its Inhabitants*. New York: Wiley and Putnam.

Wisotsky, S. (1990) *Beyond the War on Drugs: Overcoming a Failed Public Policy*. London: Prometheus Books.

Wodak, A. (n.d.) 'The Connection Between HIV Infection in Injecting Drug Users and Drugs Policy'. <www.hopkins-aids.edu/geneva/hilites_macer.html>.

— (2003) 'The International Drug Treaties: "Paper Tigers" or Dangerous Behemoths?', *International Journal of Drug Policy*, Vol. 14, pp. 221–3.

Wolfe, D. (2004) 'Condemned to Death Thanks to the U.S.-Led Drug War, AIDS is Exploding Among Injection Drug Users', *The Nation Magazine*, 26 April.

World Bank (1997) 'Confronting AIDS: Public Priorities in a Global Epidemic'. <www.worldbank.org/aids-econ/confront/>.

Yongming, Z. (1999) *Anti-Drug Crusades in Twentieth Century China: Nationalism, History and State Building*, Lanham, MD: Rowan and Littlefield.

Youngers, C. (1997) 'Coca Eradication Efforts in Colombia', Washington Office on Latin America Briefing Series, Issues in International Drug Policy, June.

Youngers, C. and E. Rosin (2004) *Drugs and Democracy in Latin America: The Impact of U.S. Policy*. Boulder, CO: Lynne Rienner.

Zaitch, D. (2002) *Trafficking Cocaine: Colombian Drug Entrepreneurs in the Netherlands*. Amsterdam: Kluwer.

Zhang, K., D. Li, H. Li and E. Beck (1999) 'Changing Sexual Attitudes and Behaviour in China: Implications for the Spread of HIV and Other Sexually Transmitted Diseases', *AIDS Care*, Vol. 11, no. 5, pp. 581–9.

Zheng, X., C. Tian, K. Choi, J. Zhang, H. Cheng, X. Yang, D. Li, J. Lin, S. Qu, X. Sun, T. Hall, J. Mandel and N. Hearst (1994) 'Injecting Drug-use and AIDS Infection in Southwest China', *AIDS*, Vol. 8, pp. 1141–7.

Zimring, F. and G. Hawkins (1999) *Crime is not the Problem: Lethal Violence in America*, Studies in Crime and Public Policy. Oxford: Oxford University Press.

Index

Index